~ GHOSTWALKER ~

ADVANCE PRAISE FOR *Ghostwalker*

"Mountain lions, also called cougars or pumas, are magnificent beings who are central to the integrity of the ecosystems in which they live. Because they are predators, they are feared and wantonly and brutally killed throughout the landscapes they call home. They surely deserve better—to be treated with respect, dignity, and compassion—and if *Ghostwalker* doesn't convince you to appreciate them as the majestic animals who they are, I'm not sure what will. Leslie Patten's book should go a long way in clearing up misunderstandings about mountain lions. I hope it will enjoy a broad global audience because the disdain and hate with which some people view mountain lions also characterizes the way in which other nonhuman predators are seen, and they all suffer from being violently killed 'in the name of humans.'"

—Marc Bekoff Ph.D., University of Colorado; member
of the board of The Cougar Fund, author of *The Animals'
Agenda: Freedom, Compassion, and Coexistence in the Human Age*
(with Jessica Pierce), *Canine Confidential: Why Dogs Do What They Do*,
and editor of *Listening To Cougar* (with Cara Blessley Lowe)

"*Ghostwalker* is a rare blend of poetry and scholarly insight, concealed mystery and revelation. This book is a journey through the eyes of a woman who, having never seen a cougar, has actually seen him better than most: with a heart wide open to receive the tales and lessons these cats hold for all Creation, especially mankind."

—Cara Blessley Lowe, Co-Founder, The Cougar Fund

"I learned more about the elusive lion in four hours curled up with this book than four decades hiking the Greater Yellowstone. Patten seamlessly knits together personal experiences, scientific research, archaeology, and legend to reveal the very essence of the lion."

—Tom Carter, author *Day Hiking Yellowstone*

"To know the essence of the lion—that is the quest of Leslie Patten as she tracks and ponders the life of America's mountain lion—a quest that will leave you yearning for the high country, on the trail of the ghost cat."

—Will Stolzenburg, author of
Heart of a Lion: A Lone Cat's Walk Across America

"*Ghostwalker* is a fascinating page-turner, sharing stories that lead us through the complicated mix of cougar admirers and the many questions about the survival of these wild cats. It is vital for these elusive ghosts of the forests to be protected and valued. Even if just out of sight, we can imagine them out there, living free to roam the landscape just as it should be."

—Lisa Robertson, Co-Founder Wyoming Untrapped

"*Ghostwalker* is an enthralling and informative journey into the lives of one of the West's most enigmatic inhabitants, the cougar. Patten deftly braids legend, biology and her own experience to guide readers through a stunningly beautiful exploration of these amazing animals, and their myriad meanings to the ecosystems and communities of which they are part."

—Wyoming Wildlife Advocates, Jackson Hole, WY

GHOST WALKER

TRACKING A MOUNTAIN LION'S SOUL

THROUGH SCIENCE AND STORY

LESLIE PATTEN

GHOSTWALKER

Published by Far Cry Publishing
thehumanfootprint.wordpress.com

ISBN: 978-0-692-16385-6

10 9 8 7 6 5 4 3 2 1

Cover and interior design by www.DominiDragoone.com
Cover photo: © Drew Rush/*National Geographic*
  A cougar patrols its territory inside Yellowstone National Park
Greater Yellowstone Ecosystem map by Charlie Beck and Mark Mahaffey
Index by Steve Rath

All photos are from the personal collection of the author or in the Public Domain, except for the following: p. 8 © Bonnie Smith; p. 22 © The Cryptic Zoo, Jamie Hall; p. 26 courtesy Gila National Forest/Wikimedia Commons; p. 73 © Peter Schurch; p. 77 & 79 © Megan Walla-Murphy; p. 81 © Reuben Weinzveg; p. 87 © Scott Davidson; p. 91 © Steve Winter, Panthera; p. 92 © Brittney Esther; p. 93 courtesy of Panthera; p. 98 © Denis Callet; p. 105 courtesy of National Geographic Topo!; p. 109 © Denis Callet; p. 114 © Santa Cruz mountains, Trish Carney, Bay Area Puma Project; p. 121 © Mark Elbroch, Panthera; p. 128 courtesy of Panthera; p. 131 © Santa Cruz mountains, Trish Carney, Bay Area Puma Project; p. 138 GIS data management and project cartography was provided by B. Cohen and J. Sanchez http://journals.plos.org/plosone/article?id=10.1371/journal.pone.0107985#ack; p. 159 © Denis Callet; p. 167 © Robert Martinez; p. 168 © Drew Rush, *National Geographic*; p. 174 & 175 © Charlie Beck; p. 183 © Trish Carney/Bay Area Puma Project; p. 189 courtesy Santa Cruz Mountains, Felidae Conservation Fund; p. 191 © Steve Winter/Bay Area Puma Project; p. 220 courtesy Mountain Lion Foundation.

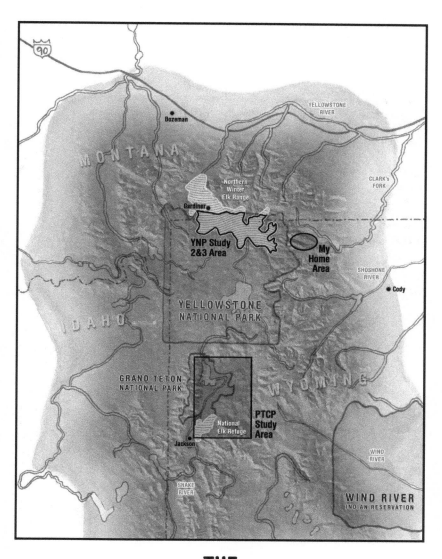

THE
GREATER
YELLOWSTONE
ECOSYSTEM

MAP BY CHARLI BECK AND MARK MAHAFFEY

TABLE OF CONTENTS

There's no one. Do you hear? It's the puma
stepping in the air and the leaves.

—PABLO NERUDA

FOREWORD

———— ✤ ————

A lot of books and articles about the puma pass across my desk. I try to read them all, but must admit I have become jaded and groan with every request for a review. So when Leslie Patten appeared with her manuscript, my skepticism flared. I had never heard her name, and braced myself for one more volume that either decried the cruelty of puma hunters or proclaimed alarm over puma threats to human welfare. I grabbed my red pen (figuratively—these days you key up "track changes") and settled into my hard-nosed critic mood. Within a few pages, I realized that I was reading, not editing. The copy was clean, and the author had done her homework. She had read the scientific literature, and had interviewed most of the best biologists studying the species. She had clearly delineated the issues affecting wildlife agencies responsible for puma regulations. This effort to this point might have resulted in a useful perspective on the status of the species in the American West.

But she reached further. She read the lore as well as the science and sought people living near and engaged with pumas—houndsmen, trappers, and owners of livestock. She became their neighbor and interviewed them with empathy finding no demons.

While accumulating this written and oral knowledge, she also went to the field. She learned to recognize puma sign from biologists and hunters, and she and her dog roamed alone through an isolated landscape bounding Yellowstone, following puma tracks and setting trail cameras in strategic places. She became an accomplished wilderness naturalist in the habitat of pumas, grizzlies, and wolves.

And best of all, she engagingly interwove her experiences with the science and lore to create the best popular treatise on pumas that I've read in decades. Her scholarship is impeccable, she tells a good tale, and she writes with a journalist's eye for clarity. Asked to recommend a book that summarizes the current state of the puma, I'll choose this one for some time to come.

I congratulate Leslie for a job well done.

—HARLEY G. SHAW
Retired Wildlife Research Biologist
Author: *Soul Among Lions*
Managing Editor, Wild Felid Monitor

PREFACE

⸺ ❧ ⸺

After living in the Canadian backcountry for an entire winter track-ing and studying mountain lions, writer and naturalist R. D. Law-rence summarized his experiences this way: "I had developed the ability almost to *think* like a lion, to recognize instantly those places that would not offer prospects of prey, or that were too tangled for quiet travel. I could 'read' tracks and tell from the width of the stride and the depth of the impressions whether a cat was walking unhurriedly—alert, but not stalking—or whether it was intent on hunting, but not yet within sight, scent or sound of game."

This book aims to empower the reader with that kind of knowl-edge. It is also meant to answer a personal question I carried with me as I followed lion tracks through every snowy winter of Wyo-ming, and one I posed to every interviewee: *"What does it feel like to be a mountain lion?"*

I live next to Yellowstone National Park, one of the greatest wildlife viewing parks in North America. People from all over the world come to Yellowstone and to Grand Teton National Park, its neighbor to the south. They see grizzly bears and wolves, coyotes and elk. Yet most will never see a mountain lion. And neither have I. I've only encountered their ethereal presence on the landscape, which left me pondering where they were and what they were up to. For five years, through serendipitous encounters with their tracks and scat, as well as following their wanderings, I gathered more anecdotal information about cougars than scientific knowledge. I grew to know their habitat and where I might find their spore. I could recognize a lion kill, and I knew where to set up my trail camera. I caught photos of males courting females, mothers with young, and males marking their territory—cougars doing what cougars like to do. Still, I never encountered a mountain lion. And even though I was learning where to find evidence of their presence, that burning question—*What is the essence of the lion?*—compelled me to dig deeper.

This book is an attempt to answer that question. In a sense, I began a hunt, but one that ends in total absorption, not in a kill. As I interviewed people, scouted for lion sign, and pondered how to focus the story, the book took shape as a tracking tale. The track in the snow or sand became the lion itself. Just as a tracker views sign from every angle—from ground level, from a standing view, in different light, and by walking around the print—I was following the crumb trail as best I could, over every substrate. Sometimes the outline was clear and at other times it disappeared. Slowly, a more complete picture emerged, driven by my curiosity of a lion's illusive nature.

My journey is this book. My initial questions were perfunctory—how do I track more efficiently, how do I make the best use of my trail camera, and what does a kill site look like? But as winter arrived each year, and I saw mountain lion hunters with dogs showing up, my curiosity grew. Why do these houndsmen hunt mountain lions? What laws do western states have to protect these animals? What are conservationists and scientists saying about mountain lions? Soon I was on a road that led to interviews with dozens of people with diverse backgrounds.

Every September, as Wyoming's mountain lion hunt season began, I picked up a hunt brochure to check the quota for my valley. Throughout the long winter, I visited the Wyoming Game and Fish Harvest Report website and watched the count tick off as cougar kills were added each week. One year I called the local office of the Wyoming Game and Fish Department to ask a biologist how they set these quotas. Why was my quota of twenty the same every year? Did they know how many lions were actually in my hunt zone? Did they know how old they were? When I found out the Department uses a sketchy method of tooth aging, suitable lion winter habitat, and hunter success to set those quotas, and that mountain lion populations are difficult—in fact, almost impossible—to count, and that the Department doesn't even attempt it, I began to wonder how hunting pressures might be changing lion dynamics in my area.

Though this book's emphasis is on my home region in the Rocky Mountains, I have included a chapter on California. Mountain lions are hunted in all the western states except California and, with that in mind, I traveled to California to use the state as a yardstick against which to judge the effects of hunting. However I soon discovered that mountain lions in California have their own unique difficulties—problems that are creeping throughout the larger landscapes of the West: human overpopulation, fragmentation, genetic bottlenecks, rodenticides, urbanization, and road density. California also shares some of the same problems Rocky Mountain states are dealing with, such as poaching and livestock predation. Two of the biggest issues for mountain lions, as well as all large predators throughout the Rockies, are habitat loss and landscape fragmentation. California has already begun to address these issues, and the way in which the state is trying to tackle these problems could be a blueprint—and a warning—for other western states. In essence, these two diverse regions are microcosms of the problems mountain lions face in the areas they now occupy. But an understanding of the soul of the mountain lion through the looking glass of this book can pave the way for tolerance and new management practices, and may even allow for lion immigration eastwards.

The stories of lions in the two states for which I present in-depth science—Wyoming and California—provide the reader with

a full view of how adaptable lions are, but they also tell the stories
of their hidden social lives and their use of diverse landscapes and
prey. The mountain lion's biggest threats come from humans. Yet
we humans are fickle, our attention wavers, and our proffers of love
and protection are grounded within the intimate sphere of what we
know, and what we can see. Lions offer none of that. To that end,
I felt the need to move beyond the science for the most intimate
stories and details. I looked to trackers, conservationists, and, to my
surprise, houndsmen. I discovered there were many hunters who
had followed the tracks of lions to the point where the lion itself
had changed them.

The majority of the personal experiences described in this book
occurred over the course of many years. Mountain lion research
in the Rocky Mountains takes place during the winter; therefore,
the reader will notice references to light-snow years and heavy-
snow years. Lastly, mountain lions are referred to by more than
forty different names in the English language alone. They are by
far the most successful predator living today across the Americas,
and their nomenclature includes names in Spanish, Quechua, and
many Native tongues. Puma, mountain lion, panther, and cougar,
are some of the more common English names for the same animal.
In this book, I roam freely, like the animal I speak about, from
name to name, mostly using puma, mountain lion, cougar, or lion.
Sometimes I just use the word "cat," and when I do, I mean cougar;
otherwise I will note which cat by name, such as "bobcat." Panther is a name specific to Florida. Catamount is an old name, referring to cat-of-the-mountain. And the large cat is also referred to as
Ghost Cat, Shadow Cat, Cat of God, Greatest of Wild Hunters,
and Spirit of the Mountain, all terms that illustrate its elusive and
illustrious qualities. *Puma concolor* is the mountain lion's scientific
name. Whatever one chooses to call them, mountain lions are no
doubt among the most majestic, noble, beautiful, and enigmatic of
all our wild predators living in the Americas.

CHAPTER 1

THE QUIET RAPTURE
OF OBSERVATION

*Once, in every corner of this continent, your passing could
prickle the stillness and bring every living thing to the
alert. But even then you were more felt than seen. You
were an imminence, a presence, a crying in the night, pug
tracks in the dust of a trail. Solitary and shy, you lived
beyond, always beyond. Your comings and goings defined
the boundaries of the unpeopled. If seen at all, you were
only a tawny glimpse fleeting toward disappearance among
the trees or along the ridges and ledges of your wilderness.*

—WALLACE STEGNER

THE JACKSON HOLE SIGHTING

On a cold wintry day in 1999, on the National Elk Refuge outside
the town of Jackson, Wyoming, a local townsperson spotted something unusual moving in the cliffs beyond the grasslands where
the elk were feeding. He pulled out his binoculars for a closer look,
and to his surprise and amazement, there was a mountain lion with
three kittens resting high up in an alcove, almost at the top of the
plateau. The outcrop, called Miller Butte, was perfect protection,
not only from humans, but also from a new immigration of wolves
that was storming the valley like a rising sea, returning to the area
for the first time since the 1920s.

It didn't take long for the townspeople to learn of the cat family. During those first days, a dedicated few from town parked on the road, set up their spotting scopes and chairs in sub-zero temperatures, relishing this fortuitous event. It's rare to see a mountain lion. Here was a chance to view a mom with her kittens—a wild cougar family—and spend hours delighting in their antics.

By the end of that first week, the rest of the world was showing up. They came in droves, more each day; a sign that read "Parking for Mountain Lions" suddenly appeared along the Elk Refuge road beside a specially plowed parking area. Photographers and nature lovers from across the globe poured into Jackson Hole for this rare sighting. For long periods, mom would disappear, only to return to gather up her kittens. Nine times over the course of their forty-two-day stay, she moved the family elsewhere to feed on a kill. The crowd grew anxious. Would the lions return to their makeshift den site? These were older kittens, and at seven months, they were no longer nursing. Soon they would grow beyond the age where they would wait, hidden, while mom traveled to make kills, returning only to gather them and take them to feed. Soon they'd be traveling with mom full time, learning the skills they'd need to feed themselves. Then one day, nearly six weeks after the lioness and her family was spotted, she and her kittens were gone, as quickly as they had appeared. Jackson resident Lisa Robertson voiced what all these newly converted local and national mountain lion supporters felt: "It was magnificent in every way. I'll never forget it as long as I live. I wish it would happen again."

The sighting of this wild family left Jackson residents awed and aware. People who had never thought about mountain lions before were now questioning what might happen to the Miller Butte lions. What were the hunting regulations and the quotas? Could the kittens be killed? And what about female lions—were they fair game for the hunt? Four months after the arrival of the lions, the Wyoming Game and Fish Department's annual lion-hunting quota went up for review. The Department changed the quota in the Jackson hunt area from five mountain lions to twelve, citing growing reports of an increase in lion sightings. Quotas in most other areas around the state were doubled as well. The Department felt there were too many lions, but in a local newspaper interview, even the Agency admitted that "it is virtually impossible to get an accurate count of an actual lion population."

The public voiced concern: there was not enough data on lion numbers; non-hunters, so-called non-consumptive users with just cameras and scopes, had no real voice in the decision process; and females with dependent young, like the Miller Butte mom who left her young to hunt, could be legally killed by hunters. The Miller Butte sighting spurred a budding awareness resulting in increased advocacy for Jackson's lions. Tom Mangelsen, world-renowned wildlife photographer, and Cara Blessley Lowe, filmmaker and author, launched The Cougar Fund, a conservation organization, the first of its kind in Wyoming to focus solely on mountain lions. And with funding from the Hornocker Wildlife Institute, a sixteen-year project studying the mountain lions of Jackson Hole began in 2000.

We value what we know and love, yet a lifetime spent in the mountains or desert does not guarantee even a sighting of the black tip of a lion's long tail. So how can we learn about an animal that is as invisible as a ghost?

✐ MY FIRST LION TRACK

The usual winter storm in the Absaroka Range of the Rocky Mountains east of Yellowstone National Park arrives from the west or northwest, deposits its snow load into the upper basin narrows, then peters out as it drifts eastward. Occasionally a Norther comes barreling down from the Beartooth Mountains, dumping an icy blanket cover over the desert and high country around Cody, Wyoming.

Mostly these blizzards bypass the rocky flats above the Clarks Fork River canyon. The flats are a curious maze of undulating granite masses, punctuated with ravines and outcrops, caves and gulches, that weave this way and that. I call them baby drainages, small, yet everywhere. A giant U-shaped peninsula three miles long and two miles wide, the area is a platform of Precambrian granitic rock that terminates in cliffs overlooking the Clarks Fork River, thousand-foot vertical walls that only mountain goats and bighorn sheep dare to navigate. Vegetation on the plateau consists of scattered limber pines and grasses, so the going is easy. The best part is that in winter, little snow falls here, and if there is snow, the exposed rock warms in the winter sun, leaving a scanty dusting—just enough to track wildlife, yet sparse enough for a biped in hiking boots. Because of the minimal snowfall, the elk, and especially the deer, use the valley and its ridges as their winter feed grounds. They weave in and out of the narrow passages in this corrugated landscape, hidden during the day, feeding at dusk and dawn in the open rocky areas. I've gotten to know the fluted labyrinth quite well.

My weekly winter hike here led, in short order, to seeing bobcat tracks in one specific area. Every few days I'd hike into these sagebrush meadows and study the track pattern in order to learn more about bobcats. I am familiar with bobcats, and I know that if they are left to run free from hunting and harassment, they are sometimes visible in fields catching mice or sunning themselves in the open.

Bobcats—and all cats including cougars, I soon discovered—are very neat in everything they do, including how they walk. They are masters of limiting their energy. Their usual track is a perfect "direct register," where they place their back foot directly into the track of the front foot. It's a cat's "lazy," yet perfect, walk, or maybe just a way of leaving as little trace as possible—neat and clean like the rest of their lives. With careful observation, I could see where they sped up or slowed down to hunt for prey. I learned what their "sit down" looked like in the snow, and I tried to figure out their different gaits and what they might have been thinking or looking at. I especially liked to track twenty-four to forty-eight hours after a storm. I learned that during a storm, animals, like humans, will hunker down and wait it out. Once the storm passed, I gave the wildlife some time to go about their business and then set out tracking. What I didn't know was that these little cats were prepping me for their much larger cousin.

A sunny, windless, twenty-degree winter day in Wyoming means a chance for short sleeves, light winter gloves, a hat, and lightweight thermals. It's always a welcome event, a chance to stretch outside and fend off cabin fever. Sunrise isn't till 7:00 a.m. in January. With a blanket of new snow cover from the previous evening, and a cloudless sky above, I readied for a hike to the granite mesas where my bobcat likes to hunt. My route consisted of a large expanse of brushy meadow, a stair-step climb up ledges on a boulder face via an animal trail to the tier above, an easy walk across slabs of unbroken washed granite past a weathered elk kill, and a short scramble over boulders to a low saddle edging a rock cliff. All in the course of only two miles. After a climb to the crest, a tight meadow expanded in a V-shape before dropping into densely timbered draws.

As I approached the saddle, I was surprised to see a set of "bobcat-like" tracks. Instead of heading toward the meadows, a bobcat's favorite place, these large prints followed along a house-sized boulder cliff to its edge, which harbored a view of the entire north country. Yet these tracks were too large for a bobcat—more than three inches wide. Immediately, without ever having seen them before, I "grokked" that these large prints must belong to a cougar. Although bobcat and cougar tracks are almost identical in shape, size matters—and size tells the truth. Their prints rarely show claws (think of a domestic cat whose claws are retractable), and although similar to a canine's, you'll know the difference once you've seen several cat

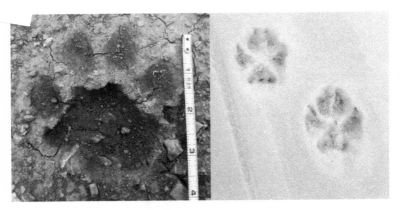

left: cougar print, right: wolf tracks

tracks. Cats have a typical "C" pattern in the negative space, while canines have an "X" pattern. Other telltale signs are the asymmetrical third toe in the front foot, the heel pad with three lobes on the bottom, and a "notch" or slight depression on the top of the heel pad. The dog family has a triangular heel pad.

As I followed the tracks, it appeared as if the cougar made her way to the precipice, paused, and looked over her vast domain. The prints took my breath away. Something deep inside me stood at attention, not afraid, but now much more alert, awed, as if the tracks were a sacrament. I was in the presence of a true predator, in fact, *the* perfect predator.

Puma concolor—cat of one color. The cat with the tawny coat that blends in perfectly with her surroundings is the quintessence of grace, speed, agility, and stealth. I've seen wolves face to face many times, only a few feet away. I am never afraid of wolves. Instead they elicit feelings of comradeship, maybe genetic recollections of an earlier time when we hunted together. Yet this print of a cougar triggered a different response. The quiet of the icy landscape penetrated my body, and my mind was still. *This cougar passed where I am standing.*

What was even more interesting was that this lion, her tracks quite fresh, was mingling within the hunting area of the bobcat I had previously spotted. Now I was doubly curious how these two felines were negotiating this space. Perhaps the bobcat was taking advantage of the cougar's hunting prowess for large prey, stealing bites from deer carcasses when the lion was full and asleep. Or maybe that bobcat skedaddled at the first smell of that cougar.

With that first "sighting," I had made contact with this magnificent animal, even if only through her fleeting imprints in the snow. Wonder and awe, yes; but also, so many new questions, as if a door had opened begging me to explore beyond and unravel the mysteries of this illusive cat—the *Spirit of the Mountain*. Pumas, numinous in their ethereal nature, and detected only by tracks, are almost impossible for a hunter to find without the help of his dogs. It is said that pumas deliberately walk on hard substrates so they cannot be tracked. The scent that is retained in visible and invisible tracks is their only tell. These animals are the most successful land mammals of the Western Hemisphere, yet our understanding of their lives is miniscule. Possibly all this appealed to my own temperament—all that is hidden is worth the effort to probe.

Soon I began making regular trips to this area to discover the wanderings of pumas, having completely forgotten about my bobcat venture. I even began to call this peninsula of rock *Cougar Flats*. I used my instincts, and especially my dog Koda's nose, to slowly puzzle out their comings and goings, their patterns and habits. A new adventure began. And where best to begin this adventure but with the melding of past and present.

LIONS OF THE PLEISTOCENE

Eighty miles from my home, on the flanks of the Big Horn Mountains, is a sinkhole barely noticeable to an animal walking along the easy incline of a boulder face. Only twelve by fifteen feet wide

Researchers at natural trap cave with protective grate

at the top, the hole falls eighty-five feet to a cavernous room at the bottom. Scientists rappel down to do their excavation work, which began in the 1970s and has gone through several rounds since; the last investigation in 2015 was led by Dr. Julie Meachin. I'm listening to Dr. Meachin's lecture at the Draper Museum of Natural History in Cody, where she is talking excitedly about a wolf they had identified in the cave that was not previously known to live in these parts.

"The wolves at Natural Trap Cave are not dire wolves, and they're not the living gray wolves that we have in the area today. But they're something totally different, and that's Beringian wolves," explains Dr. Meachin.

Meachin is talking about a time when eye-popping, enormous megapredators and huge herbivores roamed North America. Excavations in the cave have uncovered mammoths, camels, ancient long-horned bison, short-faced bears, prehistoric horses, and several cats that no longer exist—the American lion and cheetah among them. Natural Trap Cave is a window into some of the fauna that lived in the Big Horn Basin during the Pleistocene age, where the incredible diversity of mammals in North America rivaled modern day Africa. The wide array of potential prey for pumas would have included two species of capybaras, as many as thirteen species of horses, onagers, and asses, three species of tapirs, two species of peccaries, seven species of camels as well as deer, nine species of pronghorns, and three species of mountain goats and sheep. Other mammals, too big for a puma to kill, like bison, giant ground sloths, and mastodons, lived here as well.

As the last Ice Age began to melt, and humans crossed into North America, a wave of extinctions began to take place between 11,500 and 10,500 years ago. Scientists are still debating the exact cause or causes—possibly a combination of climate change, disease, and human predation—but in very short order, all of these large mammals, along with many others, disappeared. The climate warmed, the seas rose, and large coastal grazing areas became inundated, reducing habitat for the megaherbivores who went extinct. Predators, their own demise lagging behind, were now more competitive than ever, and the likelihood is that they turned to smaller sized prey, further hastening extinctions. Grasslands that once supported these megaherbivores turned into forests, changing the distribution and types of prey and leaving habitat that was more suitable for smaller predators with an ambush strategy, giving the mountain lion an advantage.

Geneticists tell us that pumas disappeared in North America during the Pleistocene extinctions, and our modern-day puma comes from a small founder population (think bottleneck) that migrated out of South America and recolonized the continent. When pumas returned, they emerged into a world that was friendlier yet with less diversity of prey. Those large carnivores that endured the change had been the mesopredators in a world of giant and fierce megapredators, but now they were at the top of the food chain—wolves, mid-size bears, jaguars, and pumas. And the paucity in diversity of fauna benefited deer, bighorn sheep, elk, and other medium-sized herbivores. Ecosystems became simpler, yet pumas were well suited for this new challenge of reduced selectivity of prey. Lithe and powerful, with proportionally large hind legs, they can leap as high as eighteen feet in one bound, or vault across a chasm forty feet wide. Good at turning on a dime, they use their tail almost like a rudder, employing speed and gravity to their advantage. Mostly solitary and highly intelligent, they can climb trees, sprint up to fifty miles per hour for short distances, or spring gracefully to a high desert ledge to escape their few remaining predators, which were reduced to gray wolves, coyotes, jaguars, and grizzly and black bears. Using a coursing, then waiting, strategy, cover is their most important ally, and cover can be found in forests or in deserts. Their retractable claws grapple prey, while long whiskers on their muzzle act as tactile organs, which help to direct the killing bite into the nape of the neck or throat. A cougar's dew claw, called the "killer claw," is a massive tendon-attached thumb that holds its victim steady. Although lions have relatively small lung capacity, sprinting shorter distances than canids, they have greater prey-capture success. This versatility explains how, from a small founder population, pumas entered the Holocene Era and were able to occupy North America from as far north as northern British Columbia down to the tip of South America, and from the Pacific to the Atlantic.

✐ LEGEND ROCK

It's an unusually warm March afternoon when I drive from my mountain home to Legend Rock, one of the premier petroglyph sites in Wyoming near the small town of Meeteetse. Archaeologist Larry Loendorf told me there were several, what he called "long figures" pecked into the sandstone wall that might represent lions. Around noon, I arrive at the Meeteetse Museum to pick up the key to the site's locked gate. Legend Rock is another forty miles south of the postage-stamp-size town of Meeteetse, but you can obtain a key there, or in Thermopolis, a larger town farther south.

I'd been to Legend Rock many years before. On that previous excursion, a friend gave me a hand-drawn map, basically a few scribbles showing where to turn off the highway onto a bumpy dirt oil-field road, with a line that said "continue for another 5 miles." At what looked like just a wiggle on my hand-scrawled map, I was to turn, navigate through the myriad of two-track roads, then "cross two cattle guards." There I'd eventually find a wide wash cut by Cottonwood Creek. Over the millennium, the creek has cut and polished the cliffs smooth with a darkened patina that ancient peoples put their mark on.

Today the drive is easy because great improvements have been made. Now there are signs and a paved road. I think I liked it better in obscurity. The small two-lane road runs east-west; the snow-capped rugged Absaroka Range creates the backdrop for a bleak expanse of desert that's been close cropped by too many cattle. Taking in the view, one wonders what drove Native peoples to this location, used over and over for 11,000 years. The creek is here, and the desert winds shear off the little snow that falls. A good winter campsite possibly? The nearby Absaroka Range is home to deer and bighorn sheep, as well as roots, tubers, and white bark pine nuts, all critical foods that ancient peoples depended upon and gathered during the summer months. The desert looks bleak, especially at this time of year, yet food can be found. A herd of antelope crosses the road. A jackrabbit bounds towards the horizon, while evidence of pack rat—a favorite food of Indians who smoked the lagomorphs out of their homes—is easy to locate among the rocks.

The site has been developed in a nice way, mostly to prevent all the vandalism that takes place in a lonely, remote area. A few years ago, a high-school student on a field trip was able to steal away from

Lion petroglyph with head missing

the group and write "No Trojans Allowed" over one of the thunder-bird images, leaving it indiscernible. Missing panels, etched initials, people rubbing off the varnish with oils from touching the stone—white man disturbances to a small area that has been intact, used in a sacred manner, for thousands of years.

The visitor center is closed in winter. I'm alone as I walk along the etched wall. Trail cameras follow my movements; placed low, they blend in, resembling path lights. I marvel at all the mysterious figures and recognize the wildlife pecked in stone. Bighorn sheep, elk, deer. These artists knew these animals intimately. I keep my eyes peeled for what might represent a cat—a slender figure, no horns or antlers, with a long tail and upright ears. But since I've never seen a petroglyph cougar, I don't know what I'm looking for. The figure could even resemble a coyote. And the spotting is made more difficult because of the thousands of years of rock art across these walls. Along with the familiar animals, there are enormous human-like etchings with unusual numbers of toes and fingers, as well as upside down figures. Some have headdresses, some horns, some originate or end at cracks in the rock, maybe to indicate a transition from one world to another. Theory has it that these drawings were either done directly at the vision quest site, or upon the seeker's return, as a way of recording their experiences. These weird figures evoke a sense of the extramundane.

I spot a very small stone animal, high up, that appears to be chasing a hare, yet the hare is bigger than the apparent cat. Maybe a coyote then? Toward the end of the panels, I notice a figure that is explained in the interpretive paper as a helper or little person. The helper is watching a large headless figure (because that portion of the rock is missing) that resembles a mountain lion, its tail pointed straight, disappearing into a crack. Nearby, and higher up, are two more cat-like zoomorphs, these smaller. One of them, quite faint, seems to be head butting a figure that looks like a spaceman with its arms and legs spread eagle. Curiously, Larry Loendorf told me that among the Crow, Blackfeet, and Shoshone tribes, he did not know of any special powers attributed to lions. While they were all fond of lion hides for bow cases, he could not recall any shields adorned with lion figures or lion-decorated tipis from tribes that visited this site. The interpretive paper from the visitors' box has no information as to how old these particular cat-like figures are. The Crow have been in this area since the 1500s. The Shoshone are thought to have arrived as early as 4,000 years ago, possibly even longer. But people were hunting mammoths 11,000 years ago in this desert, and those people, too, etched on this wall. What these figures mean is anyone's guess. In total, I counted three figures I felt were cougars. Cougars in rock art are considered a rarity for unknown reasons, maybe because they were not routinely hunted for food.

The air is still. The monotonous drumming of an oil pump sounds quietly in the background. Cottonwood Creek gurgles softly as it ambles at the base of the petroglyph rock palette. Even though it's still too early for a spring run-off, the creek runs harder than usual on this warm day. Climate change is etching its own effects on the earth in this place. I'm drawn here and don't know why. Maybe, I think, I'll feel a symbolic link to the animal I'm searching for, a connection that transcends time and space. Thus far, my project has been propelled by an unexplained motivation; maybe I'm hoping for this stone image to merge with the manifest, making the intangible more palpable.

Shrine of the Stone Lions. Two lions carved out of stone within a circle of protective boulders. Door faces east.

I finish my time along the panel and walk down to the creek with Koda. He enjoys a cool drink and brief swim while two other parties of tourists arrive to begin their petroglyph sojourn. I'm glad to have had the time to myself and head back to the parking area to drop my pack and camera. The dog is rooting around by a small arroyo on the opposite side of the trail where I notice signage. Of course, I'm curious. The sign reads "Private Property." Beyond the sign, for the first time, I notice cliffs with more dark patina, so I assume there might be additional rock art on the private lands. A faint trail leads across the arroyo; I cross and am jolted by several clear prints of a cougar, outlined in the dry mud. I do what I'm used to doing—I examine them, measuring their length and width. But in another part of my consciousness, I feel these prints are a gift and an offering. The people who performed vision quests here entered into the stone itself, aided by fasting and possibly herbs, returning with their vision, which they inscribed on these darkened walls. Here is my rock cougar, come alive, prowling ancient ceremonial cliffs. Like a prayer, the print speaks to me as if to say, *thank you for putting your attention on me and giving me voice.* I follow the tracks a short way, but just like a lion, they quickly vanish in that liminal space between antiquity and destiny.

CHAPTER 2

BROOM RIDING AND HUMAN MEDDLING

There was the wolf, the fox, the bobcat and the cougar. The cougar had a head of an Indian and his paws were hands, which made the medicine man scared. But that cougar talked to the medicine man in Shoshone and said, "Do not be scared. Don't be scared because they are spirits. We'll help you. We will help you, under one condition: that none of your people, be it Shoshone or Bannock, will hunt the cougar, hunt the bobcat, hunt the fox, hunt the wolf—and don't eat them, don't kill them. Stay away from them. If you agree on that, then the spirits will help the Shoshone Bannocks drive these people out."

—SHOSHONE-BANNOCK STORY FROM CRATERS OF THE
MOON (TOLD BY TRIBAL MEMBER LAVERN BRONCHO)

THE ONZA

It is worth a visit to the regions where cougars and jaguars still roam together in order to unearth the curious tales that once were told about these elusive animals. We enter a deeper past, a time when the house of spirits took prominence over the land of flesh.

The legend of the onza dates back to the Aztecs. Believed to be a big cat akin to a cougar, yet far more aggressive, the feline was said to roam the mountains of northwestern Mexico. Described in a consistently similar manner since the conquistadors, onzas had long skinny legs, longer tails than cougars, and were gray-brown in color with faint striping on their legs. Locals in the mountainous regions of Sinaloa and Sonora told stories of the supernatural powers of onzas. Onzas were incredibly swift, capable of powerful leaps akin to flying. They hunted at night by the light of a jewel embedded in their forehead. A few more "scientific" believers thought onzas were the "missing link" to the American cheetah; others thought they might be an entirely new species of cat—half cougar, half jaguar. Onza, from the Latin for leopard, is Mexico's Sasquatch, a creature seldom seen yet large in legend.

In 1986, in Mexico's northwestern state of Sinaloa, a rancher shot what appeared to be an unusual looking cougar, one with long dog-like legs and a very long, thin body—a female, weighing sixty pounds with a twenty-three-inch-long tail on a forty-five-inch-long frame. He brought the carcass to a neighbor, who proclaimed it was identical to the onza killed by his father years before. The onza was sent for DNA analysis. The results confirmed that this animal was a healthy puma, albeit a mutant or possibly a subspecies form. Did DNA on this one animal specimen put the mystery of the onza to rest?

J. Frank Dobie was a folklorist, writer, and newspaper columnist. He grew up south of San Antonio, Texas, on a ranch where Mexicans were more numerous than those of European-born ancestry, and few spoke English. Mexican families had homes on his father's property, so Dobie was familiar with their culture that mixed old Indian ways with Spanish tradition. In the late 1920s, the Guggenheim Foundation gave Dobie a grant to live in Mexico for a year to gather story material. Dobie used that year, and subsequent years, for pack trips to explore the vast, sparsely populated, mountainous regions of Mexico, lingering around ranches and mining camps, soaking up stories. Dobie told a tale of a jaguar hunt that turned into something quite different and mystical.

While settled in a small hacienda that he used for a home base, Dobie had the idea to find a jaguar. As a lover of animals, and a person who'd rather sleep among wildlife than kill them, he nevertheless wanted to hunt this elusive animal for its beautiful hide. He asked his friend, Inocencio, to prepare for a trip to Barranca de las Viboras, a three-day ride into rough, timbered country. Inocencio rounded up an old hound dog, named Lead, and a "fierce" Airedale, a dog with no hunting experience that a neighbor had somehow acquired. Neither Dobie's host nor any of his friends knew anything about hunting with dogs, so Dobie had no idea how Lead would trail.

The small party of two men and two dogs arrived in a narrow feeder canyon after three days of hard riding and pitched their tent along a creek named Arroyo de los Arrastres. A solitary cabin stood on the opposite bank, occupied by a Native "whose veins had never been injected by one drop of the blood of the conquerors." That night, as darkness set in, a silence lay across the land. From beyond the arroyo, Dobie heard a strange bellow that sounded like a bull calf.

The next morning, the Native appeared from his cabin and asked, "Did you hear the tiger up on the mountain last night?" Dobie joked, "Yes, he has horns about three inches long." "No," replied the Indian, and he told the party he could prove it was a *tigre*. They started off with the dogs along a narrow "coyote spine" leading to the tablelands above, where Lead took off like a bullet, baying the entire time. The Airedale bolted back for camp, tail between his legs. As they followed the dog's route, they soon came upon four large prints in the moist earth that "no mountain lion or jaguar . . . could make." Each one of the prints was as big as a saucer, and each had its outside toe missing. The other thing missing was Lead. The party called and searched, yet Lead never returned.

Between the Barranca de las Viboras and Arroyo de los Arrastres, there were no mines, no ranches, no haciendas—only two or three cabins. It was wild country, with wolves, panthers, jaguars, and deer. The party's new Indian friend, Estanislao, now accompanied them as they rode into the mouth of the steep canyon entrance. The group camped on a small bench, a place "in a solitude as primeval as creation." After hearing of a Native *tigre* hunter who lived far down the valley, Dobie asked Estanislao to fetch the man as a guide. In two days, Estanislao returned with the *tigero*. The Indian wore only a blanket under which Dobie could see great scars on his chest, with one naked rib sticking out, the wound healed, but the bone uncovered. One side of this man's face and nose were gone, so that the teeth on that side jutted out. Quietly, the *tigero* explained how he was attacked by a jaguar, saved only by his dogs.

That evening the men fell asleep next to a fire of oak and juniper. While the others slept, Dobie lay awake thinking about his jaguar hunt. He suddenly "felt" an extraordinary noise—felt more than heard, he explains—for the "sound" was like a swish in the air. The night was black beyond the light of the fire, yet Dobie thought he saw a blurry object walking away from it. He called for the Airedale, who didn't respond. When daylight broke, they looked for tracks. The soft ashes from the extinguished fire revealed the tracks of four feline feet, each with an outside toe missing, all four as big as saucers. The half-faced *tigero* said no jaguar feet grew to those proportions. Dobie and his Indian friends climbed up the steep mountain slope where the night before he'd heard rocks displaced. Halfway up, they discovered the Airedale, covered with grass and sticks. Inocencio brought out two small leg hold traps typically used for coyotes, setting them along a natural runway near the dead dog. The next morning as they climbed the ridge to check the traps, they could hear the rattling of the chains. The growling animal had been caught in both sets.

The animal they'd caught was not a jaguar, but it "looked like a mountain lion," though Dobie described it as far larger than any he'd known. Its breast was enormous, its hide turned gray with age, with faint strips down the inside of its legs. The beast was a female, and its four-toed feet appeared abnormally large. Dobie shot the animal, and the crew dragged it to a flat area by the trail, where they rested with a cup of coffee before skinning it. Within a few moments, noiseless as a drift of smoke, four sandaled Indians appeared, walking in single file, halting directly in front of the dead lion.

"It is an *onza!*" they each declared in turn. "What is an *onza?*" asked Dobie. Onza means ounce in Spanish, so this name made no sense in reference to any animal. The four men left without another word. In time, an old Indian, too slow to keep pace with the others, came along. "*Caramba!* It is an *onza,*" he too exclaimed. "Please," asked Dobie, "tell me, what is an *onza?*"

"The worst of animals," replied the old man. "Sometimes I say it is a cross between a bull tiger and a she lion." The old man continued on with a strange tale which I paraphrase below:

> In my village of Arroyo de Peñasco, seventeen years ago, there lived a witch. Strong and hideous looking, she ate "like a sow, but we never knew where she got her food." It was said she could enchant deer like a tiger and make them walk into her trap. In the village, there was a man named Ignacio who lived with his wife and three young sons. One morning, Ignacio went to look for his older boy Pedro, but Pedro had disappeared. The entire town looked all over the mountains, but no Pedro. The townspeople built signal fires around the mountainside that burned all evening, but the boy never appeared. The following day, the men wondered if the witch might know, so they went to speak with her. But once they arrived at her house, the men knew right away she'd done something with the boy. The men tortured her, just a little bit, by punching a hot wire through her ears, but she would not tell. That evening men were posted in the brush around the witch's house. At midnight, the

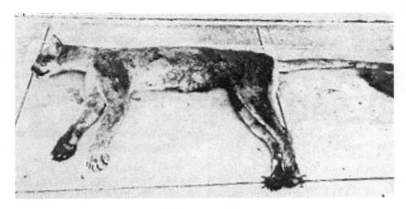

Animal claimed to be an Onza shot in northern Mexico.

door of her cabin opened and out came the witch. She
stood looking, looking, stretching her neck for a while, and
then suddenly she disappeared. I saw this with my own
eyes. We heard a sound over our heads, a *sh-sh-sh-shoo-
oo-oo*. It seemed to circle overhead, then vanish. And that
same night another of Ignacio's sons disappeared. In the
morning, we went back to the witch's house. This time we
used a fiber of the maguey plant, pulling it back and forth,
and by these means slowly tortured the witch by sawing off,
one by one, the little toe of right foot, then her left, then
her little left finger, then her right pinkie. Still, the witch
did not speak. Fearful for his last and littlest son, Ignacio
and the townsmen decided to make a trap for the witch.
They worked all day arranging the door to the boy's room
so it dropped like a trap door. They made a hole in the roof
and set a trigger. That evening, Ignacio and I waited on
top of the roof to ensure the trigger went off should the
witch enter through the trap door. We watched the sky,
and as the horned moon was about to hook a certain star,
we heard a swish of air, *sh-sh-sh-shoo-oo-oo*, then noises

in the room below. Ignacio dropped the trap door and
the thing was trapped inside. Although the baby boy was
inside the room with the witch, no one dared to enter until
first light. It was decided the witch could not carry the boy
away while trapped inside. The townsmen got ready—with
ropes, machetes, and knives. We were poor people and had
no guns. Two men stood by the trap door, but when they
opened it, what came out was not the witch, but the *onza*,
the animal you have killed. The boy was not to be found.
And the witch? That same night there were men hidden
in the bushes around her house. When the horn of the
moon was hooked around the star, the men saw her come
out. She stood looking, looking, like the night before. Then
suddenly they heard *sh-sh-sh-shoo-oo-oo*, and she was gone,
never to be seen again.

With disbelief, Dobie said to the old man, "You must have felt
pretty bad for torturing a human being so much when it turned out
that an *onza* was to blame?"

With that, the old man took his walking stick and pointed to
the four missing toes, and the holes in the animal's ear flaps. "What
more proof could you ask for?"

Although this story seems foreign to western sensibilities,
in many earth cultures throughout the world, people deemed
witches to have mystical resources not possessed by mere sorcer-
ers or medicine men. Worldwide, witches are viewed as strange
loners who remain at home while their "shadow-soul" travels the
night as an animal. In Africa, the idea of leopard-men and lion-
men—humans that transform themselves into cats and kill with
claws—is well known. Among the ancient culture of the Olmec
of Mexico, there were jaguar shamans or "were-jaguars" whose
shape shifted into jaguars at will. It is not uncommon in indigenous cultures to hear of individuals who allowed the animal's

spirit to inhabit them. The more elusive, the more obscure and nocturnal an animal, the more enigmatic their lives, the greater the power and myths surrounding them.

This surreal narrative, loaded with magic and primeval mystique, is clearly about an enormous mountain lion living in the midst of people with simple lives tied to the knot of the earth. Woven from the unseen, it presents a psychic view of the world as a bridge, through creatures and forces, to the objective world. It is also an account of the death and trapping of an old, beautiful animal that obviously lived large. Tales of witchcraft and shadow-souls lie in contrast to stories about predator pursuits in the old West: stories of wholesale wildlife slaughter. A visit just north of the border tells a different tale from our past.

BEN LILLY

Around a sharp curve along Highway 15 in the Gila National Forest, an inconspicuous road sign captures my attention. "Ben Lilly Memorial" it reads. I'm on vacation for a few days in the Silver City area of New Mexico, returning from the Gila Cliff Dwellings. I know of Ben Lilly from my mountain lion research, but I didn't realize I was in his old hunting grounds. I'm curious what this monument might look like. There's no obvious pull out or parking area, just a wide ditch where the road makes a bend. A narrow use trail marks the unadorned entrance, framed by a tangle of juniper and pines. I walk twenty-five feet and the trail ends at what appears to be a small clearing local teens use for beer parties—a large fire pit and lots of trash. Not exactly a place of honor. Poking around, I find that the trail continues, hidden behind some twiggy Gambel oaks. It takes me along the canyon forest another quarter mile to a view spot overlooking the deep ravines of the Mogollon Mountains. But where is this monument?

Behind me, an enormous granite boulder rests at the hogback's precipice. I climb closer and spot a bronze plaque embedded on its side. A rainbow of spray paint adorns the plaque along with the graffiti artist's initials. Here it is, the monument. At one time, someone carefully and artistically carved a relief of Ben Lilly's head. The plaque sports a serious looking mountain lion to Lilly's left and a smiling bear on his right. Lilly has an eagle eye on the lion, looking sideways. The inscription describes Lilly in glowing terms. Ten years after Lilly's death in December, 1936, J. Stokley Ligon of the United States Biological Survey, a good friend of Lilly's, along with several ranchers and admirers, gathered the funds to erect this memorial—an honorific gravestone overlooking Lilly's haunts where he exterminated hundreds of lions, black bears, and some of the last remaining grizzlies of the Southwest. Today, who knows the name Ben Lilly? Only this forsaken trail to a lonely defaced plaque bears witness to a time in our nation's history when men waged genocidal war on predators.

At one time, the name Ben Lilly was synonymous with a folk hero around these parts. Today, in mountain lion history, he is the go-to figure illustrating the wanton slaughter of lions in the last century. Lilly's legendary lion-killing reputation is unequaled. Killing became his life-long mission and obsession, with a focus on apex predators. He was said to have killed upwards of five hundred mountain lions, six hundred bears, as well as the last grizzly in the Gila Wilderness. Born in 1856 in Alabama, his family moved to Mississippi when he was a young boy, where he enjoyed wandering in the woods for days on end. After the Civil War, his parents sent him to military school at the age of twelve, but he ran away, living by his wits for a time, his whereabouts unknown, until his uncle discovered him working at a blacksmith shop in Memphis and brought him back to Louisiana. His uncle promised to leave him his property if the boy would settle down, work the farm, and marry. Lilly's first wife was a woman he referred to as the "daughter of Sodom and Gomorrah." It was during this time on his uncle's three-hundred-acre farm in the Louisiana bayou, surrounded by unfenced swamps, canebrakes, and woods, that Lilly found his passion for hunting along with extended periods of solitude. He preferred exploring the woodlands to working on the farm. To spend more time and wander farther into the wilderness, Lilly established a moveable camp, taking off for days, sometimes weeks, with as many as twenty-five dogs. This he called his "wild period" when he

Ben Lilly

began developing his woodcraft skills along with his eccentricities. If he returned from hunting wet and muddy, he refused to change or wash. "It's better for the health to let them dry on you," he'd tell his wife. One winter he brought home so many ducks that she ordered him not to bring one more into her kitchen. And after his wife asked him to shoot a hawk that was taking her chickens, Lilly said, "All right." He gathered his gun and didn't return for more than a year. "That hawk kept flying," he told her.

Lilly's most famous possession (of which he had very few) was a hunting knife he carried close on his belt. With his skill as a blacksmith, he fashioned many "Lilly knives" over the years from old files, farrier rasps, automobile springs, and any usable steel he could find. He gave the small ones away as gifts. But his special knife was eighteen inches long, double bladed, with an "S" curve that he tempered with panther oil. He believed this exaggerated shape created more bleeding, giving him the ability to cut his victim deep and in either direction. The knife also served as a kind of machete. The canebrakes, a vast wilderness comprised of thick, tall, cane forests in the early South, stretched for miles on end. These thickets were the last refuge for bears, lions, hogs, and other hunted animals. Lilly ventured into these swamps with only an ax, gun, and knife, cutting his way into an animal's hidden lair. He needed no compass and did not rely on landmarks or the night stars, but instead used an intuitive, animal-like sense of direction. Like a good horse, he could back trail himself through thick swamp, boasting he could stick a knife in a tree in the morning, enter the pathless canebrakes forests, and re-emerge from any direction in the dead of night to retrieve his knife.

He carried a Winchester repeating rifle, practicing his marksmanship on bees and bats, while shooting off the heads of ducks so as not to destroy the meat. Buzzards, cedar waxwings, and the last remaining ivory-billed woodpeckers were also in his sights as target practice. Once, when a local friend needed some meat, Lilly went out with him to hunt squirrels. In a short time, there were twenty-five squirrels in the sack, but Lilly had pounded them with ammunition, putting five or six holes in each for target practice. During those early years in Louisiana, Lilly was just "sharpening his horns," practicing on small animals for the deadly kill on the largest. On his numerous forays into the surrounding woodlands, he exterminated all bears from a wide area in Louisiana. His main objective was to kill bears and cougars. "I never saw a lion I did not kill or wound," was his declaration.

Ben Lilly was a compact, powerful man—all sinew. Five foot nine, he was barrel-chested, wide-shouldered, and built like a lion. His strength was famous in his home state of Louisiana. It was said he had hands "like a ham." A champion athlete, he set local jumping records and amazed townspeople with his horse stunts. One time while after a bear, he lost a shoe in the mud, but he kept running for twelve miles before catching up with the exhausted bear and dogs. He could carry a pack of 125 pounds or heave a four-hundred-pound bear into a wagon bed single-handedly with a rope. By now large predators were scarce in the Louisiana swamps, but that only honed Lilly's hunting skills, as well as his tenacity. "The Boones and the Crockett skimmed the cream," writes Frank Dobie in his biography of Lilly. "Ben Lilly scooped up every drop of splattered milk from the cracks."

At the age of forty-five, in 1901, Lilly called his second wife and three children together, kissed them goodbye, and left them everything he owned except five dollars. He was heading west for a land where the big predators remained. As he moved along, he made money selling bear meat and wild honey. His life philosophy was now well formed. He regarded himself as the policeman of the wild, "a self-appointed leavener of nature." Bears and lions specifically were, by their very nature, evil. Lilly considered it his biblical duty to set things straight by killing these "devil" animals. He had evolved into a religious fanatic, mixed with a special kind of mysticism. His tenacity and obsessiveness molded him into a superb hunter, unmatched in his ability to read track and sign. When he was trailing with his dogs, he forgot to eat and drink, sometimes for days on end. Then he'd gorge himself on his kill and the bit of corn meal he carried with him. He never kept the skins of the animals he killed for himself, considering them a worthless piece of clothing. He was on a mission, and that intensity of focus molded him into an expert woodsman. He had no coat, but piled on layers of shirts. If he was cold, he'd build a fire, push aside the coals, and sleep on the warm ground. At least once a week he bathed in a stream, sometimes breaking away the ice, then rolling in snow to dry off. The air in a town was toxic to him, and when offered a bed, he preferred to sleep outside on the ground with his dogs.

Although a killer whose laser focus was on large predators, Lilly was also a bundle of contradictions. Lilly's zealousness and religious fervor for trailing and killing bears and lions stood in stark contrast to how people described his demeanor. "His voice was so soft and his whole expression so innocent that nobody listening to him and looking at him for the first time would suspect the emphasis and stubbornness he kept in reserve," said Dobie upon meeting Lilly. To the men who knew him, Lilly was a man of complete honesty and character. He never swore, drank, or smoked, and famously rested on Sunday, his holy day. If his dogs treed a cougar on Saturday night, the animal had a stay until Monday morning. But his religious beliefs extended to the supernatural. Lilly's favorite meats were bear and especially lion, which he felt would endow him with exceptional instinct, prowess, and agility to pursue his quarry. He expected no less of his dogs than he did of himself—running them for days without food. He would go out of his way to make sure they had water before he did, took great pleasure in watching them work, and valued a dog's intelligence rather than a specific breed. Yet ultimately, they were simply tools of his trade. If a dog began running trash or quit the trail, he had no need for him, and the dog was beaten or shot to death.

As Lilly traveled west, he left behind a wake of wildlife destruction. But his folk-hero status was growing. While hunting in Texas in 1907, Lilly received a telegram summoning him to a presidential camp on Tensas Bayou for a bear hunt with President Theodore Roosevelt. Lilly, the loner who had no inclination to guide others, was off looking for bear sign when Roosevelt shot his bear that another guide located. Yet he left a great impression on the president, who later wrote about him:

> "I never met any other man so indifferent to fatigue and hardship. The morning he joined us in camp, he had come on foot through the thick woods, followed by his two dogs, and had neither eaten nor drunk for twenty-four hours; for he did not like to drink the swamp water.

It had rained hard throughout the night and he had no shelter, no rubber coat, nothing but the clothes he was wearing and the ground was too wet for him to lie on, so he perched in a crooked tree in the beating rain, much as if he had been a wild turkey."

In 1908, Lilly hunted grizzlies, mountain lions, and black bears in Mexico for three years, sending skeletons and skins back to the Smithsonian Institution. He returned to the United States, entering through the boot heel of New Mexico. Now in his mid-fifties, his predator killing career was waxing as a new era of government eradication programs for predators began. His reputation was widespread, his services were in high demand among ranchers, and he was finally well paid for a passion previously pursued only as a personal vendetta. As he scoured the landscape of these large predators, he noted stock that were dead along the way, some in inaccessible canyons. In his mind, every cattle death was due to predators. He discounted disease, malnourishment, or other causes.

Lilly recounted this story while speaking before a livestock convention in El Paso in 1928. In 1910, while following the tracks of a large brown bear across the Mexican border for several weeks, he re-entered the U.S, waiting for the bear to circle back through its range. On his return, while he was scouting for lion tracks in the area, his young dog ran off into the bushes. Lilly followed thinking the dog was chasing a rabbit, but instead found the pup was being pursued by a female adult lion. Since Lilly had intended to trade his gun for a burro, it had no ammunition. Not being one to let any opportunity to kill a lion pass him by, Lilly ran after the lion, attempting to hit her with his Winchester. The lion broke free, treeing several times while trying to avoid Lilly who was throwing rocks at her. The fifth time she treed, Lilly climbed up the small pine, grabbed the lion's tail, and both fell to the ground in a heap. Even after being harassed, the lion still made an effort to escape, sprinting downhill with Lilly running after her waving a stout stick. "I struck her on the back as she was passing around the top of a small pine log that fell down on the ground. She sprang at me. I struck her over the head with the pine stick and broke the stick in two. She came so fast that I grabbed up a large rock that would weigh about six pounds and held it tight in my hand. I pounded her on the side of her head, and she fell at my feet, apparently dead." Lilly goes on to describe gouging his knife into her and forcing his reticent dog to smell and bite the dead lion. With stories like these, probably highly exaggerated, Lilly added to the mystic of his legend.

Lilly's recounting of a lion he tracked on and off for years illustrates his persistence and tenacity. The lion had an odd track reminiscent of Dobie's onza. "In November 1912, while I was trailing six days behind a grizzly, I saw a female lion's track that was about eight days old. The left front foot of this lion made a five-toed track; she had, I judge, been caught in a trap that pulled one toe out of joint in such a way that it printed two points on the ground. She was being followed by two yearlings. This was in the Blue River country of eastern Arizona." A heavy snow blotted out all track sign, but Lilly came across the unusual five-toed lioness track again, two years later, thirty miles south of his original sighting. The lion was being followed by another set of yearlings. Lilly trailed this five-toed lioness for thirty miles. The family was moving quickly and another deep snow obliterated their evidence. For the next two years, Lilly enquired of every hunter and trapper he met about the five-toed lion, yet none knew of her whereabouts. Lilly never forgot those unusual tracks. Tireless in his pursuit, he waited patiently for his opportunity. This came in 1916, four years after his first encounter, south of Reserve, New Mexico, "a full hundred miles from where I first saw it," says Lilly. "It was pointed in the direction of the original range. It was fresh, and after following it all afternoon I killed the maker of it about sundown."

But again, Lilly exaggerates the tale, as the distance between his first sighting and where he killed the cat in New Mexico is only about thirty miles.

Lilly left behind a few writings on mountain lions. They reveal a close study of his quarry and their natural history, yet many of his conclusions were suppositional, not supported by present-day research. He took meticulous measurements of his kills. He raised lion kittens in order to study them, then killed them when they were grown. He opened up the bowels of every dead lion to learn about their diet. Although a keen observer of nature, he lacked an empathy for its wild things, relating to the natural world by violence. He was a prisoner of his own mental prejudices, unable to view nature as an impartial philosopher, but only through his lens of biblical opposites. It is difficult for us today to understand Lilly's complexities. He was a man who lived so close to the earth—half-wild and instinctual, writing checks on old bones, sleeping with his hounds for warmth—yet killing with such ease and callousness. "One lion family I followed went eight miles with only one stop. The lioness lay down under some rocks; the kittens sucked and played all around her. When I killed her, I saw that she was giving plenty of milk." Frank Hibben, who went out with Lilly on his last hunt at the age of eighty, said he still had "the same insatiable longing" to kill, much like a person who has an insatiable greed for money.

Ben Lilly was unquestionably one of the most destructive figures in North American wildlife history, contributing to the demise of the grizzly bear and the wholesale reduction of mountain lions and black bears in the Southwest. Although a few might think of him as a superb hunter and woodsman, his story is more a lesson in attitude. His lack of true reverence for life is the antithesis of our values of ethical hunting and wildlife conservation—a misguided, warped sense of nature that viewed large predators as "endowed by their very nature with a capacity to wreak evil . . . and should be destroyed." A misshapen, exaggerated product of his era, one could consider Lilly a vessel—a queer, half-crazed man who performed his executions as a service for others, for the government, and in his own mind, for God. Genocidal war on predators had been codified as our nation's God-given right, and Lilly was their proxy.

✎ ALDO LEOPOLD – AT THE CROSSROADS

Ben Lilly's plaque isn't the only one that adorns the Gila National Forest. At the Gila Cliff Dwellings National Monument lies another plaque, this one highly visible, situated directly in front of the visitors' center, honoring Aldo Leopold. Leopold is considered the father of wildlife ecology. His famous book, *A Sand County Almanac*, is hailed as an epic treatise on environmental conservation. In it he formulates the idea of the land ethic—the true connection between people and the natural world.

Leopold came to the Southwest as a young forester, fresh from the Yale Forestry School, during the infancy of the U.S. Forest Service. He was an avid outdoorsman who saw the natural world through the eyes of the narrative of that time—pushing hard to kill all predators "down to the last wolf and lion" in order to preserve deer and protect cattle. During his tenure in the Gila National Forest, he in fact hired Ben Lilly to extirpate predators. But here is where Leopold's story takes a turn, a result of two important events that would profoundly influence his perspective. The first was an irruption of deer in the Gila National Forest in the late 1920s, so severe that it caused massive overgrazing and starvation of the herds. This paralleled another, more famous deer irruption at around the same period, on Arizona's Kaibab Plateau. In both of these cases, the enormous increase in deer herds had been accompanied by intensive trapping and hunting of predators. The second incident occurred when Leopold was a young forester in New Mexico around 1909 while working on the rimrock of Black Canyon. As Leopold watched a wolf pack run through his camp, he fired several shots at a mother wolf and her pup. Climbing down from the rims, he arrived just in time to witness a "fierce green fire dying in her eyes." That moment fostered an epiphany that would take decades to evolve into a philosophy. When Leopold sat down thirty-five years later to gather his essays into a book, he had studied watersheds and erosion, visited Germany's Dauerwalds with their meticulously groomed forests devoid of predators, and had traveled to Mexico's remote Rio Gavalán, a wild landscape where wolves and cougars ran free. "It was here [in the Rio Gavalán] that I first clearly realized that land is an organism, that all my life I had seen only sick land, whereas here was biota still in perfect aboriginal health." In his most famous essay in *A Sand County Almanac*, "Thinking Like a Mountain," using story as parable, Leopold began a new conversation about wildlife and our relationship to the natural world.

> "I realized then, and have known ever since, that there was
> something new to me in those eyes—something known
> only to her and the mountain. I was young then, and full
> of trigger-itch; I thought that because fewer wolves meant
> more deer, that no wolves would mean hunters' paradise.
> But after seeing the green fire die, I sensed that neither
> the wolf nor the mountain agreed with such a view."

The intersection of these two figures, Leopold and Lilly, marked a crossroads in our nation's stance toward predators, which would take many decades to fully evolve. Leopold left the Southwest in 1924, transferring to Madison, Wisconsin, where he taught game management at the University. He died just prior to the publication of *A Sand County Almanac* in 1949.

The Animal Damage Control Act of 1931 officially formalized wildlife extermination with a federal agency, a budget, and a mission to destroy mountain lions, wolves, bobcats, and many others

predators including animals that were considered injurious to agriculture, husbandry, forestry, game, or domestic animals. Bounty
hunters, and a federal bureaucracy, now replaced farmer-colonist
mythical figures like Lilly. Along with these federal efforts, western
states placed bounties on mountain lions that individuals as well as
professionals could collect. In Montana, 1,900 bounties from cougars were collected before the state reclassified them a game animal
in 1963. In Arizona, during the fifty-one years the bounty was in
effect, 7,723 mountain lions were killed. California had more than
12,400 mountain lions turned in for bounty monies between 1907
and 1963.

During the late 1960s and 1970s, a national sea change was
taking place toward predators and wildlife. Possibly the change of
heart had to do with a less rural America, city folk who had not
grown up with the myths of hatred toward cougars, or maybe the
paucity of iconic animals remaining. Some suggest a small group of
dedicated activist women fueled the change; others postulate it was
the rising tide of wildlife research that began to alter the national
conversation—far-reaching thinkers like Rachel Carson, Olaus
Murie, and the Craighead brothers. Yet whatever the causes, a new
era of environmental awareness was ushered in during the second
half of the twentieth century.

Mirroring public opinion, Disney movies like *Charlie, the
Lonesome Cougar* (1967), *Run, Cougar, Run* (1972), and made-for-
television shows like *Lassie, Flight of the Cougar* (1967) and Marlin
Perkins *Wild Kingdom* (1963-1988) brought mountain lions into
people's homes, portraying them not as vicious man-eaters, but
sympathetic animals who raised, loved, and protected their young
just like humans. Miraculously, this force of public opinion transformed the landscape for recovery of the American lion, and within
the course of ten years, all the western states, with the exception of
Texas, reclassified mountain lions as game animals to be managed
with licensed hunts set by state game agencies.

CHAPTER 3

A LANGUAGE
WITHOUT TONGUES

. . . this sleek, amazing animal I often call the Clark Kent
of the mammal world—particularly the carnivore world—
because they really have this meek and mild type of nature.

—TONI RUTH

TONI RUTH'S YELLOWSTONE CLASS

As I left my home for the long, seven-hour drive to Yellowstone, I was grateful that the January morning was clear and dry. I was heading for the Lamar Buffalo Ranch to attend a class with Toni Ruth, a world-renowned cougar expert. In summer, the drive takes just an hour from my house to the Ranch. But in winter, the road is closed, and I'm forced to take the roundabout way via Highway 90 in Montana, a sometimes windy, icy route. Nevertheless, I was willing and excited to make the trip. I'd read several of Ruth's research papers in a large, science-focused anthology entitled *Cougar: Ecology & Conservation*. By now I'd been tracking cougars in winter around my area, and I was eager for more information. I was a novice at knowing where to find tracks, but by luck I would catch them on Cougar Flats fairly frequently. Several times I'd spent half a day following their athletic routes, only to end up in a mess of wolf tracks where I'd lose the cat's trail. I'd caught a cougar

scream on audio one winter night, and I'd accumulated many photos of cougars on my trail camera. I wanted to know more about
these cougar/wolf interactions and how to find tracks more reliably.
What kind of habitat should I look for? What were some clues as
to their presence? Ruth, I figured, could sort out and answer many
of these questions.

Toni Ruth conducted the second of three major cougar studies in Yellowstone National Park. She'd been involved with cougar
research in Florida, Texas, New Mexico, Montana, and Wyoming,
and her research had been highlighted in British Broadcasting
Corporation (BBC) and National Geographic films. While the
first Yellowstone study took place between 1987 and 1996, pre-wolf
days, Ruth's aim was to understand how wolves might be affecting
cougars, since their prey overlap. Working under the auspices of
the Hornocker Wildlife Institute/Wildlife Conservation Society,
Ruth radio-collared eighty-three cougars between 1998 and 2006.
Trudging through the deep Yellowstone snow, Ruth found that
cougars were killing mostly elk, the major prey during the winter months in the northern area of the Park, and that wolves were
scavenging or overtaking approximately twenty percent of cougar-
killed carcasses. Because mountain lions are so elusive, collaring for
the project was done using dogs. Researchers use houndsmen and
their trained dogs for this process. Dogs follow a scent trail, and
then tree the cougar. The scientists follow the dogs, dart the treed
cat with a sedative, lower her down gently, usually with ropes, take
blood samples, process other inspections such as teeth and claws,
and attach the collar.

On our first afternoon, a large stack of snowshoes appeared
outside the Buffalo Ranch's main building. "Find your size and
match 'em up." I'd brought my own, but the Yellowstone Institute
provides snowshoes if you need them. The Institute sits in the center of the Lamar Valley, poised against the low hills that square off
the meadows, with a smattering of cabins laid out in a semicircle.

A community kitchen and classroom are set apart; the bathrooms have the bonus of a heated floor. The valley is one of the coldest, low-lying, open expanses in the Park during the winter. I've taken many classes there. One winter, on a wolf-watching tour, we never left the premises; we woke up at dawn, bundled up in preparation for the sub-zero weather, walked a few hundred yards to a line of spotting scopes, and watched the Druid pack make kills while wolf #302, nicknamed "Casanova," wooed females.

Today only a lone bull bison, his head acting as a giant shovel, plows snow back and forth, exposing the dry grass underneath. Our class, all thirteen of us, pile into the Institute bus headed toward a pullout several miles away. The bus deposits us on a gently sloped open hillside—a connector route to the Garnet Hill loop trail. These trails are rarely used in winter, so we make our own tracks through deep snow downhill. Another bull stands in the distance, but Ruth guides us fifty or more yards away in a wide semicircle. Park rules require a buffer of twenty-five yards from a bison, yet Ruth's caution is well founded. The only time I've ever used my bear spray was on a bison bull during the summer rut.

Huffing and puffing down the bluff in deep snow, we finally meet the trail in the meadow below, although it's barely visible. Bison and elk tracks cover its faint outline. This part of the Garnet Hill route follows Elk Creek alongside steep talus slopes. Wide swaths of willows and alders are winter food for elk and moose; narrow, drier sections house a winter fairyland forest of Douglas fir and Engelmann spruce. I've hiked it many times in summer, but in winter the creek is mostly frozen, easy to cross.

Every so often we have to move a great distance off the trail to let a wandering bison pass. As we enter thicker tree cover, wolf tracks become plentiful. One of the class participants works as a Yellowstone wolf guide. She tells us she thinks these tracks might belong to the Slough Creek pack, their presence signaled by a G.P.S. collar. This is our second day of looking for cougar sign, and so far, no luck. After an hour of hiking, we stop for a rest at the base of a large talus slope so thick it seems the mountain is falling down upon itself. Plopping onto pre-Cambrian gneiss boulders, we pull out snacks as someone asks Ruth about cougar den site locations.

"People watch movies and think of lion dens in caves," says Ruth. "That happens, but more typically, since other animals use caves as well, den sites are in heavy vegetative cover, places that are difficult for predators like wolves or bears to get through."

We move on and the terrain opens away from the creek. We're just trying to keep up with Ruth, who seems ever vigilant for cougar sign. She heads toward higher ground and begins searching close to the rock walls that define this canyon, making for perfect lion habitat. Douglas firs teetering on the uneven icy ground hug the rocky terrain, requiring us to maneuver with our clumsy snowshoes to keep up with her. In and around this maze of trees, Ruth is leading the crowd at a fast clip until she suddenly stops. She's found what she was looking for under an enormous Douglas fir. She bends down to point out some cougar scat that was covered by snow. A scrape is nearby in the soft, exposed dirt.

"The snow is fairly fresh, so the old lion tracks were covered," says Ruth, "but I know this is good puma area, and these large trees are where males like to make scrapes. We're lucky to find some fresh scat here, too." Although Ruth is no longer involved with the day-to-day activities of the current Yellowstone cougar study, she knows the scat will contain valuable genetic information. She shows us how to collect it properly using tweezers. She had worked these prime cougar areas for more than five years, tracking, treeing, and collaring cougars, which gave her confidence we'd find some sign here.

Although we found a scrape and cougar scat, the class still hasn't seen a track. Scrapes are scent marks made most often by male cougars pushing backwards with their hind feet. This motion leaves a depression about a foot long with a small mound of debris

Ruth demonstrates how to properly collect scat

piled at the far end. Sometimes the puma will urinate or defecate on the scraped mound. Our ultimate destination is the Hellroaring Creek trail, then back up to the parking area. Just before the junction, Ruth spots fresh tracks. She moves fast to follow the tracks leading up the steeper slopes of the ravine. Following cougars is an athletic endeavor, and Ruth proves that point. It's hard for the class to keep up with her; as usual, the cougar has traveled all over the folds of the mountainside. I'm beat from a half day of hard snowshoeing, and so I retire to a rock. I'll save my puma tracking for another day. A storm is brewing and I know the hike up Hellroaring Creek trail is a heart pumper. There is no greater silence, or spirit renewal, than a winter day in Yellowstone. I'll take this moment to breathe it in, while my classmates enjoy the thrill of tracking one of the biggest cats in North America.

The following morning, Dan Stahler is our guest speaker. Stahler is the project manager for the current Yellowstone cougar study, but he's had his biologist fingers in many predator studies in the Park, including wolves. He shows us some great trail camera footage. Researchers placed cameras on a cougar scrape along a high rock precipice. It is believed these linear impressions are intended to mark territory as well as attract mates. Their camera caught not only cougars, but scores of other animals investigating these scent marks, including a grizzly bear that laid down on the scrape and napped for the day. This, I saw, was a gold mine of trail camera photos and information. Scrapes were the obvious place to start placing my cameras.

Besides learning about scrapes, the class helped me understand some of the strange behavior I was seeing on my trail camera videos, where cougars lifted their heads and opened their mouths. Cougars, I learned, have a gland on the roof of their mouth called the vomeronasal organ. The gland acts like a vacuum cleaner for smell, drawing interesting scents in for further identification. I also found that cougars are primarily visual creatures, like domestic cats, and that by hanging a shiny object like a CD or pie plate near my trail camera, I might have better luck catching one on film. I went home armed with more cougar information. Up till now, I'd watched for their tracks in the snow and followed them. My new plan was to hunt for scrapes. Now I had a new and powerful tool in my puma toolbox.

✐ MAURICE HORNOCKER

Without a doubt, the most influential cougar researcher, the father of modern cougar science, is Maurice Hornocker. Hornocker began his research in the winter of 1962 in western Montana with the support of the Craighead brothers—twins John and Frank—pioneer researchers of grizzly bears in Yellowstone National Park and inventors of the first radio-telemetry collars. Hornocker's first research capture was a big male cougar. With the aid of two houndsmen, the cat was treed thirty-five miles southeast of Missoula in the

Bitterroot River drainage at dusk. After Hornocker shot his tranquilizer dart into the tom's hip, the cat climbed even higher into an overhanging limb of a giant, old pine. The idea was for young Hornocker to climb the tree and then lower the cat down to the ground with ropes, but midway up the partially dead tree, as night fell, he had second thoughts. "This is crazy, it's dark, the wind is howling, you are a novice tree climber, and a partially (if at all) tranquilized mountain lion awaits you seventy feet above the ground."

The next morning, Hornocker re-tranquilized the cat, but when he climbed up to reach the cat and swung a rope around his leg, the half-drugged tom "came alive. Letting loose a deafening growl, he swung his huge head around the tree trunk not three feet from my face. Eyes blazing and fangs bared, he lurched his body, attempting to move from the fork." On impulse, Hornocker grabbed the cat's rope-like tail, launching him into space. The cat fell, unharmed, onto a snow drift below. Hornocker brought the cat back to his holding facilities and used the animal to develop handling techniques. After a month of tests, he released him back into the wild. Two years later, that Bitterroot River tom was killed by a hunter not far from where he was captured. "When I learned of his death I felt a real loss—he truly was a research pioneer."

The first winter of research, Hornocker tagged and tattooed thirteen lions, but by the following spring, nine of the subjects in his research area were killed by bounty hunters. Hornocker moved his study to the remote, roadless wilderness known as the Idaho Primitive Area (now re-named and protected as The Frank Church—River of No Return Wilderness Area). During the first five years, Hornocker and houndsman Wilbur Wiles trailed, treed, ear-tagged, and then followed their subjects through dense forest, steep mountainous terrain, and deep snows for more than twelve hundred miles each winter. Radio telemetry hadn't been perfected yet. The two men shot one elk and two deer during the hunt season each fall, cached the meat in various areas around their two hundred-square-mile study area where it would stay frozen, and used it for food during their long, bitter cold winter of work. The second five years of their ten-year study, when they were joined by researcher John Seidensticker, the team applied groundbreaking radio collars—the first to be used on mountain lions. Through the use of telemetry, the mysterious veil of lions' lives began to lift, revealing the enormous home ranges of toms, whose territories span mountains and deep river bottoms, while circumscribing several female ranges. The myths of hordes of lions described in Zane Grey's 1924 book *Roping Lions in the Grand Canyon*—"we stumbled onto a lion home, the breeding place of the deadly cougar canyon."—was dispelled by rigorous research and analysis. The team also surveyed deer and elk, and lions' food intake. After ten years, they found that, not only do mountain lions maintain their own numbers, they also exert a positive force on deer and forest health. Hornocker's groundbreaking research became a persuading influence for many western states to reclassify lions as big game with hunting quotas and hunting seasons. Considered the father of mountain lion research, Hornocker also set the stage for other studies throughout the western states using the same methodology. As G.P.S. technology became more prevalent and affordable, the last ten years has seen a burst of new information and insight into the lives of mountain lions.

WHAT IS A SCRAPE

Biologist Max Allen and his colleagues worked on analyzing puma scrapes in California's Santa Cruz Mountains and Mendocino County. Allen put up trail cameras on puma scrapes, hoping to find answers to research questions. How are cougars using scrapes to communicate? Why do they go to such elaborate means, rather than simply urinating as canines do? Allen set up the experiment with variables—a physical scrape accompanied by puma urine;

Cougar using a Flehmen response to take in smells more deeply

just puma urine; and a control site where he patted the ground with his gloved hand. He found that pumas were much more likely to investigate the scrape sprinkled with urine, rather than his patted dirt or the urine alone. When checking areas that had no physical scrape, pumas were equally as likely to spend time smelling his gloved pat as the puma urine. This suggested to him that pumas need the visual sign of a physical scrape to find the olfactory signal. Since pumas are primarily visual creatures, his findings made perfect sense. After analyzing more than one thousand videos of scraping behavior, he concluded that lions could distinguish not only the freshness of scrapes, but also the individual lions who made them. This knowledge is only an icebreaker; biologists are still in the dark as to what information cougars learn from scrapes.

A new and interesting finding of Allen's involved a type of inter-species communication. Scrapes, urine and feces deposits, and rolling and cheek rubbing are well known to be intra-species communications, in other words, ways in which animals communicate with others of their own kind. But Allen found gray foxes using puma scrapes in a rather odd way. Besides marking scrape sites with their own urine, foxes were also routinely cheek rubbing on puma scrapes, and doing this more frequently on the fresher ones. Cheek rubbing releases chemicals from the sebaceous gland, allowing animals to deposit their own scent, but it can also be a way of accumulating scent from the object rubbed. Since the fox cheek-rubbing visits didn't correlate with fox breeding season, or with how recently other foxes had visited, Allen believes foxes were applying puma scent for protection from larger predators like bobcats and coyotes. In other words, foxes, being the crafty animals they are, were attempting to *disguise* themselves as pumas.

For his studies, Allen sought out community scrapes. Community scrapes signal that a conversation is taking place between two or more animals. These community scrapes are placed at either high traffic sites or in a natural amphitheater where females will go to caterwaul, letting a male know she's receptive. Anna Kusler, a graduate student researcher at Pace University working with Panthera's Teton Cougar Project (PTCP), called high traffic areas "movement paths." "Over time the animals will learn those," she told me, ". . . a huge prominent spruce, for instance, fifty yards from the base of an exit, or an up and down corridor along the cliff line. Everybody gets it. They want to know who's there, nobody wants to be in the dark. They want to know the last time one of their neighbors came through. Are they healthy? Are they looking to mate or not? These are communication areas." Kusler said she even observed cougars who didn't overlap in time using the same pathways and scrape trees, even though the two cougars had never known one another.

After my class with Toni Ruth, I began to look for these scrapes in earnest. Ruth had indicated that these scent behaviors were typically under large, mature trees, which made sense, because in winter they would remain fairly dry, allowing for that visual sign to stay in place. Cougar Flats is comprised chiefly of limber pines—pines that are short and stout—with a sprinkling of large Douglas firs. I was now on the look-out for firs with a snow-free base that contained scrapes.

It was a grey morning harboring a light snowfall when I decided to investigate a broad, shallow basin, slightly hidden by a hillside

Male making a scrape

of dense limber pine. The hollow sits five hundred feet below the rocky flats where I found my first cougar print. The deer trudged an obvious path through deep snow down the forested hillside into the open area. By May, snowmelt creates an ephemeral pond, often large enough for Koda to swim in, but in summer the pond is dry clay. This meadow basin, fringed with rock, pines, and aspens, sports an impressive Douglas fir at its southern limit. I walked over to explore the dry duff its limbs protect from winter snows. Several enormous fallen branches were scattered around its drip edge, concealing the tree base from the adjacent meadow. There, beneath the tree's stout frame, I found what I was looking for—a distinct linear depression about twelve inches long with a small mound of fir needles and duff at one end. Approximately one foot away from the scrape was a covered hump of dirt. Moving the soil a bit, I saw several older cougar scats making this an unmistakable "latrine." This is where I set up my trail camera.

Max Allen was working his study in an area where only two large predators—cougars and black bears—reside within a horde of mesocarnivores. Obviously, Allen's study results cannot simply be laid on top of an ecosystem like Yellowstone, where wolves, bears, and pumas compete with each other for similar food, with black bears and grizzlies being the most common usurpers of puma kills. Pumas are subordinate in ecosystems with these top predators.

I checked my camera several times over the course of that winter and spring. The scrape attracted several cougars, one bobcat, and a few resident squirrels. A serious of photos revealed a male cougar courting a female, generously making scrapes, following her around like a puppy dog. Bears would have been asleep at that time, and there were no signs of coyotes, wolves, or foxes.

We don't have gray foxes here, but we do have red ones. Since the wolf reintroduction, I believe my valley's red fox population has rebounded, based on my own anecdotal evidence and the number of sightings. I've spotted evidence of their presence frequently—in person, as tracks, on my trail cameras—yet I've never seen a red fox on puma scrapes.

As a biologist, naturalist, and tracker par excellence, Mark Elbroch prides himself on getting to know his study animals intimately. Elbroch is the lead scientist for Panthera's Puma program. His background includes a doctoral degree that focused on puma research in Patagonia, a CyberTracker certificate for his work tracking lions in Kruger National Park, and ten books he authored or co-authored, including several on tracking. In the world of biology, he's known as "the Indiana Jones of puma research." Interestingly, for all the field work he's done with large cats, Elbroch himself is allergic to the felines.

Elbroch told me that, during his time on the PTCP in Jackson, Wyoming, he had never noticed a red fox scenting on a scrape either. Footage from my trail camera reveals that a fox, sidling up to a carcass, appears nervous and watchful, but also a bit careless and oblivious to human scent. Elbroch wonders if they might even be following pumas around in wintertime, since foxes seem to locate a cougar kill so quickly. On the PTCP, with the advantage of G.P.S. collars, Elbroch might, for instance, see a cougar make a kill at 4:00 a.m., and he would be at the site by 8:00 a.m. When the crew arrived, there'd be a fox on it already. Foxes take great risks, he told me, and, incredibly, they are rarely killed. In the five years he did field work on the Teton study, he might have seen three or four foxes killed by a lion.

Like its gray counterpart in California, would a red fox learn to use puma scent to avoid coyotes in an ecosystem that also has wolves? I wondered. Wolves chase pumas off kills, almost more for the "cat/dog" enjoyment, but they will consume the carcass. Might a puma scent, in an ecosystem of abundant megapredators, be an attractant instead of a deterrent?

I hunted around the old Douglas fir tree, pushed my way through a budding aspen forest into wind-stunted limber pines near the rims. Several smaller scrapes were visible under the trees. This, I assumed, was what Allen called a "community of scrapes." I ducked my head while traveling through the trees until the trail opened onto a rim of exposed rock and cliff edge. With the river below, this precipice faces stair-step terraces across a narrow gorge.

Every time I checked my camera, I made the short trek through the aspens and stunted pines to the bluff's edge. Just before emerging into the open, coursing around the last limber pine, old bones from an elk are scattered around, a reminder of who reigns here, the ghost king of the mountains. The perch of rock where I can easily and safely stand is a small seam boxed by vertical walls. Countless times I've stood there just to glance across the narrow gulch, to take in the endless expanse of rock, mountain, and sky. On this day, though, as I emerged from the trees, I saw a mountain goat on the other side of the chasm; a billy feeding on a ledge halfway down. It took no effort to imagine a puma slinking at the top of the mesa, eyeing that goat, settling into a crouch, ready to spring the fifteen feet in one graceful leap. I looked down at my feet glued to the flattened boulder beside the vertical drop, and there, gleaming back up at me, was an arrowhead. Obviously, another hunter had been here, along with my phantom cat, a few thousand years ago, and the mystery of this place was palpable once again.

CHAPTER 4

THE TWENTY-SEVEN-MILLION-ACRE EXPANSE OF WONDER

Unseen, you haunt the shadows
of these humped and weathered
slickrock hills—sinuous
channels choked with roots
and fallen spalls, caves,
crumbling monoliths,
gnarled and silent trees,
the obscure domain
of rattlesnakes
and staring figures
pecked on stone.

The canyon's hush
Turns dense; my nape hairs
bristle as I sense your eyes
are on me.

Only a moment—
then the disembodied stare
withdraw, as though
some ancient, waning power
had turned away
and sheathed its claws.

—LYNNE BAMA

JACKSON, YELLOWSTONE, AND HOME EAST

My valley sits on the edge of an extensive ecosystem where the natural dance of predator and prey still takes place. Yellowstone is the centerpiece, a primeval zone—primeval except for the four million visitors every year. But wildlife is essentially untouched by human development, hunting, or supplemental feeding. That makes the area a perfect refugia.

Fanning out beyond Yellowstone's boundaries, millions of acres of protected wild lands unroll in every direction, yet these dollops of federal forests and grasslands butt up against ranches, trophy homes, housing developments, and towns big and small. Outside of Yellowstone's invisible line, wolves and cougars are pursued during specified hunt seasons; grizzly bears, on the verge of being hunted, are moved from one drainage to another for misdemeanors and crimes such as killing cattle or breaking into garbage receptacles.

What's most amazing about this Rocky Mountain terrain is its topographic and ecological diversity, formed through eons by ocean, ice, and fire. Permanent snowfields tumble down thousands of feet, metamorphosing from scree into forest to the broken country of high desert. Jagged young volcanic mountain ranges transition to the oldest rock on earth in the Beartooth Mountains. These rich environments allow wildlife to travel elevationally with the seasons, and they also supply the variety of cover and habitat suitable for the different predators' needs.

Two major mountain lion studies are being conducted in the Greater Yellowstone Ecosystem—one in the Jackson area by Grand Teton National Park, and the other in Yellowstone National Park itself (see map in frontispiece). It would seem that two studies so close together would provide similar data, yet each area has distinct features, ungulate patterns, and human interferences. Navigating the data maze requires an understanding of an area's topography, prey composition and movement, as well as a knowledge of prime cougar habitat and its relation to wolves, elk, and deer.

During harsh winters, the elk herd in Yellowstone's Northern Range provides the only food for large predators. The elk herd uses the northern limits of the Park boundary, which includes Lamar Valley, but especially the broad grasslands that border the Yellowstone River corridor toward Gardiner. The majority of the herd— more than 60 percent—migrate outside the Park into Paradise Valley. Excellent cougar habitat exists along the Black Canyon of the

Yellowstone and its affiliated drainages, while wolves, the coursing predators, use the expanses of the adjacent frozen winter grasslands.

Deep snow at high elevations forces ungulates to migrate lower down, compressing the whole predator/prey dance into smaller areas. As spring arrives, elk drop their calves in the tall grass and begin to disperse across the landscape for their spring migration, surfing the green wave, following new shoots of grass and forbs into higher elevations. Bears emerging from winter dens bring a new top predator into the competitive mix for cougars. In her Yellowstone study, Toni Ruth found that bears visited 50 percent of cougar kills and bumped cougars off approximately half of those. But her study focused mainly on the effects wolf reintroduction had on cougars. Her primary finding was that the cats shifted to more complex terrain to mitigate direct interference from wolves, and that wolves pushed cougars off kills more frequently in winter when the competition and congestion between the two predators was highest.

In the PTCP in the Jackson area, lead scientist Mark Elbroch discovered several shifting effects on mountain lions as the wolf population increased. When the study began in 2000, there were nine wolves in the Jackson research area comprising nine hundred square miles (2,300 square kilometers). By 2012, the wolf population had increased to ninety-one. The Jackson study provided a perfect opportunity to see what effects the return of a top predator, after almost eighty years, would have on cougars, a subordinate carnivore that had previously ruled the roost with its rival absent.

Jackson is covered by deep snow in the winter. More than a century ago, elk migrated as far south as the Red Desert, but in the late 1800s, when the town of Jackson sprang up, houses, cultivated pastures, and wire fences blocked their migration route. Warm winters increased the size of the herds, which spent the season in the valley, but harsh winters killed thousands. A particularly harsh winter in 1889-90 killed twenty thousand elk out of a herd of fifty thousand. These cycles continued until finally, during the winter of 1909, after three harsh winters in a row, the townspeople had had enough. Elk were wandering into town, invading ranches and haystacks, and dying in such droves that one resident exaggerated the travesty saying, "It was possible to walk at least two miles stepping on elk carcasses without ever putting a foot on the ground."

Through a multitude of efforts—private, state, as well as an act of Congress—land was put aside to house and feed the elk throughout the winter. Over a span of one hundred years of supplemental feeding, the elk have lost their innate migration memory. Today, up to ten thousand elk gather each winter on the National Elk Refuge and several state-run feeding grounds along the Gros Ventre River in the study area, milling around, waiting for bales of hay to be spread across the ground each day. Wolves and cougars share many of those same spaces, selecting their opportunity. In all, twenty-three of these feed grounds exist in northwest Wyoming. In 2015, when the Bridger-Teton National Forest re-permitted the Alkali feed ground in the Gros Ventre valley, the acting Forest Service Supervisor, Kathryn J. Conant, put their rational succinctly. "Elk feeding sites have been strategically placed on and near national forest system lands with the intent of preventing elk migration through private lands that are located in historic big game winter range."

Deer, on the other hand, have maintained their age-old routes and so migrate out of the Jackson study area during the winter into drier country further south. When spring arrives, they re-emerge in the valley, dispersing in tree cover and higher open areas. Jackson cougars do not follow the deer or elk, preferring to save energy and let the wildlife migrate into the area, but they are also limited because of the lack of abundant cliff-type protection they prefer. This makes areas like the Gros Ventre River corridor feedlots, which offer cover as well as good hunting opportunities—prime cougar real estate.

Similar to what Ruth documented in her Yellowstone research, mountain lions in Jackson were also seeking out different home range habitat as the wolf population increased. These home range areas had only one safety attribute—distance from wolves. Wolves, called coursing predators, run elk in open areas; cougars are ambush predators who need cover, waiting for elk to move into the trees nearby. Choosing between good prey habitat, while at the same time seeking refuge from wolves, became more difficult as the wolf population grew, especially for female cougars with young. Males have the luxury of choosing home ranges farther from the open areas that wolves use. This is because males have very large home ranges—from seventy-five to two hundred square miles—that encompass several females' ranges. And males do not have the same calorie needs as nursing females or females traveling with kittens. Females, who have smaller home ranges—averaging forty to eighty square miles that may overlap with ranges of other females—found themselves juggling between increased hunting opportunity *and* safety from wolves.

My backyard shares the Absaroka Range with Yellowstone Park's eastern edge, and I'm just a five-hour drive from Grand Teton National Park, but my valley's physical features and winter wildlife couldn't be more different from these two areas. Yellowstone's brutal winters drive the game to find refuge north and east of the Park. My valley hosts a Yellowstone migratory herd of more than two thousand elk. The volcanic Absaroka Range, the Park's eastern high ridges, form a rain shadow, creating light snow cover. The elk herd arrives as the snow deepens in December and early January. Deer, ever faithful to their migration routes, come down from the Park's high country in October and stay till April when they head back into the Park, sometimes as far as Hayden Valley. The elk, too, vacate my valley around mid-April or early May, depending upon the snow pack higher up, to surf that green wave back into the Park.

This all means that there are several distinct differences between my valley and the two nearby research areas: I have both deer and elk during the winter; the prey animals are following their natural migration instincts as opposed to being fed supplementally in Jackson; there is good wolf habitat where the elk feed in open areas, and there are excellent bifurcated ridges, cliff edges, and craggy, tight drainages preferred by deer and cougars. But in my valley, cougar hunting is allowed throughout the winter, from September through March, with a much higher quota than Jackson has. The Jackson hunt area has a quota of three cougars; hunt area #19, a large mountainous region that includes my valley, has a quota of twenty cougars. I wanted to explore how my topographic recipe panned out for cougar/wolf interactions, compared with the Jackson and Yellowstone study. Although I'm "just over the fence" from these two study areas, I was told repeatedly that results from one system cannot be applied to another area. Each requires its own study, an expensive proposition. Yet truths can be gleaned from the research relative to cougar behavior, and I intended to delve as deeply as I could with the limited resources I had—my feet and my observational powers. But first, I needed to begin at the beginning: I needed to know what a cougar kill looks like, and how and where to find one. Winter wolf kills are abundant around the valley. They are easy to locate by scanning the winter skyline for magpies, ravens, or golden eagles circling above or gathering on trees. Cougars, though, meticulously cover their carcasses, hiding them under tree cover, in an attempt to avoid all those thieves. After Ruth's class, I started combing Cougar Flats to learn more about cougar kills.

WHAT A KILL LOOKS LIKE

A well-worn deer trail cuts a track into a canyon toward the frozen creek bottom. A light cloud cover obscures the winter sun, and a cold wind freezes my fingers and nose. I'm wheeling around limber pines and juniper bushes, occasionally stopping to pick a few berries to munch on. After several hard freezes, the soft purple berries of the junipers express a sweet and pungent taste that I've developed a fondness for. Besides a handful of swollen rose hips, too mushy for my palette, these berries are the only things worth munching on this time of year.

A lone Townsend's solitaire, watching the landscape from his high perch atop a Douglas fir, gives his persistent bell-like call. The monotonous tone rings across the granite slabs, eliciting a return call far in the distance. The bird cherishes these juniper berries in winter like I do. In these high elevations, the solitaire is among only a handful of small birds that hang on in winter. Chickadees, forever friendly, inquisitively fly lower to watch me from hanging branches. Their indefatigable cheeriness brings a reminder of simple pleasures into this raw winter landscape. Nuthatches also brave out the cold. In winters with deep snow, I've even seen both birds disappear and descend to lower elevations.

To my right is the wooded slope of the hillside, and to my left lies a layered cake of sandstone ledges with crevices stair stepping to the flat mesa above. Koda's nose seems to be in high gear, as he suddenly peels off and heads for a low, hidden bench in the rock structure. Following the dog, I squeeze through the rib of sandstone contours, where I encounter a level shelf about the size of a double bed. Koda's hard at work already chewing on a piece of leathery hide. This is my first look at a mountain lion kill. Although it's obviously old, it has all the tell-tale signs that I learned about in Toni Ruth's class: a covered mound of pine needles and dirt, hair that is sheered as if by a scissors, and a few deer leg bones left. It's instructive, for once I've seen the distinct signs with my own eyes, it's hard to forget what a cougar kill site looks like.

An obligate carnivore, sometimes called a hypercarnivore, cougars, like all felids, eat only meat, placing them in an elite category with polar bears, crocodiles, and great white sharks, among others.

As I examined this old kill site, I remembered a few things to look for. First, lions will generally cover their kills with grass and surrounding brush. Covering their kills probably helps preserve the freshness of the meat, as well as deterring scavengers. Especially with a larger kill, mountain lions like to eat and then rest nearby, which means a latrine could be near the carcass. Remembering Toni Ruth's instructions from class, I looked around the area and found an old cougar latrine nearby, covered as well. If you think like a cat, you have to think fastidiously.

Cougars enter their kill through the rib cage and start with the organ meat, which is rich in nutrients. Big cats, along with their small domestic cousins, lost the ability somewhere in evolutionary time to convert carotenoids like beta carotene into Vitamin A, so they have to obtain it directly from these nutritious organ meats. Large cats in captivity, if not fed some form of Vitamin A, develop respiratory and digestive tract infections, blindness, incoordination, listlessness, and other severe problems. Cougars pluck the fur off their prey before they start to eat, usually leaving the fur in a fairly neat (of course!) circle. Lastly, cougars and all cats kill by making precise bites to the back of the neck or the skull.

Once you've seen an intact cougar kill, distinguishing it from a wolf kill is fairly easy. Wolves and other canines like coyotes and foxes rip at the hair and skin, leaving a large mess. Of course, sometimes wolves will steal a cougar kill, and then it's hard to tell who the initial culprit was. Canines can carry bones off to far-away places. I once saw a coyote trotting along with an elk leg in her mouth, headed for her den site a quarter-of-a-mile away.

After that first experience of finding a puma kill, I began questing in earnest for more old or new kill evidence. I scoured all the draws of the mesa, discovering loads of covered mounds under trees, mainly in the wrinkled skirts of the numerous minor contours and folds. Most of them were probably years and years old, undisturbed after dozens of winters of deer activity on the flats, yet they were

Under trees, the tell-tale leftovers of a cat kill

instructive. Most of these old kills still had parts of leg bones. Lacking grinding surfaces on their premolars and molars, felids are not adapted for bone chewing, often leaving the limb bones, vertebrae, and skulls, as well as pieces of skin of larger prey uneaten. Particular drainages had more kills than other areas, leading me to believe these were deer corridors, and that the rocky, short overhangs above these finger-size gullies contained perfect ambush spots for the lion. After uncovering many ancient disintegrated kills, all of them deer, I emerged from a ravine to find a fairly fresh elk kill in open meadow. The carcass was within fifty feet of the tree line, and it appeared other predators had visited it. I couldn't be sure, but it did have some of the telltale signs of a cougar kill. It wasn't covered, but the fur had been sheared off, not torn; it lay all in one piece, not scattered, and the debris around it appeared as if it could have been covered, then uncovered. Two distinct puncture holes were on the collar bone, another sign of cougar predation. The scene recalled something Toni Ruth relayed to me about her research in Yellowstone. In those early days after wolf reintroduction, as the wolf population was increasing, and then peaked, not only did the elk population begin to decline, but also the calf to cow ratio, leaving fewer small prey for cougars. It's risky for cats to have to kill larger prey, in terms of injuries to the cat, but also because larger kills often end up out in the open where there's more possibility for detection. This means not only loss of calories, but also conflict with wolves.

"As the calf to cow ratio declined," Ruth told me, "we did see more adult elk showing up in cougar kills. And those adult elk kills tended to be more out in the open and at lower slopes, perhaps because the chase was downhill or the struggle ended up coming out of the forested landscape into the open. Those kills were more likely to be detected by avian scavengers, which then the wolves keyed in on. For some of those large kills, we had grizzly bears, as well as wolves, showing up fairly rapidly. These large kills were in contrast to something smaller that is easier for the cougar to drag into cover, or to make the kill in cover and stay where it can really be concealed."

I also found many curious deer kills that appeared as if a hunter had skillfully taken his knife and skinned the animal. By the time I found these carcasses, they were picked clean, but the rib cage had been chewed through. These kills puzzled me. No hunter would leave the carcass. At one point, I read that a lion will take its sharp claw and skin a deer like a surgeon's knife would.

When I could find fresh tracks, I started combining my cat tracking with some of these new insights. One day I was wandering the deer trails that traverse the layers of the limestone mountain that cozies against my house. I fondly call this tree-studded, layer-cake-of-a-mountain Turtle Rock because its exposed, steep, amphibian-like buttress swims with its head facing east. The snow was fresh from the previous night's storm, and in a small hollow, I encountered perfect mountain lion tracks. Cougar tracks always call for a change of course. Instead of following an easy deer switchback trail to the next level, I followed the tracks that beelined up the steep slope to a bench above, the last before the trees melt into full-on scree toward the summit. Enormous boulders, remnants of the rocky rims, lie scattered among open fir trees. The cat had chosen a route along the rim edge where she could see below and beyond while remaining hidden beneath a boulder. The terrace is a favorite pass-through for wildlife, who circle under the cover of dwarfed firs into the next valley. When I spotted tracks of several wolves veering towards the cat tracks, I wasn't surprised, as wolves will follow elk through this forest. Were the wolves pushing the cat?

After trailing the lion tracks that were occasionally obliterated by a pack of wolf tracks through numerous terraces, I discovered that the entire track mélange ended surprisingly close to my cabin in the nearby woods in dense brush. Amid the thicket, I found a deer kill, fairly fresh. I assumed the cougar had killed the deer and was quickly pushed off by the wolves. I'd missed the entire drama, which had occurred in the dead of night while I slept nearby, although I could read part of the story in the tracks. It is apparent that wolves have their eyes more on the cat than the kill. Chalk it up to the age-old cat/dog rivalry. Tracking cougars in winter, I found this to be a common scenario. One day I was tracking a cougar for several hours, only to find his prints disappear in a mess of wolf tracks. When I asked veteran tracker Jim Halfpenny about it, he told me to look up in the trees next time. That's where I might find the cougar.

⇜ THE BATHROOM TRAPPER

We're having a record year for snowfall, five-foot drifts of powder, and all my usual haunts have been cut off from hikes for now. I watched a buck yesterday expend hundreds of calories working his way through snow above his belly. He walked as if wounded, his struggle massive. With a tough winter like this, there is sure to be a lot of winter die-off of deer. In early spring, when the warmth melts patches of snow, and the green grass pushes through soft earth, deer hungrily zero in on these shoots, leaving the forbs alone. Yet a game warden told me that for the first two weeks, these new grasses are nutrient deficient, and the deer—already weakened—will starve, dying like flies. It's hardest on the fawns. A lot of winter die-off means a surplus of food for emerging bears.

One morning I awoke to find a moose and her calf standing outside my front window. I'd cut a path with my snow blower from the front door down the long driveway. The cow walked in the clearing until she encountered a soft wall of drifted snow. Now she was on her own. The cow and her calf stalled by my picture window, pondering a route, then plunged ahead into the deep drifts with ease, her long legs acting like four ski poles, her calf close behind. Moose were made for this kind of weather.

I decided to check my trail camera that's set up on the scrape in Cougar Flats. It's an easy two-mile hike to the camera, even on the foulest winter day. I load my pack and drive out to the parking area that houses the only restroom for miles around. The county keeps the parking lot plowed just for that reason. But they haven't been here this winter, and snow is piled several feet high, which means I have to park on the other side of the road a few hundred feet down.

The deer and elk have trudged a fairly deep trail that Koda and I follow through the parking lot. The journey from the parking area to the flats below, circling around trees and down a rocky slope, always has the deepest drifts. I expect that when I reach the lower mesa, where the viewscape widens, the wind will have blown the short-grass meadow clear. From there it's an easy haul to the land of rock and sky, where among those granite knobs I typically set a course to look for cougar tracks. But today these deep wildlife ruts are not leading toward the outcroppings. Instead they make a beeline toward the river, a steep five hundred feet to the partially frozen passage, with a treacherous trail up the other side. I've hiked the track when the ground is dry and clean and the creek is low in the fall. I'm not doing it today. I've got my information: the animals are staying close, the drifts too big; they are confined to moving back and forth by the highway, using the river crossing as cover, relying on the asphalt edges to heat and melt the snow, revealing the dry grasses. The deer are simply circling—highway to meadow to river to highway—finding resting spots in the cover of trees.

Koda and I turn around. I'm frustrated because the snow has not hardened up to make any route doable. We follow our same tracks back until Koda lags. When I call him, I notice he's making his own trail in a completely different direction. He's ten years old now, and has a bad front leg, but none of this deters him. He's exerting great effort to swim through the deep snow toward something he smells. There's another bench above, and we just saw a handful of deer, but I'm certain he's not interested in them. When Koda is doggedly following his nose, I always defer, for I know he will lead me to wonderful surprises. Yet I'm a bit worried he might be smelling a baited trap.

Several years ago, there was a man who trapped bobcats right near the parking area, just one hundred feet from the only winter public restroom between here and Cody. He was a lazy trapper who placed his traps all along the highway, north and south of the bridge, for miles on end. He created two trap sets near here. One he placed under a large fir by the main game trail. That trail doubled as the sole use trail to the tableland below, the one I took today. The other set he placed in a hollow on the mesa above, where Koda was now heading. Bobcat trapping season is long—pretty much all winter—and there are no fixed limits by the Game and Fish Department. At that time, prices for bobcat pelts were soaring, mostly due to demand for coats in Russia and China, with a pelt in prime condition fetching as much as $1,000. When prices are inflated due to demand, there are many more trappers—experienced and novice—setting leg-hold traps. One tree had a jackrabbit hanging as bait,

A trap set outside of Moab on a tourist dirt road that I released Koda from.
Trap is to the right of Koda.

as well as invisible scents that trappers sprinkle around, and every time Koda and I passed by, the dog wanted to lunge for the rabbit. And each time I had to command Koda to stay back. The trapping trick is to nail rabbit parts to the tree with the leg-hold trap placed directly in front of it, covered with dirt and snow. A shiny object, like a tin can cover, hangs on an outer branch as a visual cue. Cats are visual creatures. The shiny stimulates the curious cat.

It's difficult for a person unfamiliar with these traps to discern how to release his pet from one. I had practiced beforehand, and, in fact, had to release Koda from one once when we were hiking outside Moab, Utah. Trappers are required to check their traps every seventy-two hours, and during that time, animals can freeze to death or gnaw off their legs trying to release themselves.

This man, who I now thought of as the *Bathroom Trapp*er, was lazy. I started tripping that trap every time I passed it. I was tired of corralling my dog, and I was angry at this symbol of abuse. I'd seen fewer and fewer bobcat tracks over the years, and hardly any bobcat sightings. Bobcats were being killed off for greed and some foreigner's coat. This particular trap now became the focus of my resentment. Soon I wasn't just tripping the trap, I was stopping to pee outside the tree's drip line to deter wildlife.

Ultimately the day of reckoning arrived for my monkey-wrenching activities. One morning, as I began my usual rounds into Cougar Flats, I put down my personal deterrent near the tree, tripped the trap, and then continued on my way. But on my return, I noticed the trap was reset. That could only mean one thing: the trapper had come by to check his traps while I was out on my hike. I saw his large footprints, and his truck sat in the parking area. I headed home knowing that since no one else hikes this area in winter, that trapper saw my vehicle, assumed I was the one giving him endless headaches, and probably wrote down my license plate. Sure enough, a week later the game warden paid me a visit to issue a $250 ticket.

You see, I was in the wrong for touching the trap, or even for releasing any non-target animal such as an eagle or deer. Although people are allowed to release livestock or a pet, Wyoming law dating back to the 1800s protects the trapper. I knew that, and I was willing to pay the consequences, but I told the game warden that I thought the trapper should at least trap "ethically," meaning that his traps shouldn't be set next to a public restroom and trail. Apparently the *Bathroom Trapper* did move on; he wasn't there the following winter, although legally he could trap right next to that bathroom if it pleased him. But for all the times I'd sprung his trap over the years, the game warden told me that what had bothered this trapper most was that I'd peed by the trap. Is urinating in the great outdoors considered tampering with a trap? Wyoming law states that it is illegal to *"Intentionally tamper with or remove a trap or snare; or release or remove a furbearing animal or predator from a trap or snare that is set . . ."* Nothing about urinating.

I now had a personal vendetta against trapping. When the Game and Fish Commission reviewed trapping laws at a meeting in Cody one spring, I chose to voice my opinion. The Commission only discusses trapping laws every three years, so now was the time. It's a formal meeting, recorded in its entirety, and you have to be on the list beforehand to speak. Once your name is called, you're "on"—in front of a microphone. It was all a bit intimidating.

Interestingly, I was the only speaker who did not represent a group—either the Trappers Association or a conservation group. That alone seemed to command the commissioners' attention. I'd already figured out it was no use to argue before the Wyoming Game and Fish Commission for a ban on trapping. That's like arguing for prohibition all over again. I voiced my opinion for a few "minor" reasonable changes—like some visible flagging to indicate a trap or snare (I know plenty of people who've gotten their foot caught in a trap hidden under dirt), and a quota on bobcats. Even the head of the Houndsmen Association, whose members hunt bobcats with hounds, just like cougars are hunted, argued for a quota or a temporary moratorium. He saw, as did I, that bobcats were becoming scarcer, meaning they were being trapped out. Trappers of old used to know their territory, and, since their livelihood depended on it, they were careful not to kill off their opportunity. They were also not running 150 miles of trap lines. No snowmobiles either. They snowshoed in to check their lines. Most of the trappers today take any bobcat, not just males. When one pelt is worth $300 or more, greed sets in.

A representative from the Jackson group Wyoming Untrapped spoke at the meeting. The group's approach has been to start small and try to make minimal changes. Because of this, they asked that only one very high-use trail in the Jackson area—a trail used by dogs and hikers and little children all winter—be designated off-limits to trapping. One trail in the entire state of Wyoming. The commissioners politely listened to every speaker, and then announced their verdict: the laws would remain exactly the same as they'd been for one hundred years. "The town of Jackson was built on trapping," said one commissioner. *Yeah*, I thought, *and the South was built on slavery, but we don't have that anymore.*

Cougars do sometimes get caught in baited leg-hold traps, as do eagles, deer, rabbits, squirrels, and just about every other animal. This is called trapping a non-target animal—a meal is a meal. Cal Ruark, the former president of the Bitterroot Houndsmen Association and a mountain lion advocate, told me a gruesome story. As the snow was thawing in Montana, a friend of Ruark's was scouting for antler sheds when he discovered the hind foot of a mountain lion in a wolf trap. His friend brought the trap with the severed paw to Ruark.

"My friend told me the trees were all tore to hell," Ruark said. "The drag on the trap was hung up on a tree and there were claw marks on the trees where the lion had stood up on its back legs and tried to climb."

Ruark placed the trap in a milk carton—drag, foot and all—and went directly to a Montana Fish, Wildlife & Parks meeting. "I put that milk carton up on a table," Ruark told me over the phone, "and I asked the commissioner, 'What kind of foot is that in that trap?' He said, 'Is that a wolf foot?' And I said, 'You better look again. That's a hind foot off a mature tom mountain lion,' I told him."

It is illegal to trap mountain lions in Montana, and these incidental trappings are not counted toward the annual mountain lion hunt quota. No one knows how many cougars lose a toe or a foot in a trap, but in the first two years of legal wolf trapping in Montana, sixteen mountain lions were caught in traps, while thirty-two were caught in non-wolf set traps between the 2013 season and the 2015 season.

A study in Nevada, where trapping of mountain lions is also illegal, found that cougars were more likely to die if they had been captured in a furbearer trap. Injuries from traps—loss of toes, broken bones—can cause starvation and increase hunting and depredation mortalities. The study's findings suggested seasonal hunter harvest equaled that of non-target trapping of cougars. Also alarming was that females were more likely to die from trap injuries than males.

Ruark noted that there was no name on the trap, which is illegal. "That lion might have been able to get along for a little while, but he's dead now. He can't hunt on three legs. All I asked was for the Commission to count that lion against the quota. 'A dead lion is a dead lion,' I said, 'and you have a quota, no matter how they die.' And the game manager for Region 2 told me, 'Well we can't start counting all of those things.'" Ruark told me he was on the fence regarding trapping on public lands before this incident, but now he's strongly against it.

In 2016, the Wyoming legislature introduced House Bill 12, a bill that would have allowed any person with a valid hunting license to kill a mountain lion using a trap or snare. The aim of the legislation was to provide "additional tools" to reverse mule deer decline. The Wyoming Game and Fish Department has its own mountain lion management system that divides hunt areas into source, stable, or sink, and lions traveling together cannot be shot. But the state legislature can throw chaos into the system, ignoring the best science and substituting mythology. Mountain lions in Wyoming are already hunted using hounds, bow and arrows, and all legal firearms. A concerted effort on the part of the Wyoming Game and Fish Commission to reduce lion populations in 2008 has succeeded by all measurements. Adding indiscriminate trapping and snaring would have been a death knell.

Deer are an important game species, and hunting is a major source of state revenue. State agencies often advocate increasing quotas for mountain lions in order to protect the deer population. Yet study after study has shown that cougars have little effect on deer populations. Although the Wyoming Game and Fish Department doesn't subscribe to the notion that "fewer cougars mean more deer," their large carnivore biologist, Dan Thompson, told me he thought of their 2008 quota increase this way: "We've definitely seen an increase in mountain lion harvest, which is heavily driven by an overall reduction in mule deer populations across the state. Again, I think there's a notion that the increased harvest was to bring back mule deer, but it was never that way in my mindset. I felt, and this is how I justify it, that because of reduced primary prey we could have an increase in mountain lion harvest because it's a cyclical effect. But not with the notion of killing more lions to get back to where we were in 1963."

If a deer population is already low, due to habitat loss, weather, or over-hunting by humans, lion predation is mostly additive. Habitat loss, fragmentation of migration routes, over-hunting, and climate change disruptions all have impacts on ungulate populations. And now a deadly disease called chronic wasting, or CWD for short, is marching across the state of Wyoming. The disease was first recognized in Fort Collins, Colorado, in the late 1960s. It spreads slowly through what are called "prions," a little understood not-virus, not-bacteria, but thought to be misshapen proteins that can remain in the soil and water for a long time. It's a sad demise, attacking the brains of elk, deer, and moose, turning them into mush. Similar to mad cow disease, CWD fits into a constellation of comparable diseases known as spongiform encephalopathies. The point is that CWD is moving from east to west across the state, and that the disease, combined with other factors, means that mule deer, the primary food of cougars, are in the decline. In another study that contradicts the popular notion that low deer populations need a boost from higher predator harvests, biologist Michael Miller found that mountain lions were four times more likely to prey on infected mule deer with prions than on uninfected deer, even though most of the affected deer showed little or no obvious sign of the disease. In addition, removing cougars to boost deer populations can potentially decrease ungulate fitness by increasing the survival of older deer, leading to fewer young.

Boosting deer populations is not as simple as killing predators, as uninformed Wyoming legislators would like to think. Adding trapping to the mix of methods to kill cougars could decimate cougar populations, animals that already have a low density on the landscape.

In the end, House Bill 12 died in the legislature, thanks to an outcry from sportsmen's groups and the general public, but this kind of old-school, anti-predator thinking still lurks in the halls of our western state houses, driven by fear of this magnificent animal.

Koda was now out of sight on the mesa above where I stood. I knew my *Bathroom Trapper* had definitely abandoned this area, but where there's a void, another trapper might fill it. I wondered if Koda was picking up the scent of a hanging rabbit up on the bench. Since we'd had no new snow, and I didn't see any human tracks, I figured Koda smelled something else. With a lot of effort, I made it up the rocky edge through the deep snow to the bench above to join my dog, whose nose was hard at work. Soon I spied a snow-covered mound that looked like either a boulder or a juniper. I brushed the snow off, and underneath I found what the dog had keyed in on—a dead fawn, frozen and disemboweled, its spine and rib cage completely cleaned of meat. I pulled it out of the snow while Koda began chewing on the leftover ribs.

There are lots of predators around here that could have killed this deer—cougars, coyotes, wolves, bobcats and, though unlikely at this time of year, bears. Since many predators wait in the wings to get their fangs on a kill, it can be difficult to identify the main predator unless you find a recently killed carcass. But in this case, I, or rather Koda, found the fawn intact. The fawn's head was frozen thrown back, and the skin was deftly sliced, as if a knife had cut it.

This little deer was not a fresh kill, but it had been frozen and covered by the snow. It was obvious that the rib cage had been entered, as several ribs were chewed off for an entry point. I pulled its neck away from the frozen head and pushed back fur in order to examine the skull. I could clearly see two pencil-thick puncture holes, approximately an inch-and-a-quarter apart, on the back of the skull. In such a harsh winter, this little fawn would probably not have survived till spring. But the meal it provided just might save a kitten to live another day.

CHAPTER 5

CLUES FROM BEYOND THE VISIBLE

The earth remembers; the earth speaks;
the understanders of what it says are the humble ones.

—J. FRANK DOBIE

CALIFORNIA TRACKERS

Jim Sullivan, a tracking teacher in Bodega, California, lives deep in the redwoods just a few minutes from Bodega Beach. I know the area fairly well. In a former life as a landscape designer, I drove these back roads regularly to small specialty nurseries, gathering rare plants for clients. One-lane winding roads make for queasy passengers. Redwood forests are dark and wet. Eerie fog rolls in with regularity in a fairy-tale setting where the little people might be living. All redwood forests in northern California (except for the tiny, postage-stamp-size areas now preserved, such as Muir Woods National Monument) were logged beginning with the gold rush to build San Francisco, as well as all the towns and equipment needed for those projects. These trees may look tall, but they are, at most, one hundred years old, just babies for redwoods. Pastures, liminal spaces that once were old-growth forests, are now used by hobby ranchers, as sun sanctuaries for homes, or, as gentrification marches on, for home vineyards.

Sullivan's home is not far off the highway, but the road is narrow, even at times yielding to a redwood along its edges. This winter the rains have returned, and today it's pouring and the forest is darker than its usual inkiness. Finally I turn down a long dirt driveway and park behind his Subaru per my instructions. I've forgotten to bring rain gear from Wyoming, so I pull my ridiculous ski-jacket excuse for a raincoat close and run toward his A-shaped cottage just a sprint away from the main house.

Sullivan came recommended to me by a mutual tracker friend as someone who knows about the lions around here. Sullivan is thin, and tall, with a wide smile and graying hair. I like him immediately, and his manner puts me at ease. His cabin is modest. He opens the door and we are immediately beside a kitchen table. Paintings cover the walls. Bones, tiny jaws, bird skulls, and various earthy knick-knacks cover the table. A man after my own heart—he's got half the outside inside, and right where he eats.

A fourth-generation native Californian, Sullivan grew up here hunting and fishing, joined the infantry, and was sent to patrol the Korean DMZ after the Korean War. A border where no humans are allowed, 160 miles long and only 2.5 miles wide, the DMZ has unwittingly become a protected zone for wildlife. Although off limits to hunting, Sullivan, as an officer, had a permit. On one occasion, he tells me, he saw the biggest cat track of his life. "I was just blown away, and it reawakened my sensibilities about tracking." Now he teaches tracking classes in Sonoma County. "I'm just amazed at the interest in tracking now. I was born and raised here and couldn't find a tracker or even a tracking book. Now it's like tracker central." His classes fill quickly.

Although he's hiked these hills since he was young, the first time Sullivan saw a mountain lion was in the late 1990s. Cougars were probably extirpated by the 1930s in this county. It may not

Tracking in mud along the California coast with Jim Sullivan

have been until after cougars were permanently protected from hunting in 1990 that they began recolonizing the coastal areas. Sullivan tells me he's had at least six "hardcore" sightings and a handful of "that's a tail." Most of the six sightings occurred when he was landscape painting in a field. "Painting is like tracking. Trackers are visual thinkers and so are painters. There's a lot of cross-training and sensitivity," Sullivan tells me.

"I was walking across a large meadow and saw two little spotted kittens come out from behind a tree just ahead of me. One made a circle and went back in, then the second one did the same. Then a dog came out. A great big, stiff-legged, brown dog. It was really confusing to my mind trying to put that together. Then the kittens came out again and went back in, but the second time, the dog didn't come out. Suddenly the mom burst out, at a full-on gallop, with her tail flying, and ran right past me and out the gate. The dog came out again, hair up, and stiff-legged. I knew that dog because he'd given me trouble before. He was very territorial."

Sullivan's quirky nature is expressed in his painting style. He likes to find a spot that inspires him—occasionally in other people's meadows—and sets up an old ironing board as his easel. On another occasion, Sullivan was painting in a neighbor's meadow when he heard a noise behind him. Running up the hill at full speed were two hunters, decked out in orange and carrying their rifles. "Sorry to come on your property mister," they told him, "but there's a couple of bulls chasing us up the hill." It was late afternoon and the sun was low, throwing long shadows across the meadow from the tall redwoods at its edges.

Sullivan paints the full picture for me. "Out in the middle of this meadow, all of a sudden, all three of us see this cat, at full gallop, coming out of one of these shadows, just like a weasel, with its tail flying. We were all just dumbfounded and about thirty seconds passed before one of these hunters said, 'Shit, that looked like a mountain lion.'"

But here's where Sullivan's brilliance as a tracker shines forth. "I think what happened was when [the men] got chased up, they flushed out that cat. The cat then came up in the shadows along a hedgerow by the meadow border. I'm sure the cat crawled out on its belly all the way along that hedgerow. And then it got in the shadow and came out in the field. When it came to the end of the shadow, it said, 'Oh, screw it, I'm a lion, I'm just gonna run out there.'"

Sullivan's tracking philosophy naturally combines cognitive science and tracking, spirituality and practicality. Tracking is what we humans have done for millions of years in order to feed ourselves. It's in our DNA. "All the different things you do in tracking," Sullivan tells me, "took place at a time when our neo-cortex was forming. Our brain is designed to work that way because it came into being as a neo-cortex, at least in part, in order to solve tracking problems."

Sullivan describes how, in tracking, you view a track or series of tracks from several angles, and things change depending upon your perspective and also your presence and other presences.

"I've studied a lot of science, and one thing that's important to understand is that things don't follow laws. Laws are like a grid we put on it in order to understand what's happening. So, making a statement like 'wolves are a certain way or bobcats are a certain way'—you have to do that, it's necessary—but it's just a grid you're putting on to what the animals are actually doing."

Trackers hold the world from a different point of view. A person whole-heartedly immersed in tracking might tell you that it's a way of looking at the world that they can apply to every part of their life. For instance, I've heard trackers speak about "tracking their emotional reactions" in the same way a Buddhist practitioner might express sitting and "allowing what's arising." Trackers have told me that tracking is a metaphor for learning anything. Most people have laser focus, forming their opinions based on one way of looking at a situation. Tracking teaches a person to view a track, or any situation, from, for example, the eagle's perspective all the way to your eyes-on-the-dirt perspective, then to walk around and see a track from every side. Trackers learn their information from questions rather than from conclusions.

Meghan Walla-Murphy traveled the world to learn tracking, from South Africa to Montana to California. She now teaches tracking classes in northern California. Walla-Murphy happened to be working on a project in Colorado at the same time Mark Elbroch was on his Garfield Mesa mountain lion study, allowing her the rare opportunity to accompany Elbroch's crew while they investigated a fresh lion kill. Because the pumas in this study wore G.P.S. collars, the crew could discern a kill at 4:00 a.m. and be on the site by 8:00 a.m.

Walla-Murphy had an interesting "tracker awareness" story she related. "Kill sites are incredibly informative," she said. "It's a wonder how something can be so disturbing when it's occurring—everything goes quiet, and you can almost feel that impact, as if it were the epicenter of an earthquake—yet it draws all these species that are partaking in it. We're speaking of apex predators, and our culture has such a fear and horror of death, yet it's a very fertile time on the landscape. Everybody is there. You've got the ravens and the vultures, the coyotes and the foxes, the maggots, the flies, and on and on. When I come upon a kill I like to map it. Literally draw it. I make concentric circles that go out from the carcass."

I asked Walla-Murphy to describe her drawing methods. I thought I'd adopt this technique. "Begin by putting your killed animal, deer or elk, in the center of the paper," she explained. "Then walk out from that spot in larger and larger concentric circles, noting on the paper what you discover—a blood trail, a scrape, a gut pile, a scavenger's scat." She maps everything on the page.

Data from the PTCP in Jackson produced a scientific paper documenting thirty-nine scavengers at lion kills, more than any other study worldwide. Easily abandoning kills to larger predators, mountain lions can share up to 39 percent of a kill without having to kill again. This illustrates the ecological importance that pumas play in the food web.

The ability to get into the mind of an animal develops by putting in your "dirt time," trailing and tracking. By following an animal, the tracker sees how it moves, where it goes, whether it wanders or travels directly. I had an experience once in that deep way when I tracked a black bear in the fall for several weeks. I was mostly curious about what the bear was eating. But that curiosity led me on an adventure I couldn't have anticipated. I followed the bear around the nearby forest, looking at every scat. I saw where he bedded and, one morning when the bear had walked up my driveway, I saw where he'd torn apart large logs looking for maggots. He moved seventy-pound rocks with ease and climbed up steep slopes, clawing at enormous squirrel middens, leaving squirrels to chatter at me as I followed his sign. At night, after my day of tracking, I'd lie down and feel like a bear. I even dreamed bear dreams. I told Walla-Murphy this story.

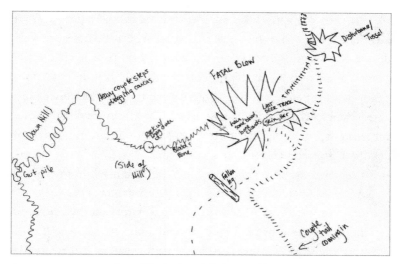

A small portion of the site kill map

"Imagine if someone were following you," she said. "Seeing where you eat, where you shit, where you sleep. Those are all very intimate, vulnerable experiences. So now when you're following an animal, you are intimately intertwined with that animal's life. What happens for me when I'm trailing an animal for any length of time is that I start to move like that animal. I go under things that I'd normally go around for instance, or sometimes I'm even on all fours to get somewhere. There's an empathy for that animal that emerges and comes forward."

Our awareness is not limited to what we know using just our five senses, Walla-Murphy tells me. When she's tracking, quiet, her mind's not chattering away or filled with all the potential distractions of the world. That's when all those other sensory awareness tools of her body and brain are able to come forward. One of the most important things she's learned through tracking is to trust her body more than her mind. She gets cues, responses, and danger information from her body, and when she doesn't listen, she finds herself in a situation she'd prefer not to be in.

Jim Sullivan approaches the question of animal empathy from a different angle. He tells me that some South African trackers describe the feeling as "taking the animal into your heart," while others call it "putting on the skin of the animal." But Sullivan once again demonstrates that he can easily combine cognitive, cutting-edge science with ancient Native insight. "It all comes down to mirror neurons," he says, "and mirror neurons are interesting parts of cognitive science that relate to tracking."

"I've never heard of this," I tell Sullivan and ask him to explain.

"About 40 percent of your muscle neurons are what they call mirror neurons. Mirror neurons entrain with another person's brain. They do that by reading body and audio language and then constructing what that means into an image. I can look at you while you move your thumb, and the thumb map in my brain will move."

According to neuroscientist Vilayanur Ramachandran, Director of the Center for Brain and Cognition, and Distinguished Professor at the University of California San Diego, mirror neurons are subsets of the brain's motor command neurons. These command neurons fire when a person performs a specific action, like when I reach to grab an apple. And just as Sullivan notes, these subset mirror neurons fire when I watch *you* grab an apple, as if I'm adopting your point of view. Dr. Ramachandran describes it as a virtual reality simulation of the other person's action in my brain. These mirror neurons aid with imitation and emulation. But there's more. There's another kind of mirror neuron that's involved with touch. If I watch another person being touched, I can empathize with that person, but the only reason I don't actually feel that touch myself is because receptors in my skin create a mental barrier. That way I won't be confused. I can empathize, but I'm not thinking that it's actually happening to me. Yet if you anesthetize my arm, or if, say, I have a phantom limb, and then I watch another person being touched, that skin barrier is removed, and I will experience that person's touch in my mind; the barrier is

Walla-Murphy teaching a class

dissolved. Ramachandran says that, in fact, we are all connected by our neurons and that there is no real distinctiveness from my consciousness and another's consciousness. "This is not mumbo jumbo philosophy," Ramachandran says, "it emerges from our understanding of basic neuroscience."

This is what Jim Sullivan considers critical to his understanding of getting inside the mind of the animal through tracking and trailing. Making two distinct circles in the air with his index fingers, he says, "One is your mind and the other is the animal's mind." He redraws the air circles, this time making them partially overlap. "You get pretty substantially in there, but not all the way. You know the things you need to know. You don't know the soap opera with the animal's girlfriend maybe, but as a tracker you are looking at the intention. You try to know where the animal is going; it's subtle. For a comparison, two cars come to an intersection. No one makes any bodily or verbal signs, but you negotiate who goes first. Somehow you work it out."

Jim Sullivan

The crux of the matter, Sullivan says, is how you conceive of the self and the spirit. Again, he alludes to cognitive science, which describes how we are not in direct contact with reality, but always a fraction of a second behind.

"Your eyes are hit by three hundred billion photons at any second. Before you see the picture, it takes a fraction of a second to process it. Let's say you touch your body. You don't feel it instantly. You have that gap. This is true in everything mental. We're always running a little behind reality. So, we are not living in real time, we are living in deep time. The model our brain creates from our input and our memories is the self. When you start thinking of it that way, and you start thinking about getting inside the mind of a cat, it gives you more access."

This goes back to the mirror neurons. Our brains can extend those *empathetic neurons* beyond simply touching and observing, to reading, putting in your "dirt time," and dreaming about an animal. When I spent those two weeks tracking the black bear, I dreamt about bears almost nightly. Perhaps I was processing the learned information through my subconscious, non-verbal, mind, or, as Walla-Murphy might say, trusting my body more than my mind. Listening to Jim Sullivan made me think of Native peoples dressing in the skins of the animal, dancing and imitating the movements and actions of the animal they wished to hunt or venerate. Keresan shamans of New Mexico, for example, put on bear paws and became bears. What better way to learn about the animal than for your neurons to reach out, touch, imitate, and emulate.

We go back to cats in our discussion. "Cats are intellectuals," Sullivan says tongue-in-cheek. "They're visual predators. They scheme." He returns to his thoughts about mountain lions. "A cougar sits up on a hill and watches that deer go down to get a drink of water around four o'clock every day. When it gets hungry, it sets up, and ambushes that deer. I think you learn to track from all the *tracking* animals, like wolves and cats. But tracking to me is more the awareness than anything else."

⌒ WHEN YOU FIND A FRESH KILL

On this blustery spring evening, patches of snow hold fast along the tree line by the creek. The first thing I see are fresh lion tracks in the snow, nestled under a small copse of trees, leading to a dead deer. It looks as if the deer was hastily and lightly covered with bits of fur and grass. The head and neck are exposed, and when I bend down to examine it, there's an obvious puncture wound at the base of the head. It appears as if the lion had begun to pluck the hair from the rib cage in order to enter it. Did Koda and I disturb his dinner? Now I'm a bit nervous, and it's not because I'm worried about the lion watching me—which I'm sure he is. I'm nervous about bears—grizzly bears. It's April and they are out, and here is a nice fresh meal they can knock the lion off of. I fondle the handle of my bear spray, maybe just to remind myself that it's still there,

Fresh deer kill I found covered and only partially eaten

and I take a wide view all around the meadow with its surrounding wooded slopes. Of course, a bear could run down here within minutes, but I'm satisfied by telling myself that caution is my best friend. This gives me the idea that maybe I can see the cat hiding somewhere. The steep hillside adjacent to me is bare until halfway up. The forest sets in at that point, thick, but with very little underbrush and mature Douglas firs. After examining the tracks in the snow that remain in the gully, I decide the cat must have headed east and upslope. If I make a deliberate and wide switchback climb up the hillside, maybe I'll catch a glimpse of him. Of course, this is a fanciful notion. Cats are too sneaky for me, and besides, maybe that cougar hightailed it up to the top of the crest.

A storm is moving in fast; the skies are breaking open in claps of thunder. I'm in a meadow, and powerful bursts of lightning are finding their way toward the pass. It's time to move out fast. I return, keeping cover through the trees as the rain begins to come down in a torrent. These kinds of storms usually move swiftly, and I decide I'll wait it out. But Koda will have none of it. "Get out of here. Get out of here fast!" he barks. And I remember my car and the two-track road it's parked on, and how that particular dirt road turns quickly into a muddy mess. I might survive the storm, but I won't be able to navigate the road if I don't hurry back.

A few weeks later, I was speaking with Marilyn Cuthill from Craighead Beringia South in Jackson. I had cougar questions for her, and I slipped in my story of the fresh kill and my search for the killer.

"Next time," she said, "take a tent and sleep out there for the night. You'll see the cat then."

Hmmm. Sounds like a good idea, but not during grizzly bear season.

———— 𝕧 ————

Jim Halfpenny is a mammalogist with an impressive and varied résumé. He has tracked and taught wildlife classes as well as led scientific expeditions all over the world. I first met Halfpenny at a tracking class given through the dude ranch in my valley. We walked the river bed, making track plates while looking for grizzly tracks for three days. We found a very large canine track, which I assumed was a wolf. Halfpenny had me take multiple measurements that he took back to his office and plugged into a computer model he designed for just this purpose. At the end of all the analysis, he confirmed that the track was from a large dog, not a wolf. Halfpenny approaches tracking with a meticulous and scientific eye, leaving no stone left unturned. At his center in Gardiner outside of Yellowstone National Park, Halfpenny maintains a library that houses hundreds of plaster casts of tracks that he and his students have found over the years. I even saw a few casts of Bigfoot that people had sent Halfpenny to analyze. He considers these questionable tracks.

When I described my find of a fresh, cougar-killed carcass to him, he told me about his "one-hundred-step rule." While working in the Boulder, Colorado area, he received a phone call from a woman who had a cougar-killed deer in her backyard. Halfpenny was at her house within hours, inspecting the deer and doing a necropsy; he discovered that the deer was pregnant. He chained the deer's leg to a tree. He took one hundred steps away, sat down in the wide open and waited. When the cougar returned, she saw Halfpenny sitting there and began to pull that deer into denser cover.

"Now I've handled this deer, I've moved this deer, I've chained it to a tree. She knows I'm there, no question about that. She grabs the deer, she's got it stretched out while it's chained to the tree, and she's pulling for all she's worth. The deer's in the air, then she lays it down and looks at it like, 'Shit, I don't understand this. I just killed the thing and I can't move it.'"

Halfpenny watched the cougar into the night and throughout the weekend, filming the scene as well. At one point, two mature kittens came in to feed. Over the course of the weekend, Halfpenny and his crew saw a whole host of animals arrive to feed—foxes, coyotes, domestic dogs, and cougars. "It was like they were waiting at the edge. One would leave and the other would come in, and there were multiple cycles of this."

I asked Halfpenny about his one-hundred-step rule. He told me that he absolutely wouldn't recommend this for just anyone, but that it works for him, and he's photographed many cougars this way. The trick is to not be in a tent, or a blind, but to take those one hundred steps and to stay in the open where the cougar can see you.

Canadian author and naturalist R.D. Lawrence described a similar experience. Lawrence watched a tom cougar kill a deer while he sat on a rise two hundred yards away. Once the animal began eating, Lawrence "walked down to the valley and stationed myself at a place about one hundred feet from the kill. The Ghost was already eating when I arrived, but apart from lifting his head to give me a cursory inspection, he remained undisturbed."

What was particularly interesting about the bulk of Jim Halfpenny's cougar tracking stories was that, solely through tracking, he encountered cougars and was able to film and photograph them.

He never uses dogs, but he reads the stories in the track and persists in trailing over steep and rugged terrain that cougars navigate easily. In Colorado, Halfpenny tracked cougars that were using old abandoned mines. One cougar he was following dragged his prey down, up, and over a steep ravine to the mine opening. Halfpenny crawled through the small mine entrance and found that the tunnel opened into a large room, complete with a sandy beach and a clear lake. Inside was the carcass the lion had preyed upon. "That cougar beelined 540 yards across bad terrain. There would have been easier ways to go, but it would have been out of a straight line. The cougars know every mine there. The Front Range is a massive home of mines. I've seen kittens in those mines that I know were born there."

One tracking adventure began with a call from a woman who saw a mountain lion around her yard in an exurban area. With two inches of fresh snow, he followed the lion's tracks for quite a distance until he came upon the cat—just fifty yards ahead. "I knew the tracks were fresh, but I was surprised I was that close. About that time, [the cougar] looked up over his shoulder 'Who are you? What are you doing following me?'" Halfpenny cupped his hands, moving them in an arc to how the cougar moved. "Then he went boing, boing, out of there no more than 100 yards, stopped and looked back. 'Who are you? What's going on here?'"

Like a lot of animals, this cat was making a big letter "C" instead of running straight into the bush. Halfpenny figured out what the cougar was up to, and cut across to intercept him, but when he got to the tracks, they suddenly stopped and then disappeared. He looked up, and there was the cougar in a tree, looking down at him. Halfpenny backed off, but he photographed the cat while it languished above.

Drawing on his extensive experience with cats, Halfpenny had one closing thought for me. "All the cats are quite happy to tolerate people and curious about what people do. Cougars are very curious and you hear all sorts of stories of cougars stalking people, but I don't think that's true very often. I know from my work in Boulder they're very tolerant to be around people as long as we don't kill them or destroy their habitat."

———— ⚘ ————

Tracker Matt Nelson told me an interesting story that corroborates Halfpenny's experience of cougars' tolerance for people. The story comes from a period when Nelson worked with Mark Elbroch on a cougar study in Colorado on a private ranch.

Every morning the researchers studied their G.P.S. data in order to discern if a cat had made a kill the night before. Their goal was to mount trail cameras at the kill site as soon as possible, in order to collect the maximum amount of data. By the time they reached the kill site, the cougar was usually gone. Both experienced trackers, Nelson and Elbroch devised a plan to see the cat. They'd sneak quietly into the kill site on their approach.

"And sure enough, we started seeing the cat. We'd watch a mama creep out with her two kittens, and slink away from us. When we returned to the office, we'd look at the G.P.S. data. We could see she had walked out a little, waited for us to leave, then walked right back to the kill."

I asked Nelson the same burning question I'd asked many of my interviewees: "Do you have a sense of the essence of a mountain lion?"

He replied, "I think all that we've learned, and all that we see with this technology, is only a scratch in the surface of what a cat really is."

Nelson's answered my question with a story of one cougar followed in the Colorado Garfield Mesa study. A female lion left her kittens in one spot and traveled straight down the mountain. Her journey took her ten miles, up and over steep terrain, and when she finally arrived at her destination, she immediately made a kill. She didn't veer off her trail, she didn't tarry, but she walked

Cougar tracks under water

a straight line. She fed for a while, then walked directly back to gather her kittens and brought them to the kill site to feed.

"I got to thinking about it." Nelson told me. "What's the motivation here? Why did that cat just beeline? There were all kinds of game and tracks and other animals in the area that she walked through. But she went straight over there for some reason and made this kill. Even with all our technology, we can't understand that at all. Is there a mystical aspect there? Did she pick up something off the landscape that said 'there's an animal on that other mountain that needs to be killed?' Or was she just merely walking? I have no idea. We can see where she went and what she did with our technology, but as far as an understanding of the animal, in my opinion, we can't understand that motivation through science."

CHAPTER 6

THE HOUNDSMEN

I realize now that as a young hunter, my intent was not
merely to kill for food . . ., but was rather my clumsy way of
reaching toward something that enchanted and mystified me.

—JOE HUTTO

✎ F51 AND HER KITTENS

No story better illustrates the additive nature of hunting on mountain lions than that of female F51 and her kittens. While the **F**[emale] and **M**[ale] before their numbered identities gives researchers an impartial way to track them, the difficulties cougars encounter in order to survive in the wilds are very real and personal and can be heart wrenching.

F51 came roaming into the PTCP study area around Jackson, Wyoming, from parts unknown, establishing her newfound home range within the territory of dominant male M21. In 2011, at the age of four, she gave birth to her first litter of five kittens. M21 already had several other females in his territory he guarded over, including F61, a third-generation Jackson female. She became a new mother within of a month of F51 with a litter of two kittens, her first at the age of four years as well.

Mark Elbroch's team had a big surprise in store for them when, in early 2012, trail camera footage showed the two families hanging out together. The norm is that cougars are solitary animals, except during mating season, so the crew thought these two adult females might be related, perhaps sisters. The team didn't yet have their genetic information.

As the winter of 2012 dragged on, the two families were spotted together several more times, usually around kills. Sometimes F51 made a kill while F61 and her kittens shared her meal; other times F61 would make the kill and the extended family of cougars showed up. Elbroch describes F51 as the "hippy" mom—lots of love, but less discipline—while F61 had a more careful and disciplined approach to kitten rearing.

Two of Hippy Mom's (F51) kittens died of unknown causes, possibly because of the hardships of winter, or possibly because her litter was large for a first-time mother. But three kittens, two females and a male (M36, F59, and F88), did leave their natal range, each with a different story. Kittens can stay with their mother for up to two years, but they usually disperse at around eighteen months. Although dispersal in cougars, a cryptic species, has been hard for scientists to study, researchers agree that dispersal assures males do not breed with their mother or sisters. Both male and female mountain lions leave their mother's home range, but males travel much farther than females, looking for a large void in the landscape that is unclaimed by another dominant male.

All three of Hippy Mom's kittens dispersed at fourteen months, still on the early side, heading into a Wyoming winter to fend for themselves for the first time. Daughter F59 was killed a few months later by a dispersing two-year-old male puma. According to the necropsy report, he showed severe signs of starvation—"all his ribs, pelvis, and leg bones were all showing through his coat." His last prey had been a porcupine, which may have caused injuries and limited his hunting ability. When the male disperser encountered the young female alone, he killed her, laying atop her carcass and consuming her over four days.

F51 and her young cubs on elk carcass

The study lost track of the male kitten (M36) who may have successfully dispersed. Interestingly, Hippy Mom's third kitten, F88, was adopted by her support parent, F61, when she was ten months old. After having spent many meals together, the young cat left her birth mother to live under the umbrella of F61's old-fashioned puma rearing style. This may have ensured her success, for she dispersed with her half-sister, F97, months later.

The father of both litters, M21, was the dominant male in the territory; he died of rodenticide poisoning. Rodenticide poisoning is a common killer of predators in urban and exurban habitats, so finding the poison in M21's blood in this vast wilderness area was unexpected. Rodent poisons move up the food chain, killing predacious birds like eagles and hawks, as well as scavenging ground predators and other predators, like pumas, that eat rodents, and M21 frequented an area with several large ranches.

A new male, collared and designated M29 by the study team, moved into the area. In the fall of 2012, he sired new litters for

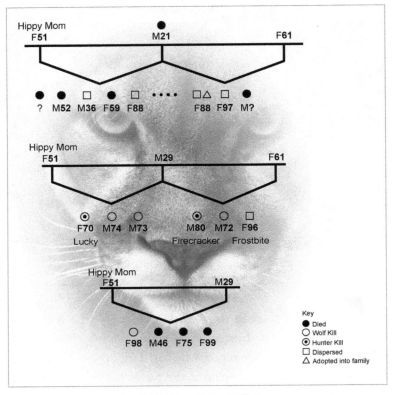

Genealogy Chart for F51

both Hippy Mom and F61. This time, Hippy Mom had a litter of three kittens, two of which were killed by wolves. When the study began, wolves were just beginning to show up in the valley, but by 2012, wolves were having a bigger impact on kittens, especially those younger than six months, and usually when traveling to kill sites with their mothers. Hippy Mom's remaining kitten, F70, was dubbed "Lucky" by the study crew, for obvious reasons.

Lucky and her mother headed high up into the cliffs after their traumatic encounter with wolves, taking refuge in a cave. For eight days, mother and kitten huddled near the rocky ramparts, and when

F51 and cub at kill

Hippy Mom began hunting again, she stayed close to her cliff retreat for more than a month. Unfortunately for Lucky, M29 mated again with her mother and she was forced to disperse at the tender age of nine months, bereft of the complete schooling she'd need to hunt on her own. Two months later, Lucky was killed by a hunter.

Hippy Mom's third litter of four was born in November 2013. Underweight at birth, and facing winter temperatures as low as -35°F, one male kitten died from exposure. In January, a female kitten was killed by wolves. The remaining two female kittens (F75 and F99) were healthy and practicing their pouncing skills when tragedy struck on April 1, 2014.

Responding to a mortality signal, researchers found Hippy Mom dead at the base of a hill. They could read the scene etched in the snow. She had encountered a new male in the territory while traversing through a narrow chute in the cliffs with her kittens. Her mate, M29, had been killed by a hunter, and a new male was slowly moving into the now vacant space. The stranger was feeding on a kill he had made when the mother cougar suddenly appeared. There was a fury of fur and claws, the two rolled down the hill sixty or seventy feet, and then wrestled at the bottom where the biologists found her. Her two kittens, now orphaned, ran off to hide. For Elbroch the scenario of this new male as the instigator didn't make sense. First, the male had already courted and mated with several females in the area in the last few weeks, so it seemed only logical that he would consider Hippy Mom as a potential mate. Second, researchers had never seen video footage of an intruding male attack and kill a female in their study area. From the snow and other evidence, it was clear that Hippy Mom was the aggressor, striking M85, perhaps to defend her two remaining kittens. Or perhaps the traumatic losses of her last litters to the elements, to wolves, and to hunting pressures led to what we humans understand as PTSD, a well-known phenomenon in elephants. Previous trauma and stress created untold psychic disturbance, leading Hippy Mom to act in an otherwise unnatural, aggressive manner.

In studies in the Greater Yellowstone Ecosystem and the Garnet Mountains of Montana, only thirteen of twenty-two independent kittens between seven and twelve months survived, a 60 percent survival rate. The odds for F75 and F99 weren't good. They moved east, away from where they were raised, into an area unknown to them. They traveled together, scavenging on carcasses, playing, nuzzling and comforting each other. Elbroch and his crew had high hopes for them at first. "In about a month the fawns will start to drop," he said. "If they can get into fawns, that would be awesome."

But soon they became separated, possibly by wolves. For two weeks, they were apart. Kitten F99 found an old winter kill she was picking apart. Then, at one point, while down at the river, she began calling and calling, hoping to contact her sister, F75. In the vast landscape of the Gros Ventre Range, there seemed little chance of the two finding each other again, yet they did, and they spent the remainder of F75's life together. She died shortly thereafter at nine months of age. When the researchers found her body in an old bed used by the entire family, her adult canines were just beginning to erupt, but they hadn't yet pushed her baby teeth out. These milk teeth are too small to puncture the hide of larger prey, and she died of starvation.

A scientific study does not usually interfere with wildlife, and the policy of the Wyoming Game and Fish Department does not permit it. But in this case, after reviewing the circumstances of F75's death, the study team asked, and received, permission to feed F99. The study's goal was to keep her alive while her teeth matured and she could perhaps learn to hunt, while also drawing her away from residences and roads where she could get into trouble. They dropped the hind leg of a road-killed moose near her G.P.S. location. This was a big boon for the kitten, the team said, and "just like that, she became a different cat."

The study fed her two more times, and F99 started adjusting to her life as a mountain lion, looking for prey, and trying to hunt on her own, rather than usurping old carcasses. Michelle Peziol, a professional tracker and biologist with the study, told me her own story of tracking the whereabouts of F99.

"I would go to these [G.P.S.] clusters and she wouldn't be doing normal mountain lion behavior. It wasn't easy to figure out what she was doing. For instance, she slept out in the open, and mountain lions don't do that. I couldn't find out what she was eating either, as it seemed she hadn't eaten anything in weeks. Then I started finding scats and pulling them apart, and that's when I discovered she was living on grasshoppers and pocket gophers. One time I found the tip of a tail of a marten she had eaten. Plus, we have videos of her hunting and trying to catch a squirrel. The other thing that was very interesting was that mountain lions have a territory. Female mountain lions have smaller territories that butt up to other females, and there's the male that shares a territory with maybe five females. This mountain lion kitten was traveling distances through three female lion territories, just wandering, out there lost, searching for food, not staying in one designated area."

In the end, this little survivor was killed by porcupine quills at sixteen months, almost five weeks after she had killed and fully consumed the carcass. Although F99 looked healthy when the study crew found her body, an autopsy revealed that quills had entered through her chest, migrating into her entire chest cavity wall, wounding her lungs. One lung had completely collapsed.

What's astonishing is that after three litters—a total of twelve kittens—only two of Hippy Mom's progeny survived to disperse successfully: F88, the kitten that was adopted at ten months by her allomom F61, and M36. Both were from her first litter of five. A video capture of F88 and her half-sister, F97, both one year old at the time, show the two kittens with a live, maimed, newborn fawn that their mother provided as a teaching lesson. The kittens are nervous at first as the fawn cries out. As the footage continues, it's apparent they both are inept and inexperienced at how to kill this animal, initially spending time batting it. Finally, after watching each other for hints of how to proceed, one of the cougar kittens picks the fawn up by the neck, tentatively delivering the killing bite. What's evident in this video capture is that one-year-old kittens are still not fully equipped to hunt on their own. In 2018, the PTCP did their final estimate on kitten survival from all the data compiled during their research. Out of one hundred kittens, fifty-one will live to six months of age. After six months, the chances of predation by wolves and bears are greatly reduced, but humans, starvation, and other causes will kill another 37 percent of those young lions, leaving thirty-two kittens out of one hundred to reach dispersal age at eighteen months.

While dispersing cougars from the study are rarely heard from again, making it difficult to gauge their success, we know for certain that F97, F61's daughter, had three kittens of her own in the Jackson area. That would make her a fourth-generation Jackson cougar.

Females can breed successfully approximately every other year. Yet a female living a long life in the wild may produce only four or five young that survive to adulthood over the course of their entire breeding life. And though sexually mature by the age of two, F51 and F61 had their first litters when they were four. In the Yellowstone Park Cougar study, Toni Ruth's data from Phase II indicates that female and male cougars who live the longest have the greatest success in producing offspring. What does this mean when we add in hunting pressures on females? On dominant toms? With all the difficulties of rearing kittens to dispersal age, plus the obstacles facing dispersing sub-adults, what role does human hunting play on survival rates? These questions, and others, prompted me to find answers from biologists, state managers, and from lion hunters themselves.

⌐ I MEET ROD BULLIS

It was inevitable that I'd get to this—wanting to talk with a houndsman.

From my vantage point, it all just looked like easy killing rather than actual hunting:

1. acquire some good dogs, either trained, or do the training yourself;
2. drive or snowmobile around roads till you find a fresh track;
3. put the G.P.S. collars on your dogs, let them smell the track, then let them loose while you sit in your car drinking a hot coffee;
4. when the G.P.S. shows the dogs had stopped for a sufficient period of time, drive to the closest access point with the least amount of exertion;
5. with the dogs baying, the cat would be resting high on a limb when you arrive. Now shoot it, skin it, and bring back the trophy;
6. repeat 1-5 for your next tag. My hunt zone offers two tags a year. Outfitters just require that their client has a tag.

Sleeping lion

This was my view of the hunt, which made it even more imperative that I speak with some actual lion hunters, but how? I didn't know any houndsmen, I had no contacts for any, and besides, after some soul searching, I realized I was just too biased to be an impartial interviewer—I was always rooting for the lion. Even if I could find a lion hunter that would consent to being recorded, no one wants to be judged by the interviewer. I knew my subject just wouldn't open up. I needed a friendlier opening, a baby-step path to enter the cougar hunter's point of view. It would take me two years of pondering this off and on to come up with an idea for access.

Over many thousands of years, mountain lions developed the strategy of climbing trees to avoid wolves. If you watch videos of mountain lions who are treed by dogs, most appear very content, for they perceive they've foiled their adversaries and can just wait it out. Eventually the "wolves" will get tired and move on to other business. Sometimes a lion even seems to fall asleep in the tree. Shooting a lion out of a tree is easy; it's the chase that's hard, especially on foot, and it would be downright impossible without dogs.

Several people told me stories of out-of-state, wealthy clients telling outfitters, "I don't have time to go looking." In these cases, the outfitter trees the lion, then calls his client on a cell phone while the dogs keep the cat treed. The rich man flies out, drives/walks to the location, and shoots the cat. The cat could have been sitting in the tree for days, adding additional stress to his slow demise. This is certainly not the way every outfitter operates, but it does happen.

I don't like the idea of trophy hunting at all, but I have more respect for hunters who pit their skills against an animal in a fair chase. The Boone and Crockett Club does not condone the use of G.P.S. collars to harvest a cougar and does not consider it "fair chase." They will not score a cougar as a trophy if the animal was hunted and killed using G.P.S. technology.

What, I wondered, was the attraction here? The houndsmen's bond with their dogs? Why would a hunter, after one trophy lion, continue killing cougars year after year? What lengths do outfitters go to for their client's money?

It was September and cougar hunting season was just beginning in Wyoming. One day, I was driving on dirt roads in the mountains when I recognized a woman I'd spoken with at a U. S. Fish and Wildlife meeting on grizzly bear delisting. I'd approached her during the break after she'd told an interesting personal tale during her public comment. She was advocating delisting the bear. I, on the other hand, had spoken in favor of keeping grizzlies on the endangered species list. Yet her bear story was compelling, and I was curious to know more. As we spoke, I realized she had formed a number of opinions about wildlife, especially predators. In the course of conversation, I told her I enjoyed tracking cougars in my area and was curious to know more about their lives. Her face hardened as she informed me that she was an expert on cougars and knew more about them than I could imagine. Those kinds of calcified statements about wildlife are always a red flag for me. The man or woman who has the most extensive knowledge and experience is usually the most humble. Their depth of knowledge has led them down the path of the greater mystery of the infinite unknowability of the natural world. Later, a friend told me the woman I'd met hunted cougars for the government agency Wildlife Services, and was an outfitter as well. She definitely wasn't fascinated with cougars for the same reasons I was. We were coming from different planets.

And here she was today, stopped with her truck at a campsite pullout, returning from hunting with her dogs. I watched as she skill-fully dealt with her dogs, her posture exuding a confidence in outdoor living. Clearly, she knew her stuff, but it confirmed to me how biased I'd be in a conversation with her about hunting cougars. Yet that gave me an idea. Why not find a hunter turned conservationist?

I decided to call Penny Maldonado, Executive Director of The Cougar Fund—a conservation organization—the first of its kind in Wyoming to focus solely on mountain lions. I asked Maldonado if she knew any cougar hunters that fit that description. She told me about Rod Bullis, who, along with several of his friends, had worked hard trying to convince Montana Fish, Wildlife, & Parks to reform their mountain lion hunting policies in order to ensure healthy populations into the future. Bullis seemed the perfect per-son to enter into a dialogue with about cougar hunting. When I reached Bullis by phone, his southern drawl hinted at his birthplace, yet he told me he'd been living in Montana for his entire adult life, since his college days. Bullis began framing our discussion by lay-ing out the various reasons people hunt cougars: commercialization (outfitters who make money off of their clients), livestock depreda-tion, and recreation. Bullis said that one of the reasons for hunting cougars for recreation was what he called an "opportunity." "Believe it or not," Bullis continued, "there are a lot of people out there that if they have the legal opportunity to kill something, they'll do it."

He went on to describe what cougar hunting had meant to him.

"For me, the most enjoyable times of my life I spent on the trail—with a friend and with a few dogs—in the winter and in the snow. My old hunting partner, who's deceased now, he told me when I first started getting hounds to hunt with—and this is important—'Rod, you'll learn a lot about yourself.' Now this is key to me."

A retired cougar hunter, Bullis was old school. A forester by profession, he worked for the U.S. Forest Service for thirty-eight years all over the state of Montana. After that, he managed private lands for another ten years before retiring. Having worked on seven different ranger districts and all over the West on fire suppression, he'd probably seen it all when it came to hunting and hunting ethics. I say he is old school because he aligned himself with a generation of cougar hunters that didn't use technology. They trained their own dogs, lived out in the wilderness in winter, and followed their dogs, as well as the lion's tracks, on foot. The first time Bullis ever saw a cougar, he wasn't even hunting, and he didn't have dogs with him. He had snowshoed thirty miles into the Bob Marshall Wilderness working on a snow-course reading for the Forest Service— a sixty-mile round trip. On his way back, he walked up over a small rise and there was a female lion with her three kittens eating on a spike elk she'd killed. When they saw Bullis, the cats ran in all different directions. Thinking back to his partner's statement, I was curious to know what kinds of things Bullis had learned about himself hunting cougars.

"It's below zero, you've got snow, you find a track and turn your dogs loose on it. You never know where you're going to end up at. It's kind of like a first date. For instance, when you have to wade the river, you gotta figure out how to do it, not frostbite your feet, and then—I've been in a river crossing at sub-zero—you find out if you have the physical and mental ability to do it, and the necessary skill to dry yourself out, to keep from getting badly hurt. Do you have the ability to spend the night in the forest where you can get underneath a tree, build yourself a fire and a cubby and stay there? Do you have the ability to find your dogs when they're lost? I never used all this new technology that's available today. So you learn about the skills and confidence you possess, and if you have the courage to implement them."

Bullis's description of trekking through snow and cold, following dog tracks, even staying overnight if necessary, prompted me to reveal my opinion of modern cougar hunting, probing for his response.

"That's what I don't understand about cougar hunting today," I told Rod. "With all the technology—G.P.S. collars, good snow machines, radios, unlimited cell or satellite service—what's the attraction? It just seems like killing to me." I was being straightforward and wondered how Bullis would take that.

"I'm really glad to hear your observation," Bullis responded. "With the kind of technology there is today—the poor cougar. He's out there, the way he was since the Ice Age. These new guys turn their dogs loose, wait on their snowmobile or in their truck, look at their laptop, then drive to the closest location to make the kill. It's pathetic. Makes it too easy. Technology has replaced connectedness to nature, and instead you've got connectedness to your device and don't learn much. Cougars are habit type animals. They cross the same place and once you learn their patterns you can almost guess what day they'll come through. With two people, you'd have one person follow the dog tracks, and one person follow the cat track. And you really learn a lot."

As I'm speaking with Bullis, I'm visualizing a completely different kind of hunt and understanding the attraction behind it. He's learning not just about his own skills and limits, but gathering knowledge about the animal. He's matching his skills against the cougar, and, he tells me, he never shot a lot of animals. "But I did chase a lot, caught a lot, and photographed a lot. I have taken some.

"I remember climbing trees, poking lions out of them, and then chasing them again. You also find things in the forest. I couldn't believe when I found a beaver that a mountain lion had caught, skinned out, and ate. Or the times I found cache kills. Or treeing a lion whose tail is frozen off. There are all kinds of things that you see in the forest when you're out there. Those are experiences that very few people will ever have."

Several times throughout our conversation, Bullis repeated two values he adhered to—"You learn a lot about yourself" was one, and the second, most important, was what he learned about mountain lions. "I wanted to honor the animal because cougars are a high life form." Bullis's southern twang is still evident when he says *high life form*. "They have social structure. They have cross-generational caring. I know that there are grandparents of cougars that assist in the rearing of the dependent young. I know that. You know, killing a mountain is not a big deal to do. It's a big deal to a mountain lion, but a mountain lion in a tree is a pretty easy target. I can't stand to watch these guys on TV shooting lions out of a tree; it's like shooting at a can. Hold them up [dead], and taking pictures of them. I am pro-hunting, but I don't like this blood and guts thing."

I pressed Bullis to tell me more, to explain why people would want to kill cougars year after year. Isn't one trophy enough?

"Some people just want to hunt for the thrill of the kill. That's the dark side. It's not me. I knew a co-worker and he was one of those hunters that if he had a license, he was going to kill it. He probably killed, in his entire hunting life in Montana, probably forty mountain lions. Every year he took as many tags as they'd allow him. And I asked him one time *why*. He said, 'Well, if the Fish and Game doesn't want me to kill one, then don't sell me a license.' And then there's peer pressure. I've seen it in the field. If there's more than two people together, a kind of panic takes over. Group think. That's why I never hunted with more than one person and why I like to spend time talking with the old-time hunters, and even some new time hunters, the people that value themselves and the experience, but even more so, value the animal."

I was beginning to understand how Penny Maldonado, a conservation advocate, had found an alliance with these houndsmen. Bullis surprised me when he asked if I knew Toni Ruth. When I told him I did, he replied, "If you know Toni Ruth, then you know the 'top of the top.' She was Maurice Hornocker's last graduate student."

Bullis expressed one problem with some of the houndsmen today in a nutshell: they've lost the historical perspective. When Bullis began running dogs, there were few cougars in Montana; bounty hunters had been killing them off for more than fifty years. Houndsmen, along with the agencies, wanted to increase cougar numbers. Bullis told me that hunters today think there have always been this many cougars, and always will be. Outfitters take their clients into a drainage and clean it out. "We'll just go into another area," they say. Without understanding cougar biology, their low density on the landscape, and their history, a houndsman's viewpoint is inherently flawed.

HOUNDSMEN TURNED ADVOCATES

Bullis encouraged me to speak with several other cougar hunters he knew, and he gave me their contact information and an introduction. It was through Bullis that I was introduced to Cal Ruark, a mountain lion advocate and former president of the Bitterroot Houndsmen Association. Ruark began hunting cougars in high school, when there were fewer than fourteen toms and even fewer females left in the entire Bitterroot Valley. The bounty programs had cleaned them out. The Bitterroot Mountains are a rugged, glacier-carved range running north and south between Idaho and Montana. On both sides of this mountainous border is the Selway-Bitterroot Wilderness. Steep ridges dominated by raw, granite peaks, deep canyons, and thick coniferous forests characterize this trailless area seldom visited by humans. "That country is standing right on its nose," Ruark tells me, describing its precipitous geography. When Ruark was growing up, the few mountain lions that existed were on the west side of the valley. There were no cats on the east side. And

once those few toms were harvested, he says, their tracks disappeared.

Ruark's hunting area was in the Selway-Bitterroot Wilderness. He set up camp the last week of elk hunting season in Idaho, then snowmobiled fifty-five miles from where they plowed the road to his base camp. He'd spend anywhere from two weeks to two months hunting cougars from his camp. Every year from 1963 through 1990, Ruark wintered in the Wilderness Area. In those thirty-seven consecutive years of winter hunting, he tells me, he only took five cats. He tracked and admired them more than anything else.

After speaking with Ruark on the phone, I drove to his home near Darby, Montana, for a visit. The Bitterroot Range forms a massive chain, a force of drama on the landscape that erupts into steep cul-de-sac canyons amidst towering peaks. Seen from the highway that runs along its base, the mountains are a formidable, yet inviting, presence. I'm riding with Rod Bullis as my guide, who tells me that the Bitterroot Valley was once a series of farms and ranches, split by a small, two-lane road. Today there are new tract and trophy homes, seemingly endless small towns, and plenty of traffic from commuters who want a bit of country living outside of Missoula. Across the Bitterroot Valley, on the eastern skyline, are the Sapphire and Rattlesnake Mountains. "The valley is a sink zone," Bullis tells me. "The quota is twenty-five cats. There's just no way a cougar can disperse across to the east with that kind of quota."

As we turn up the driveway toward the ranch Cal Ruark manages, several old hound dogs bark to greet us. Inside the modest home, three Pugs bark and sniff, jumping excitedly as Ruark's wife offers us coffee and freshly picked raspberries. A stocky, strong man, Ruark is approaching seventy, yet he still takes care of several hundred acres of hay fields and helps organize the local rodeo.

Ruark tells me he's gotten out of the cougar advocacy business. It was eating him up. The latest Bitterroot study, completed several years ago using DNA from harvested cats along with darted, treed cats, reported extremely high population numbers, off the charts for what is accepted as average in the western United States. But the houndsmen say the quotas are too high, the study is skewed, and the cats are overhunted. Ruark's heart is now in the rodeo. He shows me the flyer that advertises Darby's summer rodeo activities and a video clip of a thirteen-year-old bull bucking a rider off within seconds—a monster bull that no rider has yet mastered.

"We can go out afterwards and I'll show you one of our champion five-year-olds. He's really friendly. Likes to be petted. But if you get on his back, watch out." He quickly gets to the point of our visit. "So, you want to know about cougars. I have a whole room full of information." Ruark points to a door behind the kitchen. "I think I've read just about every study ever done."

Ruark's demeanor becomes wistful, and his voice softens as he begins talking about his time in the backcountry, trailing cougars with his dogs, camping in frozen winters for years on end. "I just enjoyed it so much. The thrill that I get a kick out of, even today, is when I look down and find a lion track in the snow or the mud. It just does something to me, and especially if it's a big ol' mature tom. It's like, God, I don't know, there's just something it does to me. Not like I want to kill it. I always think about all the places that cat's been and how it lives. That's what I've enjoyed about cat hunting more than anything else. Turn those dogs loose and following those dogs; and the places that cat goes. It's just interesting some of the places they go. Those old toms will strike up a ridge and go up two or three miles, then dive right off into the draw, and come back along the river."

Ruark trained all his dogs himself, ran them on a leash, and delighted as they weaved their way through thick brush, avoided elk tracks, and negotiated vertical rock ledges. They kept their noses to the lion track without being distracted by other wildlife tracks, which houndsmen call "running trash." For him, it was all about the life of the cougar and the experience of raw wilderness. Year after year he spent winter months in the Bitterroot-Selway Wilderness. Soon he had a young family and began to return home in time for Christmas. But after the holidays, he was out in the winter backcountry again. When his son turned seven, Ruark began taking him on hunting trips into the Selway until Christmas break was over. Earlier Ruark told me a story over the phone about a hunt with his young son. I asked if he could elaborate on the details.

Ruark's son Todd was nine years old when they camped that winter at White Cap Creek. It was a cold day, -30°F, as they began trudging through deep snow up a trail paralleling the creek's trajectory. Ruark's son looked down and saw they were now eighty yards above the wide creek bed. Father and son could see a few small cat tracks running along the dry creek bottom.

"I assumed they were two bobcats running together, which bobcats can do quite often. So, I turned the dogs loose. I told my son, 'This will be good for those dogs.'" In other words, he was giving the dogs some tracking experience. "We went around a ridge and you could hear the dogs along the creek bottom, treeing. 'That's really good for those dogs,' I told Todd. 'Let's just leave them down there and let them tree for a little bit.'"

Ruark and his young son retraced their steps down the switchbacks towards the creek bottom. When they finally arrived, they found these weren't bobcats at all, but two lion kittens who had cut back around the tree line into the creek drainage to join their mom who had a third kitten with her. While three of the cats were in trees, they found one little kitten dead on the ground.

"That kitten had its ears froze off, and the hide on all its feet was gone. And its tail was froze off also because of that cold snap. I think the only reason the dogs got the kitten was because it couldn't climb. I had an out-of-state Idaho tag with me, which at that time had cost about $250 or $300. I told my son, who was about nine years old at the time, 'I'm gonna punch my lion tag and I'm gonna place this little kitten in the tree and that's my mountain lion tag right there.' You know, that taught my kid something he still believes today. He'll always remember when I put my tag on that little kitten. It would have been real easy for me to leave that kitten on the ground, walk off and that would have been the end of it. But in my mind, my ethics, I knew that was the way it was supposed to be."

Ruark's love for mountain lions and everything he learned by trailing them on foot over the years is evident as our conversation continues. "There's still so many things we don't know about them, their social structure for instance. You stop and think about how they run into each other and mate, or take care of those kittens. A mountain lion to me is just an amazing animal. I love 'em. It's just something to see them in the tree, or in the rocks or wherever you get them bayed up. I don't care if it's a spotted cub or a 160-pound tom. I stop to think about them and, I'll tell you, I'm at the point— and have been at this same place for a long time—that I can't pull the trigger on them. I just can't make myself do that."

Rod Bullis and Cal Ruark were instrumental in arranging for Toni Ruth to come to the Bitterroot area twice to conduct educational seminars. These seminars were frowned upon by Montana Fish, Wildlife & Parks, as well as by the Ravalli County Fish and Wildlife Association, the oldest fish and game club in the state of Montana. Ruark tells me, "They were saying all we wanted to do was kill all the calf elk, mule, and whitetail deer and let the lions run rampant. . . ." But Bullis and Ruark intended to help educate

Mating pair

lion hunters. "So many people that run cats don't know anything about mountain lions. At fifty pounds or less, they're dead if they lose their mother. Their chance of survival is zero. Actually, if they get up to sixty-five or seventy pounds, the chances of surviving without their mother is still pretty slim. A lot of people think a mountain lion has a litter every year. There's just so many mistruths out there that people don't understand."

Ruark is a big advocate for not hunting females at all. Females reach sexual maturity at around two years, establishing a territory before becoming sexually receptive. Females can come into estrous at any time of the year, which means that if a female loses a litter, she can mate soon thereafter. For a solitary animal with broad territories that can cover hundreds of miles, this might have been one of nature's survival strategies. When a female is receptive, it's usually the male that seeks her out, staying with her for from three to ten days. Copulation is quick, lasting less than a minute, but they make up for this with frequency—copulating fifty to seventy times in a twenty-four-hour period during their stay together. R.D. Lawrence, Canadian naturalist and writer, spent a winter studying and tracking cougars in the Selkirk Mountains in British Columbia, where he described hearing the famous "caterwaul," an eerie sound that echoed in the forest during the stillness of winter. Lawrence hunted for the source and found it came from a female lion in estrous. After a time, a male responded and they spent time mating and eating a kill together.

All this vigorous mating is believed to stimulate ovulation, as cats are thought to be "induced ovulators." Approximately three months later, the female lion will find a secluded and safe location to give birth to her litter. Kittens will normally stay with their mother for eighteen months to two years before they disperse. Then the female comes into estrous once again. Given this interval, females are usually somewhere in the cycle of either caring for young or pregnant.

As a practical matter, most of the old-time hunters I spoke with agreed: females should not be hunted. But some Montanans believe there must be a quota of one female lion. Unlike Wyoming, where a lion's gender is not counted towards a quota, Montana has a limit on the number of female lions that can be harvested in any given hunt area. The rational is this: with a female quota of one, hunters who kill a female cougar during the "boot season" will actually report it. Once reported, the female quota will be closed for the entire season in that area. Boot season refers to "boots on the ground," meaning elk and deer hunters can carry a lion tag with them when they hunt in the fall. If they see a lion, they're allowed to shoot it. But without the benefit of treeing a lion and inspecting it closely, there's absolutely no way to tell if it's a male or female. "If you don't have a female quota of at least one, the hunter is likely to leave the dead female in the woods. With a female quota of at least one, the hunter will report it, and that shuts down the female quota for that zone," one houndsman told me.

The key to sustainable lion populations is to make it illegal to kill females. Research in Wyoming showed that, during the winter months, mothers were away from their cubs about 50 percent of the time, and probably longer than that if the cubs are under six months old. Hunter education is also crucial. Many lion hunters don't understand the basics of mountain lion biology. Researchers have found that up to 75% of treed female cougars would not be recognized by houndsmen. Mistaken sex identity results in a female kill rate of 47 percent across twelve hunting states. Three out of four of these harvested females would have dependent cubs or be pregnant.

There are also complaints about the high quotas in Montana on male lions from ethical old-timers. Grover Hedrick, a houndsman with a vast array of cougar knowledge, not only from a lifetime of hunting, but also from time spent working with wildlife biologists, had this to say about the area around the Bitterroot Valley in Montana: "Fish and Game puts out a lot of male permits. If you have several dominant cats, they kind-of control their population. But if you keep shooting the dominant cats, yes, you get a lot more cougars, but their average age is maybe two years for males. They're killing males before they even disperse, and it's dispersement that keeps a unique gene pool—the cats travel. They've shot them down so far in [the Bitterroot Mountains] that there aren't many dispersing cats. Transient cats are just not coming through. If they're killed any younger than that, you can't tell the sex of the cat because he's not old enough."

It's not easy to tell the difference between males and females. Jim Halfpenny explained, "If you have one up a tree and you can see the hair is going around the nipples, then you have an idea that it's a female. In cougars, if the male is not producing sperm, the testes are somewhat abdominal and may not show up." "People think, 'Oh I can see testes,' but it doesn't work that way. In a female, the vagina is very close to the anus and hidden under the tail. On the male, you often see the penile opening which is farther down. In a tree looking up, if you are there for long, you're probably going to pick that up. Now you can get some hints on the size of the head versus the shoulder, as the proportions are different on a male, but it's not easy to tell."

One cougar hunter, a friend of Rod Bullis, told me about a time he confronted a Montana game manager—an anti-cat, more-deer man. During a meeting, the Fish, Wildlife & Parks representative said, "We lucked out this year. We didn't kill any females with kittens."

"Well that's BS," the houndsman told me. "They shot about fifty females that year. You know, every study has shown that a female of breeding age either is pregnant, has little kittens, or has big kittens. They don't breed every year. Since they keep their kittens for eighteen months or two years, most of the time they have kittens of some age. And since they are not with their kittens all the time—they quit lactating after two months—there is no way to tell. The brown spots around the tips from lactating do stay for a while."

Grover Hedrick spoke with me about an incident that happened during a study he was working on. He treed a female, and she had brown rings around her teats, yet there were no kittens with her. The lead biologist didn't think the female had kittens.

"I told him, 'Well, you see that brown ring around there? She has to have smaller kittens unless she's lost them.' [The biologist] collared that female and when she made her next kill, researchers went in, and yes, she had two bobcat-size kittens with her. A guy hunting would want to be very careful or you'd kill a bunch of kittens too."

Ruark and I wrapped up our visit with a stroll to his Brahma bull's pen. Sure enough, the bull loved being petted by Ruark. Then Ruark did something I won't forget—he wiggled the bull's downward facing horns back and forth. "They're called banana horns. Just the way they grow. Floppy and soft." Then he added, "But don't try getting on his back."

DOGS IN WOLF COUNTRY

I was still curious about hunting mountain lions in wolf country. In January 2005, an outfitter with five dogs was hot on the trail of a mountain lion in the valley where I live. High up in the treed slopes, our local wolf pack had just killed a bull elk. The pack's pups were feeding on the elk while babysitter wolves watched over and protected them. As the houndsman's dogs worked their way up the thickly forested mountain incline, they inadvertently encountered the pack. Jason Morrison, their owner, thought the dogs were so concentrated on their task that they didn't see the wolves coming at them. His $3,500 ten-year-old hound dog was killed. Wolves are territorial and especially will not tolerate other canines in their area.

That was one of the first attacks on lion hounds by wolves in Wyoming, and it resonated in the nearby Cody area. "It took the wind out of everyone's sails," said Morrison. Coincidentally, the incident took place the year I bought my cabin. For many years after the attack, lion hunters were hesitant to run their dogs up here, so I saw very few. Then in 2012, Wyoming sponsored its first wolf hunt. Eight wolves were taken in my valley, along with many in neighboring hunt areas. Suddenly, the cougar hunters returned.

Although the wolf hunts lasted only two years until the fall of 2014, when Wyoming's wolves were relisted through a court order, the hounds and hunters continued to come. Maybe they thought we now had fewer wolves, which wasn't the case. Or maybe the Morrison dog was a distant memory. At that time, the hunt zone around my cabin extended far out into the desert where there are no wolf packs. Cougar hunters didn't need to return to the mountains, but they did. It wasn't because the hunters needed freezer food. Although occasionally a hunter will eat the meat, it's rare, and don't let a lion hunter tell you they consume their kills. They just don't. So why did they return despite all the apparent risks?

Montana cougar country lies predominantly west of the Continental Divide where wolves share the landscape with the cats.

Treed cougar

There are few cougar hunting opportunities there without facing the threat of wolves. Although Wyoming has different topographical configurations, many areas in the state have optimal lion habitat. Yet only northwest Wyoming has wolves, and lion hunting throughout Wyoming has success with high quotas. So why go into wolf country if it can be avoided? And what is the method of keeping your dogs safe, if there even is one?

Grover Hedrick worked on the second Yellowstone National Park mountain lion study with Toni Ruth after the wolf reintroduction in the mid-1990s. These were the first wolves to enter into the United States, and without first-hand knowledge of using dogs in wolf country, Hedrick asked some friends in Alberta, Canada, what they'd recommend. Hedrick is very protective of his hounds, and his Canadian friend's advice was to use bells on his dogs. The tinkling sound, they told him, might be just "too much of a human sound for the wolves. Those wolves are extremely protective of their territory, and they'll come for a long way to kill barking hounds." In the Park, all travel is on foot, no use of snowmobiles. That meant the crew was snowshoeing sometimes ten or twelve miles a day, while the dogs waited under a tree three or four hours till the scientists caught up. One time, Hedrick tells me, those bells did save his dogs during the Park study.

"The wolves came in, and they circled. They made a trail about seventy-five yards away from the tree, but they wouldn't come in on the dogs. There was just enough banging going on—they weren't comfortable."

All the old-timers I spoke with in Montana knew hunters whose dogs were killed by wolves, although none of them had that misfortune personally. For Hedrick, it's always been more about his dogs than killing any cats—"I haven't shot a cat in over twenty-five years." If the terrain allows, he will scope out the area with his snowmobile first to see if there have been wolves around. Hedrick tells me, "I was in the Bitterroot Valley a few years back and I had a big tom track. The wolves had been there and left, went a different direction than the cat had. I thought, 'I'll snowmobile a half-circle to make sure they didn't come back in.' Well, they'd come back in up on top, so I wasn't going to run it. When I came back to the parking area, there was a younger guy with three hounds, getting ready to run. I said to him, 'I don't think I would.' 'Well, they left,' he said. I told him they'd come back in again. Maybe he didn't believe me, because he turned loose and they killed all his dogs."

If you're going to hunt cats, I was told, wolves are just part of the scenario. "In wolf country," Hedrick says, "you just have to run more than two dogs. When the odds are even, they'll probably do something, but when the wolves are outnumbered, they'll drop back and howl, and probably won't do anything."

Dan Thompson, large carnivore biologist for Wyoming Game and Fish, did his doctoral work on cougars in the Black Hills. During his research, he ran his dogs after plenty of cougars in a region with no wolves; now, living in Lander and working in northwest

Young cougar inspects camera

Wyoming, he has the perspective of cougar country both with and without the complete suite of top predators. "We definitely know there're some changes that have occurred. Just behaviorally, in running cats, I see they do things different to get away from dogs. They're a lot trickier if there are wolves around, and it's more difficult to get a lion up a tree." Thompson gives me an example. "In the Jackson area, cats were running more than you'd expect, and it's not from hunting pressure. Going through downfall, zig-zagging, they were doing things behaviorally a lot different."

Speaking with these old-time houndsmen, I heard stories that make for campfire nights: a cougar in the Canadian winter swimming across a river of ice floes; the hunter who was forced to sleep in a makeshift shelter at -37°F; a lion that swam three-and-a-half miles across Fort Peck reservoir, snarling at fishermen along the way; or the hunter who followed the cat's tracks twenty miles on foot into the maze of Montana's Pryor Mountains after his dogs took off. He found his dogs, but not the cat.

These men had learned to love their quarry through a lifetime of experience, running their dogs for more than thirty years. Most had killed few cougars. For some, it was all about the dogs; for others, it was about being outside for months on end all winter long. They all lamented how different it is today when you don't have to follow your dogs. But for all of them, it came down to the magnificence of the cat, its athleticism, grace, intelligence, and power.

Many of the houndsmen told me how the outfitters changed the ethics of hunting decades ago by pushing for higher and higher quotas. Because they can charge their clients prices upwards of $6,000, many of today's outfitters hire men to drive snowmobiles on trails twenty-four hours a day looking for fresh tracks. No individual hunter can compete with these outfitters, and greed drives the quotas higher and higher each year.

Rod Bullis and I continue our conversation. He's helped me understand the roots and customs of mountain lion hunting in the West, and he knows full well that if that tradition is to continue, he and others like him with similar ethics will need to advocate for real change, as well as education of younger hunters. I've come to admire how he and his friends work tirelessly to reinsert the idea of fair chase and ethical release, as well as advocate for lion science to guide management policies. As Bullis repeatedly reminds me, "They are a really high life form. I know that. I just know that."

CHAPTER 7

THE DEADLIEST JOURNEY

From there he headed upward again and ran on for
miles. In every valley and along every rushing stream
he found the scent of man. The slope he had come to,
upon crossing the divide, was settled by ranchers and
cattlemen . . .The scent of man was upon every trail he
crossed, beside every spring, and on every ridge. Through
that night and until daylight flooded the mountains the
king cat wandered on, ever searching for a domain free
from the enemy he hated. But he found no such haven.

—RUTHERFORD MONTGOMERY

COUGAR KITTENS

All that was left was a shriveled, leathery hide, a few hanging
bones, one foot, and an intact skull with its skin. It appeared to be
a very large bobcat from the size of the head, but all the features
were misshapen. I first soaked the skull for several days in water
to soften the hide, and then I skinned it. The dermestid beetles
had already eaten out the brains. I cut off as much meat as possible
and placed the skull in an ammonia and water bath for more than
a week. I cleaned the skull a second time, soaking it in a solution
of H_2O_2 and water. Once dry, I took my first good look at the

small skull, which appeared oversized for a bobcat. I could see milk teeth but the permanent teeth hadn't quite poked through. I used my skull book for guidance to take more than ten measurements. In every category, this skull was slightly larger than the book's biggest bobcat measurements. I learned something important in that measuring process: I didn't need to go through all that trouble to determine what I held in my hand. With the upper jaw intact, I should have noticed a tiny, extra pre-molar directly behind the canines which hadn't quite emerged. Cougars have three pre-molars while bobcats have only two in their upper dentition. This was a cougar kitten skull. And it was found not far from my house, up on rocky scree.

By using a chart on tooth eruption, I determined the kitten was around three months old. How she died remained a mystery, but in the first five or six months of their lives, kittens are at their most vulnerable. Predation, starvation, and loss of her mother are all possibilities. And the fact that this young kitten would not have been able to reliably climb a tree for safety until it was five or six months old added to the many recipes for disaster here.

Newborn kittens are born with their eyes and ears closed, barely able to move. They weigh little more than a pound and are completely dependent upon their mother's skill in finding a protected nursery site. Dens are usually in dense vegetation, spaces amongst boulders, or intense log jams. Typical litters contain two to four kittens, clothed in reddish to gray-brown coats with black spots and black rings on their tails. Within two weeks the ears are open, along with sky-blue eyes, and they begin to move awkwardly about, exploring the rock overhang, brushy thicket, or pile of boulders that serves as their den.

At approximately four weeks, the kittens are engaging in mock battles and play, venturing out to explore their surroundings. By eight to twelve weeks, the kittens are weaned and on the move, leaving the safety of the nursery. They begin to lose their spots,

Puma kitten

which fade to dapples at roughly nine months and are barely visible on their hindquarters by fifteen months. Although at two months they cannot yet climb trees, they are capable of negotiating rugged terrain and will accompany mom on her hunting rounds. When she goes off to hunt, she will hide her kittens, gathering them again to feed on the kill. This is a very vulnerable time in the kittens' development, for their presence at kill sites can attract predators like wolves, coyotes, and bears.

By the time the cubs are five months old, they can quickly climb trees to evade predators. Their eyes turn from blue to brown or amber-gray, their spots fade to lightly mottled, and the kittens are surprisingly big. I shared a video I took of a mom and her kitten with a biologist, and I was stunned when he said the kitten was six months old. The kitten was more than half the size of his mom. Although they look big, the kittens are highly dependent upon their mother's hunting skills throughout their first year. She must kill a deer every four days to feed three kittens. The span

Approximately five month old kittens

between six and eighteen months is a very important time for the cubs because they learn the art of hunting and killing prey. They are exploring their natal range and learning how to deal with potential enemies. Mothers will bring live and dead prey for off-spring to practice on. Hippy Mom's orphan, F75, exemplifies the importance of these critical months of instructions. F75 was just losing her milk teeth at nine months, and she didn't have sufficient canine strength to puncture a larger animal in order to survive. She was physically immature, and her training as a hunter was by no means complete.

By eighteen months, sub-adult male cougars can easily out-weigh their mothers and may weigh as much as 150 pounds, the average weight for an adult male. Females are considered reproductively active adults by two to three years old. Because they need to disperse farther and set up their own territory that includes other females, males are labeled adults at three to four years of age. Both sexes are capable of breeding at around twenty-four months. These sub-adults are embarking on the riskiest journey of their young lives as they look to set up their own home ranges.

DEATH OF A DISPERSER

It was another droughty winter with little snow. By early April, snow at the east end of the valley had disappeared, signaling it was the right time for my annual hike to the Shoshone Sheep Eater bighorn sheep trap. It's a hard, steep, uphill climb with the sheep trap hanging along a narrow shelf on the rims of an enormous massif I've named Far Cry Mountain. There are remains of at least four sheep traps along the high reaches of the limestone cutouts. This particular trap is not only intact, it also has an impressive view of the entire valley. High ground, rocky ledges, cliffs, scattered pines, bighorn sheep—all making for good lion country. No doubt the illusive cat shared space with these Native peoples, hunting the same animal.

The hike is strenuous, an unrelenting, uphill slog traversing open meadows with folds where limber pines suck up snowmelt. Elk and deer use these south-facing slopes as their winter range. Once beyond the lower two-thirds, the long slope transforms and steepens into a series of three or four benches. Above these step-like perches, the mountain is a large flying buttress of rock and rim.

The sheep trap I'm after today is accessible only by braving a narrow animal trail along a vertiginous drop. Shoshone Sheep Eaters, so called because their main food was bighorn sheep, used dogs to herd sheep downhill along a V-shaped series of logs into these traps and then bludgeoned the animals to death.

Once I reach the first set of benches, I'm tired and I decide to spend time exploring. I haven't gone far when Koda takes off, climbing straight uphill on terrain loaded with loose scree. I can't see another bench above, only limber pines folded into rock and nasty, eroded, small gullies. He smells something, and that's my sign to follow. Koda quickly disappears high up on a small ledge obscured by trees. It appears he's found a carcass and I'm slightly annoyed that I've exerted myself just for his pleasure to chew on a deer leg. But once I'm within view of the dead animal, I see a long tail. It takes my brain a few milliseconds to figure out that this is a dead cougar.

Temperatures are still below freezing most days and nights, so there are no bugs on the carcass. Only the birds have opened the skin and picked at the insides, as well as the eyes. But the rest of the lion is still intact—the legs, head, and hide. Did wolves do this? I examine the small ledge where the cougar met his demise. Ten feet away, nestled against the nearby hillside, is evidence of a cougar-killed deer. The remains, only fur, lie neatly collected and slightly covered, a telltale cat sign. I take a closer look at the dead cat. It's obviously young—too small for a mature cougar. For some reason, the tail seems to be about half the size it should be. When I examine the head, I can see puncture wounds in the skull. One possible scenario is that this young cat, probably a dispersing male, made a kill while moving through another male's territory; a fight ensued, and the younger cat lost his life.

I volunteer in the Draper Museum of Natural History at the Buffalo Bill Center of the West, and I carry a permit that enables me to collect dead animals. The skull of this cat would be a nice addition for the museum's collection. I have a knife, my backpack, and even some large baggies, so I could take the skull back down with me today, but I decide to return with better equipment, such as gloves and a mask, just in case the animal was diseased.

In 2007, Eric York, a wildlife biologist working in Grand Canyon National Park, died from the plague. York was a skilled biologist who spent years trapping, handling, and collaring mountain lions. That fall he was monitoring ten collared lions around the Park, while also collecting data on bighorn sheep, black bears, bobcats, coyotes, and other species. The previous summer, two of the

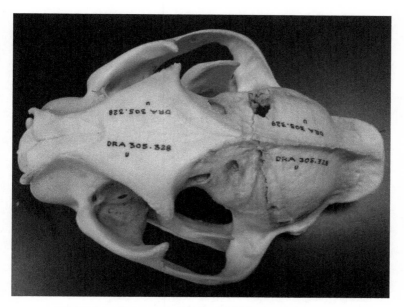

Skull I found now at the Buffalo Bill Museum of the West

female collared lions in the study had kittens, which York captured and ear tagged. At the end of October, York found the mother of one of these litters dead. He brought the mother's body back to his garage and performed a necropsy. When he opened up the lion, a wave of invisible plague spores filled the air in the garage, infecting York. He went to bed thinking he was coming down with the flu, which kept him from contacting anyone. Three days later he was dead from pneumonic plague. Cougars, as well as housecats and bobcats, can contract the disease by eating an infected rodent or by being bitten by a flea carrying the disease. It's the exposure to the animal's lungs that is dangerous for humans.

In the early years of Panthera's Teton Cougar Project study (at that time called the Beringia South Teton project), three cougars died of plague, including a mother and her kitten. While plague is not endemic to this country, it has been seen in a variety of species in the western United States. Plague is an acute disease that kills rapidly. The mother lion that was found dead appeared healthy. She wasn't just skin and bones. In her Yellowstone study, Toni Ruth found cats that died from plague, but she also found cougars that had antibodies to the disease.

I knew the story of York's death, and even though every sign pointed to the fact that this young cat had been killed by another cat, I couldn't be certain without skinning the animal. Without a pair of gloves and a mask, I had no intention of touching this cougar. I thought back to the article about York, and the admonition that the spores lie in the lung cavity. Birds had already eaten this cat's organs, but the cougar's cavity was open, and fairly fresh, so I didn't want to take any chances. I was in a maze of look-alike ledges and a hodge-podge of platforms and benches, so I placed cairns in obvious locations to mark my way as I descended.

Spring arrived in earnest as I planned my return to the carcass. I knew no one would find it, so that didn't worry me, and since it was a long, difficult hike, I had delayed my return by a few months. I told the game warden about the carcass and showed him my permit. If I hadn't had a permit, I'd be required to take the skull to the Wyoming Game and Fish Department and purchase a tag. With my well-placed cairns, the carcass wasn't hard to locate. This time I'd taken my G.P.S. to record the proper information for the Draper. But the weather had warmed enough that the carcass was full of maggots and dermestid beetles. The normal procedure for bringing dead animals into the Draper is to put them in the freezer for three days to kill everything living on the animal. Instead, I decided to put the skull into a garbage bag, place it outside my cabin, and let the bugs do much of the work before I brought it in. I might like wildlife, but insects are not my thing. Normally in the lab at the Draper, we skin the dead animal and remove as much of the meat as possible before giving it to the dermestid beetles. With all the meat and skin left on this skull, the process with the bugs took months, instead of weeks. In the fall when the sheer volume of bugs had diminished, I pulled the skull out of the bag and washed it off. I cleaned the remaining meat off the skull to ready it for our colony of beetles at the Draper. The final procedure for cleaning up a skull involves a soak in hydrogen peroxide, some fine scraping work by hand, and then labeling with a pen. After we had finished all the preparation work in the Draper lab, the puncture wounds in the young cougar's skull stood out.

Male mountain lion territories are usually immense, overlapping with territories of several females with which they breed. These dominant males spend time patrolling their land, looking for intruders and checking to see if one of the resident females may be in estrous. Yet even in a landscape as large as the Greater Yellowstone Ecosystem, my young disperser's presence must have been detected by the resident male.

For young cougars, the urge to leave their mother becomes overwhelming at some point. Recently the PTCP explored the question of what exactly stimulates dispersal in lions. The Panthera Project followed two kittens, male M80 and female F96, nicknamed Frostbite because she lost parts of her ears and the tip of her tail in winter. On April 1, 2014, both youngsters dispersed at nineteen months. The male traveled northwest, never to return, while Frostbite returned several times to feast upon her mother's kills. Finally, she made her break and established a territory southeast of Jackson.

What was interesting was the behavior of the male kitten before he dispersed. Now larger than his mother, M80 was becoming a petulant and independent teenager. In a series of photos posted by the PTCP on Nat Geo's Cat Watch, we see son M80 using his weight to lean against his mother, pushing her off a dry bed under a tree. Mom swats, nips, and hisses. You may be bigger, she seems to say, but you are still my son. "He took any abuse she doled out without contest, and we never witnessed M80 acting aggressively or violently with his mother," notes Elbroch.

M80 using his weight to lean against his mother F61,
pushing her off a warm dry bed where she lays

Mom F61 nips and cuffs her son, but he has won

The story of M80, the dispersing male, doesn't end there, and it points to the many hazards for these young cougars. That fall, a twelve-year-old boy hunting with his father killed M80 near Butte, Montana, two hundred miles from the M80's mother's home range. M80 was only twenty-six months old. Although a sad demise, what was amazing about M80's story was the great distance he traveled to establish his own home range.

In their analysis of what triggers dispersal, the PTCP concluded that a combination of parent/offspring conflict and the necessity for females to conserve energy for their next litter drove mothers to act aggressively with their kittens—hissing, swatting, and generally making their offspring feel unwelcome. What parent doesn't look forward to their unruly teenager leaving the house!

⟶ WHAT PORCUPINES, GUNS, AND HIGHWAYS HAVE IN COMMON

Global Positioning System (G.P.S.) technology has allowed scientists to see into an animal's world like never before—where it moves, how long it stays in one place, its migration patterns, and its bedding preferences—as well as documenting movements of dispersing individuals. Geographic Information System (G.I.S.) modeling and G.P.S. collar analysis requires that researchers log more time sitting at a computer than they do slogging out in the field. In speaking with Mark Elbroch, he told me he considers himself an old-fashioned research biologist. That translates into watching for cougar G.P.S. cluster data, hiking into the field as soon as possible to set up cameras, and then analyzing the scene in real time through track reading. "If there's a kill there, we mark it down. If not, we don't. It's proven to be a great way to do the work because of what we're learning and how we're changing the way people view mountain lions."

This sounds simple, but following cougar routes, especially in winter, can be grueling. Michelle Peziol, PTCP's Manager, told me how she, Elbroch, houndsman Boone Smith, and team biologist Connor O'Malley, went on a winter capture, fully expecting to be back in time for lunch at the office. The lion was "on a kill two hundred meters away from an easy snowmobile ride thirty miles from the main road." F49 was high up in the Gros Ventre Mountains with a failing collar that needed to be changed. With the scheduled winter road closures just days away, the team was under pressure to get the job done. As they rode higher, the snow deepened, and it was very apparent there was no game at this altitude. The lion was living with her six-month-old kittens near the headwaters of the Gros Ventre range. With little food available, the crew wondered what she was still doing there.

The capture crew parked their sled near the kill site and began their trek on foot. The dogs located the family's whereabouts, and they circled in, only to find that the family had killed a porcupine— "not a clean kill, it was a mess, there was stuff everywhere." The capture crew successfully treed the mother and one kitten; her second kitten was dead with more than three hundred porcupine quills in it. "At six months, it should be hitting about thirty-five pounds, maybe a little bigger if it were a male," Smith told me, adding to the story, "and this little cat was obviously not. I believe it weighed in at about fifteen pounds."

By the time the crew got the mother collared, it was dark, with a storm rolling in. And with all the circling and weaving during the chase, one of their three dogs was now missing. Peziol and Elbroch hiked back to their sled, while Smith and O'Malley went to find the missing dog. The men followed the dog's tracks until the blizzard began raging, covering his tracks. All Smith could hope for now was that the dog had settled down for the night in a safe place where the wolves wouldn't find him. Separated, each team independently realized they needed to spend the night, and each built a fire to stay warm.

By 3:00 a.m., Elbroch became concerned that his office staff would be worrying about them. With almost zero visibility, he and Peziol found the snowmobile and headed for their truck parked on the highway. As Elbroch drove through the blizzard, Peziol clung to Elbroch with one hand and to the dead kitten with the other. In an instant, the trail took a sharp turn, plunging the snowmobile into a giant snowbank and sending Peziol flying through the air holding the porcupine-laden kitten. With a lot of effort, they righted the snowmobile and

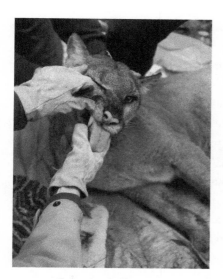

Scientists collaring a
sedated mountain lion

made it back to the trailhead. After a few hours of sleep in the truck, Elbroch returned for Smith and O'Malley. He found the errant dog on the road east of where they had caught F49, wallowing in four feet of snow. In my conversation with Michele Peziol, she wondered aloud why F49 would have been living with young kittens so high up, where the only food was small prey. Possibly she was trying to find safe refuge from the valley's wolves, Peziol mused.

Through this kind of intensive field work, Elbroch learned something about mountain lions that, in the fifty years people have been studying lions, no one had said before: dispersing lions disproportionally hunt small prey, and, in particular, porcupines. These young dispersers, inexperienced at killing and cautious about being hurt, exploit small prey and practice their new hunting skills as they look for a new home.

Porcupines, though dangerous, are slow. They weigh between twenty and forty pounds and make a highly nutritious meal of meat and fat. In a study in Colorado, Mark Elbroch reported that a dispersing male-turned-resident killed thirty-nine porcupines in four months before moving on to larger prey. Another female disperser in Wyoming killed twenty porcupines in 2 1/2 months. While P3, a twenty-month-old male, was on the move looking for a home, more than a quarter of his diet consisted of porcupines, with a measly 8 percent from deer and elk. Four months later, when P3 established his home range sixty-five miles from where the team captured him, the percentages flip-flopped, and more than 32 percent of his diet came from deer and elk.

I was surprised at the number of porcupines these young dispersers were eating in the Jackson area—surprised because there has been an unexplainable, massive decline in porcupine sightings across the West since the late 1990s. Field biologists from New Mexico to Canada have been reporting declining numbers, but no one has a handle on why this is occurring. Low elevation porcupines seem to be doing fine, but mountain porcupines are nowhere to be found. While cougars might reduce an area's population, they don't prey on enough porcupines to account for their massive declines. Speculation among researchers involves a combination of many things from habitat loss, disease, increased predation, and shooting. Climate change has killed entire forests of prime trees porcupines need for food. The increase in fires in the West has only added to their loss of habitat. Unlike other rodents, porcupines produce only one offspring a year, so their populations never become very large, and it is easy for mortalities to knock a population down quickly. This docile, slow-moving, well-armored rodent is evidently a sensitive animal.

Old-timers in my valley tell me that porcupines were once numerous here. By the 1950s, a concerted effort by the government to reduce their numbers made use of strychnine-laced blocks. In 1972, the use of toxicants was banned on federal lands. But scientists can't explain their recent scarcity.

In the ten years I've lived east of Yellowstone Park, I've only seen porcupines in forested areas twice. Yet in 1972, while backpacking in Grand Teton National Park, I had a close encounter with one. I had no money to buy fancy gear. My friends and I slept under the stars with only our sleeping bags for protection. Crawling into bed, my boots came off first, and they were carefully laid by my head. We were already deep in the backcountry, and I was awakened in the middle of the night to a distinct chomping sound.

It seemed to be coming from behind me. I popped my head out and looked around. The crescent moon cast slight shadows on a large rock near where I'd laid my boots, but it was too dark to make out any features. Tired from the long day of hiking, I concluded the noise was of no consequence and went back to sleep. After a few minutes, when the chewing sound commenced again, I realized that the stone was a new addition to the landscape. I raised my head just in time to see a shadowy "rock" waddle away. The next morning, the ankles of both boots were entirely eaten away. The culprit had been a porcupine. A trail ranger informed us they'd been having trouble with porcupines destroying outhouse seats. Poor mineral metabolism, and a generally mineral-deficient diet, drives porcupines to seek salt. Even though chewed up park benches, trees, and outhouse seats made modern man consider porcupines a nuisance, views on porcupines were once quite different. Native peoples long regarded the animal with respect and admiration. A minor animal spirit, the porcupine represented caution and self-defense. The animal supplied food and provided quills used for decoration on clothing and medicine bags. Stories were told about travelers who noted the location of a porcupine in case they were in need of food on their return.

Although many animals—including coyotes, bobcats, and black bears—will eat porcupines, only cougars and fishers are proficient at killing them and willing to forego the potential pain to continue trying. In order to kill a porcupine, the predator has to get the quill-pig on its back so that their vulnerable soft belly is exposed. That's not easy to do with an animal that has more than thirty thousand quills, each up to four inches long. Although a porcupine does not actually throw its quills, it does swing its tail with a slap at its attacker. The quills have a mild antibiotic compound that reduces the risk of infection—the only "positive" in this dangerous game. The quills are tipped with barbs designed to go in deeper and deeper as the victim moves. I've heard of quills going straight through an arm and coming out the other side, but quills can work their way into an animal's organs or bones, killing the predator even months later. Young cougars bat porcupines with their large paws to turn them on their backs. Some lion dispersers will improve their hunting skills and move on to kill larger prey.

Lion dispersal is critically important for genetic diversity, as well as for geographic expansion. Females tend to stay close to their birth mother's range, while males need to find an empty slot devoid of a dominant male. The odds are tough for dispersing males, who roam much farther than females. Occasionally there are reports of a female who roams far afield in search of new territory. One such young anomaly, dubbed Sandy after Sand Creek in British Columbia, where she was captured and collared, surprised researchers by making a trek all the way to central Montana, a 450-mile journey. The B.C. study was initiated to determine whether lions were a threat to public safety after Sandy and two other lions showed up near the community of Cranbrook, B.C., preying on urban deer. Instead of sticking close to home, the ninety-pound female took off on an adventure, navigating forested edges of farmlands and ranches, staying out of sight of the general populace. She killed deer along her route, and after nine months, she settled in the Big Belt Mountains east of Helena, Montana. Sandy's journey made international news, but just fourteen days after her story made headlines, her life was cut short by a legal hunter. All too often, a disperser's story has this same sad ending.

Young dispersers face many obstacles fending for themselves for the first time: roads, people, development, hunters, and dominant males. While M80 and Sandy lived in the vast Rocky Mountain wilderness and were able to travel hundreds of miles to find a territory, 46M had different obstacles to deal with when he dispersed, at the age of two, from the Santa Cruz Mountains in northern California. This cougar was a collared male in the Santa Cruz Puma project, and his travels were easily documented.

Following his instincts, 46M crossed the mountains and even navigated busy Interstate Highway 280 unharmed, only to find himself trapped in the city of Mountain View, California, a town that hugs congested Palo Alto, bordered on the northeast by San Francisco Bay. The young cougar traveled for hours unseen, visiting backyards and finally hiding beneath a bush in front of a house, where neighbors spotted him. That evening he moved to a parking garage, hunkering down underneath a car. Police cordoned off the apartment complex until California Department of Fish and Wildlife arrived, tranquilized the cat, and moved him back to the mountains. A Department spokesman said, "This was the perfect textbook example of how to rescue a mountain lion." This rescue occurred in 2014 and the Department was happy to make that pronouncement, as other mountain lion dispersals hadn't gone so well for the lion. In 2010, a confused female lion found herself in the area of Shattuck and Cedar streets in Berkeley, California. Berkeley Police pursued her as she jumped several fences and ran down streets. Police finally shot her as she took refuge in the back yard of a home. In Half Moon Bay, in 2012, two very young lion kittens, the size of house cats, were shot to death by the Department. After that incident, California legislators enacted Senate Bill 132 in 2014 requiring the Department of Fish and Wildlife to use only non-lethal methods to remove mountain lions, unless there was imminent danger to human life. In response, the Department created what's known as a Response Team Approach, a step-by-step guide to dealing with human/mountain lion interactions, categorizing them into four types: sighting, livestock conflict, potential human conflict, or public safety. This Response Team Approach describes what actions will be taken, based on the advice of mountain lion experts, and who will be responsible for taking those actions. In just two years, this new directive has saved more than twenty-five lions that would have been killed otherwise, releasing them back into the wild instead. The Humane Society of America has called this proactive California approach a model that all states should adopt. As cities and towns expand into exurban areas, and mountainous regions are dotted with more and more houses, young dispersers are vulnerable in their quest for a new home.

DISPERSERS EAST OF YELLOWSTONE

When I learned that my valley was a major corridor for young lions leaving Yellowstone Park, my curiosity about dispersal piqued. I'd recorded a young cougar on my trail camera all summer. He looked emaciated, although I found one successful deer kill hidden in the nearby woods. One afternoon my neighbor was working on his irrigation ditches when he heard a noise. He turned in time to see his Labrador Retriever, Boots, facing off with a cougar. He yelled and waved his arms, and the cougar ran up a tree. I'll bet it was the same lion as the one on my trail camera.

August passed into September without another incident, but as deer began pouring into the lowlands after the first big fall snow, this inexperienced, and hungry, cougar got into trouble again. My neighbors were inside their home eating dinner when they heard a strange, whining sound coming from their front yard. Racing outside, they encountered the same mountain lion from the irrigation ditch incident, but this time the lion was holding Boots's head in his mouth! Throwing rocks and yelling, they scared the cougar away just in time to save Boots's life. The dog had such deep punctures in his skull that tubes had to be inserted in order for them to drain. With antibiotics, and, after a few weeks' rest, Boots did recover.

Meanwhile, the Wyoming Game and Fish Department was contacted. They laid out baited cage traps, hoping to trap the troublesome lion, probably a young male. The lion never returned, and the traps were removed. A few weeks later I caught two thin lions on my camera, probably sibling dispersers traveling together.

Boots' cougar

Dan Thompson did his doctoral research on mountain lion dispersal in the Black Hills of South Dakota. I asked him how these lions knew which way to travel. Thompson told me there are a lot of different hypotheses to explain how young cougars chose a dispersal route. "Mountain lions are very visually oriented, so that comes into play. We had a male that dispersed to Canada. There's one chunk in the prairie you can see [from the Black Hills] if you are going toward Canada." If a visual cue is their primary honing device, then most of Thompson's lions followed that pattern. They'd make a loop in the Black Hills into the Bear Lodge Mountains, a small satellite range of the Black Hills. From there, they'd springboard in many different directions, most destined for the Rocky Mountains visible in the distance. A female, the first one Thompson ever collared, went as far as the Denver area and lived there for twelve years. On the other hand, Thompson's theory is that the reason many of his eastward bound lions kept traveling wasn't for lack of food or habitat, but lack of love—no females to be found. Considering that mountain lions once inhabited all of the U.S., this indicates dispersal is more random until a lion finds a location where all his needs are met.

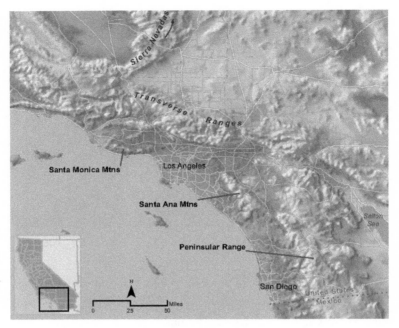

Topographic map depicting location of Santa Ana Mountains,
eastern Peninsular Ranges in southern California and adjacent regions.

As if sub-adult dispersal isn't treacherous enough for cougars,
studies done in California reveal how urbanization can make matters worse. Biologists Ken Logan and Linda Sweanor compared dispersals in their ten-year New Mexico study with those in southern
California. In the sparsely populated area of the San Andres Mountains of New Mexico, lions were using mountain/desert/basin inter-
faces temporarily before dispersing to mountainous patches on the
other side of the basin. In contrast, cougars born in the Santa Ana
Mountains of southern California found few corridors to aid dispersal out of the mountains because of a burgeoning human population
at the mountain's base. Out of eight males in the California study
who attempted dispersal, only two survived to adulthood and established home ranges thirty-five to forty-seven miles from their birth

area. And it took the California cats twice as long to find suitable home ranges than their New Mexico counterparts.

One researcher told me he still frequently hears, even from other researchers, "Well if you still have dispersals, then you must have an abundance of mountain lions, because these are extras." That's not true. Males must disperse; it's in their DNA. A biologist looks at both emigration (movement out of a study area or home range) and immigration as well. What's troubling about the Jackson cougar population is the 47 percent drop in the population since the PTCP began in 2001. The vacancy left in the Jackson landscape by the death of Hippy Mom F51 is still unfilled. No immigration. In addition, uncollared cats caught on summer trail cameras are not sticking around to form home ranges.

Young teenage males looking for a home are often the ones that get into trouble. Hunters prefer large trophy males. By killing off a dominant male who is maintaining an area, a large hole is left for teenagers to move in. Mature male lions regulate the cougar population within their home ranges by keeping the juvenile males out. When the older lions are killed off *en masse*, younger sub-adults, the teenagers, are more prone to human conflict as they jockey for territory, resulting in increased livestock predation. And a higher population of younger males can lead to infanticide as these newcomers seek to acquaint themselves with the resident females and force them into estrus.

The most dramatic example of how dispersers can keep even a declining population alive on 'life-support' is in Texas. Texas was the Lone Star holdout—the one exception to the 1970s' sea change that transformed the status of lions in the western states. Texas listed mountain lions as "varmints," non-game, unprotected animals that could be killed year-round regardless of sex—trapped, snared, shot or poisoned, no bag limits, no reporting necessary. Texas has the least amount of federal land of all the western states, a measly 2 percent. In the 1990s, the Sierra Club made a concerted effort to change the status of mountain lions in the state, but ranchers and landowners fought back and won, retaining their non-protected listing. Biologists I spoke with still remember that decision as if it were just yesterday. Since then, although the demographics of Texas is changing, maybe a hopeful sign for mountain lions, the problem is that lions are no longer on the public's radar.

The population of cougars in southern Texas is struggling—in-bred, with low populations, there is a bottleneck of genetic refreshment. In contrast, the lion population is holding on in the Trans-Pecos region, (everything west of the Pecos River), a vast, sparsely populated region of desert, big mountain ranges, large old ranches, and Big Bend National Park. Immigration from Mexico and New Mexico supplies new blood into the area. Without this immigration, the lion population in Texas would be completely exterminated today.

Although there are many older, uninhabited, ranches in the Trans-Pecos region of Texas, there also are game farms—large ranches where rich people come to hunt deer, paying up to $3,000 for their hunting excursion. Lions eating deer are eating the ranchers' commodity. Ranches hire private trappers, most of whom are quite skilled and are even able to anticipate which foot the lion will place into the trap. They don't use dogs or bait. Texas has a 36-hour trap check rule only for fur-bearing species, which means that unprotected species like mountain lions don't have a trap check time limit. Some trappers use old fashioned, large, bear traps, leaving them out for a month or more before checking them. This means that a trapped lion dies of starvation. This unethical trapping is legal under Texas law. With the hodge-podge of private lands, and backwards management, mountain lions face a grim future until Texas state laws change because of public sentiment and pressure.

A light snow fell one night, making for perfect tracking the following morning. I'd never hiked to the terminus of Cougar Flats, so today that's where I headed. I was anxious to find an access point to the Clarks Fork River, a thousand feet below. A few locals had told me there was one. From the views I'd seen, and the couloirs I'd encountered, I imagined this magical trail to be full of breathless handholds, vertical clefts, and narrow rims.

As I approached the flat's end point, large, unbroken slabs of easily traversed granite quickly turned into a jumbled, rock maze with gullies and defiles spilling toward the river below. The snow was deep in the drifts along the tree line where I spotted prints of a family of three cougars, a mom and two large kittens. I followed their tracks around large boulders until they disappeared into the steep, wooded forest beyond. I knew that must be the access into the Clarks Fork Canyon I'd been told about, but the snow was deep, and I didn't know what lay beyond those trees, so I decided to wait until the snow melted.

The following spring I set out with Koda. The seasons transform the plateau, and not just because there's no longer a blanket of snow. Cattle run here and leave their cow pies everywhere. The deer and elk have moved to the high country, along with the lions. When I approached the shelterbelt of trees where I'd seen the tracks of my cat family the winter before, it wasn't the steep slide I'd imagined. Instead, a wooded gully led a quarter mile to a dizzying cliff edge. Surely the cats had found another route in the forest. I backtracked up the canyon halfway, locating another approach around a large rib of rock that led to a small clearing with a view. I walked along this open, boulder-strewn hill to a ravine. The gully was a narrow fold of tight pines, and very steep. I could not have used this route in the winter. But now, the sharp incline was easy to navigate, especially by hanging onto trees on the way down. The ravine was short and led to a large rock platform. I easily scrambled to the top for a view. Before me was the secret of the dispersal route. I stood a thousand feet above a confluence where two vast adjacent valleys narrowed, tumbling their creeks into the mighty Clarks Fork River. One creek marries the Clarks Fork River in a waterfall, which wasn't visible from my position, blocked by a towering column of granite. Ledge upon ledge, a folio of rock fell before me as a series of stairs and a swath of treeless talus slope, making for an easy descent to the river below. Now I knew why the lions were so prevalent on this side of the creek canyon. Upstream of that massive gorge, I knew the canyon narrowed into what river runners call "The Box," twenty-three miles of rushing water navigable by only the most dare-devil kayakers. A series of hard portages, one a mile long, is mandatory and, if neglected, death is almost certain.

This canyon is considered the third deepest in the United States. At this location, a thousand feet below from where I'm standing, "The Box" untangles itself, cliffs widen, and the river slows into an easy class IV waterway, with an open river basin. Four miles downriver, the walls of the canyon fall to the desert floor in what is known as the Beartooth Front. The mighty river, flush from snow-melt in the spring, continues through the desert on its journey to the Montana border. Before the great melt in the spring, the river, though cold, can be crossed. Lions are excellent swimmers. This must be their age-old dispersal route down into the desert. This was the only promising topographic route down—easy for a cougar and manageable, though strenuous, for me. Once in the canyon bottom, they could find not only deer, antelope, and small game, but also arroyos for secret travel, cliffs and badlands for cover, and a visible route to the Pryor and Bighorn Mountains to the east and north.

When I learned of this secret corridor, confirming my suspicion that lions were using my valley as a travel route east, I began collecting mountain lion scat and bed hairs. I took G.P.S. coordinates and stored the scat in labeled paper bags in a cool area. If I could find them, the white underbelly hairs of a lion would be the best source of DNA material. I contacted Dan Stahler, who I'd met at

Toni Ruth's Yellowstone Institute class several years back. Stahler told me how to store the material properly, but since my area is outside his study area, jurisdiction for permissions become more complicated, as other agencies besides the National Park Service would then become involved. My hope was to understand whether these dispersals in my area were coming directly out of Yellowstone Park. The Draper, which has a fine collection of predator specimens, may someday be a place to analyze the DNA in my assemblage of paper bags.

In 2017, I did receive a clue about dispersals east of Yellowstone Park. The Yellowstone Cougar Project collared only three cougars the previous year: a large adult male that was killed by another male in the Park, an adult female, and one of her male offspring. The young male, M201, dispersed, spending his summer exploring the high ridges and drainages of the Absaroka Wilderness on the eastern Park boundary where the Park elk graze. He made an elk kill on Saddle Mountain, then continued south, exploring ridges and drainages until he got to the Buffalo Bill Reservoir, which lies along the highway to the east entrance of the Park. When he saw human habitation, he hightailed it out of there, traveling north until he reached the wild basin where I live. Along the way, he fed on deer, elk calves, cottontails, and marmots. He'd become a good hunter. He was looking for his own niche. Crisscrossing the valley's dirt road several times, he made an elk kill up a small satellite drainage, where, on December 1, a hunter shot and killed him. He was a naïve, young cougar, just looking for unoccupied territory, trying to avoid humans. Dispersing mountain lions have the hardest journey of all.

CHAPTER 8

THE ZEN OF MOUNTAIN LIONS

*Pumas are such masters of invisibility that even
when we researchers began to collar and collect data
on them, only a little of their mystery was lost.*

—HARLEY SHAW

COUNTING COUGARS

The stretch of landscape from Shoshoni to Cheyenne has about the same interest as the clickity-clack of a train on the rails, punctuated only when the lovely cottonwood-lined Platt River comes into view. Wide open desert space, much appreciated by pronghorn, transitions in slow motion from extreme desert to broken country bordering the foothills of the Laramie Mountains. This range, thirty miles west of Wyoming's capital city, is part of the Rocky Mountains. Yet one wouldn't know that from the rolling short-grass prairie surrounding Cheyenne at the western edge of the Great Plains. From the Wyoming border south, it's not far to the front range of Colorado, where fourteen-thousand-foot peaks beckon.

I'm on my way to Estes Park, Colorado, a small gateway town nestled next to Rocky Mountain National Park, this year's site for the twelfth triannual Mountain Lion Conference, attended by researchers, environmentalists, and state game managers. It's a chance to present the latest studies and research on lions, but I'm not thinking about that during the long, eight-hour drive. As the miles roll by, I find myself pondering these large desert expanses between the high mountain ranges of the Colorado Rockies and the Laramie Range to the south, and the Bighorn Mountains and the Black Hills far to the north. Although dispersers move through, there are also resident lions making a living here on this landscape, especially those traveling discretely through badlands and arroyos, using river bottoms and coulees. And pronghorn—the swiftest resident land mammal, with the longest documented migration in North America—lives on these lands as well.

To my surprise, Toni Ruth's Yellowstone study in the early 2000s collared a cougar that had a taste for pronghorn in Yellowstone Park. Newborn fawns, vulnerable and hidden in high grass, would be the easiest to prey on, for adult pronghorn have high-powered vision and tremendous speed. But Ruth's pronghorn killer didn't kill only young fawns. In fact, pregnant adults, and adults with fawns, were her specialty. Cougar predation on pronghorn is fairly rare. But in the case of Ruth's pronghorn-killing cougar, antelope comprised a major portion of her diet, an even rarer occurrence. I wondered how a lion kills the swiftest animal in North America with precision and regularity.

The evolution of the pronghorn's swiftness is now up for debate. For a long time, scientists maintained that the amazing speed of the pronghorn, which can run up to sixty miles per hour for long periods, coincided with the evolution of an American cheetah. Bones found in Natural Trap Cave in Wyoming—long limbed with a shortened skull—were similar to cougars, yet just different enough that researchers assumed they were related to their African cousin. But in the 1990s a more complete specimen was found in a cave in West Virginia, confirming that these cats were actually cougar relatives, not cheetahs. In 2010, new discoveries in Arizona suggested that these ghost-cougars frequented caves and pounced from rocks

A group of male pronghorns

on a now extinct species of mountain goat. At this point, the real reason for the pronghorn's speed became muddled in controversy, requiring additional work from researchers to unravel mysteries of long extinct animals. Our present-day pronghorn was the last survivor of a much larger, diverse family, wiped out, along with their cougar predators, during the Pleistocene extinction ten thousand years ago.

Toni Ruth's pronghorn killer reveals how our modern-day cougar can take down a pronghorn, probably using her ancient instincts. This female lion had the broadest dietary range of any of the cats Ruth studied, and, with it, a lot of confidence. She was a very successful mother, despite the fact that her home range had one of the highest overlap with wolves, and bears frequently stole her kills. Pronghorn tended to show up in her diet when they were migrating from the lower elevations around Gardiner, Montana, up across Mt. Everts, and south of the Blacktail Plateau in Yellowstone Park. Most of the pronghorn she killed were moving through forested areas during their migration and a large majority were either pregnant or just having their fawns. Coyotes like to comb the sagebrush for newborn fawns, and Ruth assumes the pronghorn might have been seeking out forested areas to avoid those pressures. "Every one of [those pronghorns that were preyed upon were] in the forested landscape during that migratory and fawning time," Ruth told me. "We had a pilot up in the air doing a predation sequence on this female lion that specialized on pronghorn. He watched her jump out of the forest into this little meadow system on a pronghorn and kill it."

The YMCA in Estes Park that's hosting the Mountain Lion Conference is an enormous complex, with dozens of buildings that include housing units, several large lecture halls, dining areas, and even a store. After the first morning, with more participants in our workshop than expected, the Conference moved to a spacious lecture hall that could house the two hundred-plus participants.

Mountain lion researchers are increasingly looking to the laboratory for answers to disentangle long-held questions. DNA is being used to identify at-risk populations of cougars, particularly in California. With that in mind, I wasn't surprised that the first half-day of the conference was devoted to mountain lion genomics. Several people secretly admitted they used that time for a break. Many old-style biologists, doing hands-on field work, have not quite moved into the fast lane of DNA analytics research with its new lingo of "microsatellite loci" or "heterozygote excess." But as DNA research advances, it may unlock secrets and possibly predict the future decline of genetic diversity for cougars living in isolated areas, leading to extirpation.

Kyle Gustafon, a post-doctorate researcher in the Wildlife Genomics and Disease Ecology Laboratory at the University of Wyoming, laid out an astounding presentation on lion populations in California and Nevada. Genotyping almost one thousand specimens, he found ten fairly distinct populations, some with lots of genetic diversity (healthy), and others with more limited diversity that could possibly decline further unless immigration occurs. "The primary factors acting as barriers to gene flow were roads, specifically interstate highway, and geographic distance." The more roads, the less genetic diversity, which implies a greater need for connectivity, that is, safe passage across highways. The mountain lions in the Santa Ana Mountains south of Los Angeles, face the greatest problems, and lions once extirpated won't recolonize. Gustafon emphasized that cougars are an umbrella species, and loss of genetic diversity in cougars could be indicative of larger scale losses within other species.

Many in the crowd are hopeful that DNA will help with the most perplexing problem of all—population numbers. Surreptitious animals who exist in low densities on the landscape, cougars are hard to quantify. The "gold standard" for counting mountain lions involves a direct count of radio collared animals. But that is expensive, so researchers and agencies are always looking for faster, cheaper, more accurate methods to count lions. As Peter Alexander of the PTCP demonstrated, trail cameras cannot be used to identify individual cougars. New methods using biopsy darts for DNA tissue show promise, but these methods must be carried out over the course of many years. A recent snapshot study conducted over one snow season between December 2012 and April 2013 in the Bitterroot Mountains in Montana demonstrates that controversy. Using DNA from harvested cats, as well as from live, darted cats, the researchers combined information on habitat, search effort, and likelihood of encounters in a model called spatial capture recapture. Although their methods reduced time, effort, and cost, their controversial results showed one of the highest lion densities across the West. Because age cannot be determined through DNA samples, the study acknowledges that this inflated figure incorporates young dispersers. To make a simple comparison, a snapshot study, as opposed to a long-term population study, is akin to taking a count of people going through a turnstile at a shopping center in one day, or one week. Are you counting those who went to a sale? Or are you counting people who live in the town? Or are you counting only those who work at the center? It is difficult to know who the cougars in the Bitterroot Mountain study are unless you "recapture" them in your DNA survey—are they transients or residents? This is why capture and recapture is considered a reliable count method.

I asked houndsman Grover Hedrick his opinion of the results of the Bitterroot Mountain study and why their density numbers came out so elevated. "This study incorporated two things that they never incorporated before. One was a number for undetected cats, and the other a number for transient cats. The transient cat numbers weren't used before because it can increase or decrease a population. If you have a high density of cats, then you have no transient cats staying because the territories are all filled up, plus you have the two year olds that are kicked off, they're leaving. It's an easy sell because they can say, 'We'll shoot these cats down and transient cats will come back in so we're not doing anything.' In my opinion, they blew the population numbers way out of proportion. I've hunted in the East Fork of the Bitterroots for forty years. I probably put 250 miles on my snowmobile last year and found two or three cat tracks, so there can't be that many."

I was curious how researchers could collar every cougar in an area, as they did in Toni Ruth's Yellowstone work. Hedrick illustrated the methods for me using the Garnett Range study in Montana as an example. This was a very thorough study where the study team attempted to collar every mountain lion. The study employed several houndsmen during the five years Hedrick worked on it, and, except for a few transients, Hedrick said they managed to collar every cat. "You see a cat track and you get the receiver out. If there's a possibility that it was a cat without a collar, you'd run the dogs." The "receiver" is a telemetry receiver, a hand-held unit with an antenna attached that receives a signal from the animal's collar. Cougars sometimes did get treed several times, especially when the cat was down in a gully and the houndsman couldn't find them with their receivers. "By the stride, the track size, looking at the toes, you can usually tell a female from a male. If we had a mature female in the area, most of the time you can get a beep on them. If you see a male track in there, and you know the day before the dominant male was forty miles from there, you know you've got another male. Then you run that."

Hedrick also discussed another study that employed DNA darts. The Blackfoot Study, which he worked on with two other houndsmen, began collecting DNA samples to determine population size. The plan was to divide the study area into three units, with one houndsman per unit. Within each unit, the houndsman's job was to tree every cat, and a biologist would shoot a hollow biopsy dart into the mountain lion. The dart falls to the ground, and the tissue sample is collected. The lion is allowed to go free without a collar or ear tag. After a houndsman finished treeing every cat within his unit, he'd rotate and go to the next. In that way, all three houndsmen worked every unit, treeing as many cats as they could. Hedrick said that "at the end of the study, 80 percent of the DNA'd cats were caught by all three houndsmen. That just shows if you wanted to pound an area, one houndsman could kill 80 percent of the cats in one winter."

YELLOWSTONE'S COUGAR STUDIES

Beginning in 1987, Yellowstone National Park initiated the first of what was to become three separate cougar studies, conducted over the course of twenty years. Their intention was to encompass the entire arc of the effect of wolves on the landscape and on cougars specifically. Cougars, along with wolves, were part of the Yellowstone Park predator control program in the early part of the last century. Wolves were completely eradicated from the Park, and, presumably, cougars were too. Bounties in the surrounding states kept Park populations low by limiting immigrant cougars. As bounty hunting was replaced with trophy game seasons outside the Park in the 1970s, Park policies also changed, and cougars slowly began to recolonize. In 1996, wolves were reintroduced into Yellowstone. Grizzly bears have been on the Endangered Species List since 1975. Grizzly bears' rate of reproduction is low, but their numbers began to increase by the mid-1990s, adding to the changing predator dynamics.

The first Yellowstone National Park study was conducted prior to the reintroduction of wolves, when the elk population was high. Kerry Murphy was the lead researcher, working under the auspices of the Hornocker Wildlife Institute. Designed to understand the budding cougar population in the Northern Range, this study made heavy use of radio collars.

With a lapse in-between, the second phase of research was conducted from 1998 through 2005, right after their reintroduction of wolves into the Park. Led by Toni Ruth, this study was also "collar heavy," with intensive field work, and DNA analysis of hair and blood samples. Ruth analyzed how cougars were coping and adapting to the presence of this new top predator.

Murphy's pre-wolf study saw cougars recolonizing, with young dispersers arriving and jockeying for space. With plenty of territory and no competition from other predators, male home ranges tended to be large. By Phase II, the wolf-reestablishment phase, although females were using similar home range areas as in the previous study, there was more overlap among the ranges. Suitable cougar habitat had filled up, so with females crammed into core habitat along the Yellowstone River system, male home ranges decreased by half during the time of Ruth's study.

Dispersal dynamics also changed from the first to the second study. As a general rule, if there are resources and habitat available, daughters like to set up shop near their mother's home range, while males are always programmed to disperse far away. But with the core habitats full, males and females were dispersing out of the study area, a big difference from Murphy's findings in Phase I.

The first phase of the Yellowstone Cougar Project used private and public lands outside and inside the Park, encompassing elk herd habitat in Yellowstone's Northern Range. Toni Ruth began by attempting to overlap with Murphy's study area, but ultimately, since cougar density had increased somewhat, and they wanted to focus where the most overlap with wolves occurred, the study concentrated on territory inside the Park.

I contacted Toni Ruth with the hope that she would remember me from her Yellowstone cougar class in 2015. I'd read her published scientific articles, and I knew she was working on a book about her Yellowstone research. But there still were gaps in my understanding of the second study results compared with Murphy's. In addition, I understood that she had her fingers in the third leg of research presently being conducted in the Park. As Executive Director for the Salmon Valley Stewardship, Ruth's free time was at a minimum, and I was lucky to slip into her busy schedule on the phone.

What had been good habitat before wolves, was now vital, core refuge habitat after wolf reintroduction. I asked Ruth about kitten survival. I was curious because I knew the PTCP documented a low survival rate, and her study had a much higher survival rate. First, she told me that it's difficult to compare survival rates between two studies as they may use different yardsticks of data analysis. But comparing her study and Murphy's pre-wolf study, her kitten survival was somewhat higher, due to infanticide during Murphy's. I wanted to know more about infanticide. It's been documented among male cougars, but I wondered how prevalent it really was and what might trigger it.

"[Infanticide is] relative to stability in the population. So, if we don't have wolves and bears in the system—let's just remove that from the equation—we have cats in the pre-wolf time frame where you've got turnover in adult males. There are new males coming in and there is this younger age structure, so there's jockeying for territory. And in that time frame, you do end up with elevated infanticide." Ruth went on to make a comparison with African lions, when a new male arrives who is not familiar with the females. He wants to take out the kittens she had with another male so he can breed with her more quickly. This is also a phenomenon we see in human-hunted cougar populations, Ruth told me.

"If we compare Murphy's study to ours, without wolves in there," Ruth continued, "I would expect we'd have had even higher kitten survival in the conditions that we had—just because we had a stable population, not much infanticide, and kittens also wouldn't have been dying from competition." One fascinating adaptation Ruth found in Phase II was that, compared to Murphy's study, females were keeping their kittens an average of five months longer before kicking them out to disperse.

"Exactly how much wolf predation on kittens did you find?" I asked. With the intensive collar work, Ruth would have a good handle on how kittens died.

"We didn't have it occur that much. In total, we had eight cats killed by wolves, five of those were kittens, and four of those kittens were within one litter. The other fatalities were three adults." Ruth explained she knew kittens were likely to be killed by wolves because adult females need to kill prey more frequently when they are raising kittens.

During her research, the wolf population in the study area peaked at ninety-eight wolves per 1000 km2 in 2002. To put that in perspective, at times they had one wolf pack with nearly forty individuals, including pups. Even with that high wolf density, cougar populations remained stable.

Factoring in all risks to kittens along with predation, PTCP saw a much lower kitten survival rate, and I wondered what factors Ruth thought might account for the differences in the two studies, since both took place in the Greater Yellowstone Ecosystem with wolves and bears as top predators.

"One of the differences in our landscape is that there isn't high human influence. We were also dealing with a very heterogeneous landscape; there are areas on the Northern Range that are just great for wolves—big open plateaus—intermingled with secure habitat for cats. I'm sure human activity influences how carnivores are moving in that Teton landscape, particularly when humans are hunting cats in winter as well. But also, one of the things that cougars do well is seek out refuges from competition with their main competitors, and in a lot of instances they're relegated to areas with lower prey density. But for cougars, they're able to do well in those lower densities because of the attributes of how they hunt. They don't necessarily need the same density of prey as their competitors. As long as the habitat provides them refuge and there's enough prey in there, they can co-exist."

"That would be an interesting thing to look at between our study and others—the heterogeneity of the landscape, how the prey were using that, and that intermingling with humans as well."

I asked Ruth how many cougars she saw during her study years in Yellowstone, *not* including the collaring work. "Three!" she told me. That's not many for someone tracking cougars all winter long for six years.

I wondered about the differences in cougar habitat in the Jackson study versus the Yellowstone study. In addition to topography, Jackson has winter elk congregated in feed grounds, effectively pulling prey out of the mountains and concentrating them. The feeding grounds converge wolves and cougars into tight areas, driving competition between them for habitat selection, especially for female cougars with kittens that need to kill more frequently. Would those differences account for at least some of the high kitten losses, and the 47 percent drop in the Jackson cougar population over the last several years?

I posed the question to Boone Smith, the houndsman for the Jackson study who is also a biologist. I sat down with Smith during a break at the Mountain Lion Conference. Having grown up and hunted around the Jackson area, he knew both cougars and the landscape extremely well. Smith had watched the cougar population drop over the later years of the PTCP as the wolf population grew. He told me the Gros Ventre area used to be great for tracking cats. During winter 2009, they treed nine cats and collared six in four days. "This is how good the Gros Ventre was: we never went more than two days without running a track. That winter was the very best. And in contrast, the last two years of the study, we would go seven, eight days in between finding a track that was maybe four or five days old that we didn't think was a collared cat."

Smith narrowed it down to habitat. "I think they just can't compete. The Cody area (on the east side of Yellowstone Park) has some great cougar habitat and a lot of it. The Gros Ventre has some too, and there are a few spots, like the ledges, the rocks, and the steep areas, that are ideal for them, but there's just not a ton of it. And guess where our residents hang out, right there."

As the data slowly came in and the PTCP crew waded through their analyses, Elbroch told me that "human hunting came out as a much stronger influence on cat survival than wolves in every recent analysis," just as Ruth had suggested. Although habitat quality plays a critical role, the probable tipping point in Jackson's 47 percent drop is a lack of protective refuge from hunting in their unit, as well as overhunting in the surrounding units that provide new immigrants.

Finally, I asked Ruth what she felt was the highlight of working on the Yellowstone Project. "I got to see places there that I would never have seen or discovered, only because of cats. Getting to know those individual cats so intimately was gratifying, because we got to monitor some of these cats throughout the entire study, follow them day to day, and learn about them as individuals. Really, they become like family members. When one dies, it affects you. I also can say I've never been a fan of collaring; it was necessary for the

Rocky prominence dotted with mountain goats near my home.
Good lion country.

questions we were answering. But for me, probably the other high-light, was that at the end of the study, the pronghorn killer, who we knew really well, was still alive. We had studied her almost the entire study—and getting to take that collar off and send her on her way, to live the rest of her life without following her or a collar on her neck—that's probably one of the most satisfying things for me."

The third phase of The Yellowstone Cougar Project, launched in January 2014, began with wolves as a recovered population. The ways in which cougars have changed their use of the landscape had been well-established, so the team's questions needed to be different.

Colby Anton is a personable young man who laughs easily and has a unique ability to move effortlessly between small talk and complicated scientific lingo. His youthful looks belie his experi-ence. Anton surprised me when he said he'd spent more than ten years doing field research, covering almost the entire gamut of large carnivores in North America—grizzlies, black bears, wolves, and cougars. He came on to the third phase of the Yellowstone study at its inception, working with guidance from researchers Dan Stahler, Toni Ruth, Michael Sawaya, and Howard Quigley. For his doctoral work, he has been spending the last few winters in the Park, snow tracking to determine cougar population density. The snow tracking DNA work was first explored by Sawaya during Phase II in Yellowstone to see if it was a viable method to identify individual cougars noninvasively.

As Anton's doctoral work revved up, the second phase of the study kicked in using accelerometers, a type of Fitbit® that is installed into G.P.S. collars that captures fine-scale movement dynamics of collared individuals. At the Mountain Lion Conference, Anton gave a morning presentation on DNA genotyping errors based on his Yellowstone work—another difficult, genetic-heavy lecture. Afterwards I sat down with Anton to unravel his Yellowstone genetics work, but I found myself being plunged deeper down the rabbit hole of cutting-edge, fine-scale cougar research. I should have known that Yellowstone National Park researchers, working in an ecosystem with the full suite of predators in North America, would be at the forefront of innovative research.

The movement and size of the elk herd in Yellowstone's Northern Range has changed since Ruth's study. Now 60 percent of the herd uses land outside the Park in winter—the reverse of what was previously documented. In winter, the Lamar Valley used to be full of elk, but now they congregate in smaller clusters, taking advantage of the trees as protective cover. Over the course of Ruth's study, the Northern Range elk population averaged around 9,500, with its peak in 2000 at more than 14,000 elk. Today the elk population has stabilized at approximately 5,000. This is considered the probable carrying capacity, since the wolf population has stabilized along with it. This is important, because in winter, in the Park, cougars and wolves share primary prey, which is elk. Anton's study, Phase III, is completely contained within Park

Two cougars

boundaries, with Mammoth/Gardiner on the west, and Mt. Norris in the Lamar Valley on the east end.

The population analysis methodology is simple and elegant, employing a combination of many hours of field time and twenty-first century laboratory work. The goal was to find cougar hair, the gold standard for DNA analysis. Beginning each January, the study set up a ten- to twelve-week sampling season. During the first three years, they worked five days a week in the field. The first year, Colby Anton had two field technicians with him, but as the study progressed, their efforts increased, and they added more field techs. In the fourth year, 2017, Anton rearranged his staff in order to exploit any good weather that might fall on a weekend. That winter he had nine field techs including himself, rotating through their study area seven days of the week. Transects were established along drainages and cliff edges, places where one might expect to find a cougar. With so much field tracking, the crews perfected the art of finding lion hair—a highly difficult task. Anton described the exhilaration of tracking a mountain lion, understanding its movement down to the minutia.

"It's something I feel like I've finally gotten good at, finding really small remnants of cougar sign. These are highly elusive animals that occur at low densities, and we're taking a 650-square kilometer area and trying to reduce it down to a single hair. You're on a snow track and the way you see the environment totally changes when you're tracking a cougar in the wild. It's really a special experience. You're following this animal as it's moving through the landscape at a very fine scale, every step seeing how they're using it and the decisions they make. And at every end of the stick you start to check for hairs, you start to get good at knowing what kind of substrate will catch hair."

I showed Anton a trail camera video I took of a mother with two kittens. The mother was rubbing vigorously against a large fir tree. When I went to search for hair on the bark, I found nothing. He explained why.

"At the ends of these trees, the bark doesn't catch hair very well. Ends of sticks, if they're shaped the right way, catch hair. Or rose bushes, they are the best for catching hair. Juniper and sage bushes don't catch hair well. You get good at staying on your animal's track and knowing where to allocate most of your energy to take a closer look for hair samples."

"Aren't you getting a lot of duplicate animals, out there every day, year after year?" I asked him.

Anton said that's what you want—a lot of "recaptures." Recapture, either through DNA or through treeing a previously captured cougar, is the most accurate method for population counts. This is because capturing a cougar for a second or third time in a given research area will confirm that he, or she, is a resident adult and not a disperser traveling through. Anton explained that when using hair strand DNA, the more DNA points across a landscape for a cat, the better the model can project space usage across time and space. There's only so much area across a landscape for home ranges. The better you can predict space usage, the better the model can estimate average home range size, which can help determine the number of individuals using the study area.

Since DNA samples can't determine age, Anton's count will be for the total population of cougars, including juveniles and kittens. There will be some statistical magic here since Ruth and Murphy were able to age their cats through intensive collaring, and Murphy's studies extended beyond the Park. Putting together the estimates for growth rate for the third phase, combined with the population estimates for Phase I and Phase II, then extrapolating the time in between all the studies, researchers can look at the cougar population growth rate over the last twenty years.

In addition to the non-invasive and low-cost advantages of this kind of fieldwork, Anton explained its primary advantages for the Park. "We're looking to assigning a growth rate to the population of cougars on Yellowstone's Northern Range. We can do that through estimating not just adults, but all individuals. And the growth rate tells you whether or not the population is decreasing, stable, or increasing." And that's the "Golden"—to know what's going on over time, not just a snapshot of one year.

During the third year of Phase III, the research team began their accelerometer work, collaring wolves and cougars. Anton's advisor in Santa Cruz told him to collar adult males since they don't have the reproductive complications that females do. Pregnancy, lactation, and additional hunting to feed kittens requires tremendous energy allocation. But that's a tall order for researchers when it comes to cougars, because, by their very nature, there are more females on the landscape than males. Thus far, seven cougars have been collared, but only two of those collars are still on cougars in the field. Stuff happens. A female they re-collared lost her collar after only four days. One of their collared adult males was killed by another male, while their only other collared male, a young disperser, was shot in my valley on a legal hunt last winter. Anton plans to continue collaring efforts as the study continues. The G.P.S. on the collars sends data to a computer via a satellite several times a day, but the accelerometer data stays with the collar until it falls off. The collars are set with a remote maximum "blow-off" timer, and then are collected in the field.

So, what does an accelerometer do, and what kind of information will the Yellowstone study be collecting and analyzing from it? Anton explains it to me in lay terms.

"The simple explanation is that an accelerometer acts just like a Fitbit®, those little wrist bands they created for humans to measure steps and speed, and it correlates that to calories consumed at the end of the day. But our accelerometer measures movement at sixteen or thirty-two times a second, so it gives us very fine-scale movement signatures. They were largely built off of the surge in cell phone technology." I could relate to this because, although I've never used a wrist Fitbit®, I do use my cell phone to measure mileage and calories consumed. Every cell phone seems to incorporate a health app nowadays.

"We're looking at calories consumed, and we can measure that in several different ways." Anton explains he can look at calories consumed over different time periods, whether that's hourly, daily, or seasonally. Further, accelerometer signatures enable him to correlate behaviors like running, walking, or feeding surges that are tied to the G.P.S. clusters to the accelerometer movements. I asked Anton if he's gotten any information back and analyzed it yet. He told me he had, from animals that died and from several others where the blow-off worked.

"I'm in the midst of analyzing it now. These data sets are enormous. We had a female where the collar was out for 13 months, and there were over a billion accelerometer readings for this one animal."

"You have some special program for this?" I asked.

"You do it through specialized coding software," he said. "A lot of this was figured out by my predecessors. The researchers on the Santa Cruz Puma Project have been working with this data for a long time, so they have code that I can then manipulate to do what I need."

Chris Wilmers of the University of California, Santa Cruz, is the pioneer of this work. Wilmers, along with Terrie Williams of the Integrative Carnivore EcoPhysiology lab at UCSC, helped figure this out first in a lab, and then translated it to field data. Wilmers says, "Energy expenditure is the lifeblood of an animal. If they're burning more calories than they're consuming, they'll die. And without enough surplus calories, they'll never reproduce successfully."

But in order to correlate the output of the accelerometer's data, Wilmers and Williams needed to figure out what the animal was doing that triggered the patterns, the amount of oxygen any particular movement consumed, and how much the collar was moving in response. Williams had done treadmill science with wolves, and even river otters, but wild cougars were a different thing. After three years of searching, she found a veterinarian named Lisa Wolfe who had raised three pumas. It took ten months—and "a lot of meat"—to train the cougars on a treadmill, but once they figured it out, "they were brilliant," Williams said. The collared cats were in a Plexiglas enclosure, running, walking, or resting on the treadmill as a videotape was running. All the while an oxygen analyzer measured how much oxygen they consumed during each activity. That measurement is the VO2, the correlate to calories consumed.

Wilmers found that energy expenditure in cougar hunts were almost twice what was thought in other models. And lions that abandoned their ambush strategy to hunt in more open ground burned more calories. This had implications for animals living in disturbed sites where humans have altered landscapes. This initial research, along with the research data from collared animals in the Santa Cruz study, coupled with an animal's body mass, helps Anton through the series of equations to give him his end goal of calories consumed.

"One of my hypotheses is that in wintertime, while wolf and cougar energetics may be the same, the differences in the way they budget activity and use the landscape may contribute to that. Wolves are going to be traveling a lot more. But when you see wolves traveling in deep snow, they're almost always conserving their energy by moving in single file. The animals in front break trail for those behind, and they switch off sometimes. They're energetically very efficient. They use the landscape so well."

To study their movements, Anton used accelerometer collars on wolves as well. At this point, the study has applied an accelerometer collar to at least one male in each of the Northern Range wolf packs, including two interior packs. Anton will then compare the cougar data with his collared wolves. With this information, he can begin to parse the differences in energy economics over the course of a day, or over a season, like in the intense Yellowstone winters, where calorie costs are consequential.

Anton continues outlining the differences between these two predators' energetic differences. "Cougars, on the other hand, as a mostly solitary predator, are having to find different ways to be efficient with their energy. That means not traveling as much, which could suggest staying to rocky areas that have less snow pack and relying on their cryptic hunting abilities. That's an example of the seasonal differences that I want to look at. I've never done anything like this before. It's a different lens you're looking through to examine the same carnivore or landscape that I've been seeing for a while."

How cutting-edge is this research? Anton tells me he ran into David Mech, the godfather of wolf research, in Yellowstone. "Mech was really excited. 'Oh man,' he told me, 'you're at the forefront of this. Nobody's ever done this before.'"

Anton tells me they had an adult cougar last year with four young kittens who killed marmots almost exclusively for nearly twenty days, without killing any large ungulates. "Getting at this fine scale data, being able to correlate adult female cougars, what they're killing over what intervals, and the biomass that they're consuming versus the energy expenditure over time, and how that correlates to litter size, kitten survival or what age their kittens are . . . I think we'll find out some really cool things."

As the interview comes to a close, I began to show Anton a few more of my trail camera videos of cougars, but he had one more, very important, thing to add.

"A lot of our larger goals and motivation for doing this work is to fit it into the larger Yellowstone story. And the way that Park research and management is moving towards is looking at Yellowstone as a community and not as single species projects, but actually coming together and looking at it more from a community dynamics perspective. What we're trying to do is take that cougar piece and add it to the greater puzzle of what's going on with the Yellowstone wildlife community. We're in a unique position of being able to answer really interesting questions in the coming years on what's going on in this complex system. Not just what's going on with wolf/elk dynamics, but what's actually going on within the diverse carnivore community, and how that impacts their prey."

✎ THE SOCIAL STRUCTURE OF LION COMMUNITIES—THE GOVERNORS OF FIEFDOMS

In every interview I conducted, the PTCP team members emphasized how social mountain lions are, how "everything we thought we knew before wasn't necessarily the case" relative to their social interactions. I just couldn't wrap my head around what Mark Elbroch and his team members meant. One biologist on the team said, "F49 will share with F47; then F47 will share with M29; M29 shares with M68. Mark calls it a network." How did these food sharing interactions constitute a community, or network, of social interactions?

Eventually, I got my chance to learn what was behind those broad, brush-stroke references. Mark Elbroch was detailing his work on cougar social interactions from the PTCP at the Mountain Lion Conference in a concise, twenty-minute presentation. His research data revealed a startling and new insight into cougar social dynamics.

Elbroch used thirteen specific collared pumas in his study because they overlapped in time and area. He then devised a series of hypotheses he wanted to test. First, he needed to test the consensus explanations for puma social interactions—resources, kinship, mating. But he developed three alternative hypotheses as well. Using a tool called Network Analysis, developed for the social sciences, he formulated questions about the nature of these interactions. If Puma A tolerates Puma B, would that make Puma B more tolerant of Puma A? This he called direct reciprocity. He also tested for two kinds of triangulation of tolerance. One is a hierarchical triangulation, where one individual receives all the benefits of that tolerance from the other two individuals in the system. The second kind of triangulation would be where all participants benefit mutually.

Two factors come into play in the Jackson study. First, winter is harsh and long. Second, the main diet in winter are large prey animals, not something a puma can consume in one quick feeding. That makes for increased tolerance at feeding sites with elk kills. Because more than 60 percent of mountain lion social interaction occurs around kill sites, that's where Elbroch placed his cameras. Applying his Network Analysis software tool to all the interactions, over the course of four winters, he found that a pattern emerged.

Amazingly, mountain lions do have a network. Every one of his thirteen collared lions either exhibited tolerance, was tolerated, or both. And even more astounding, these interactions were clustered perfectly within the home range of each male. Elbroch referred to the entire structure as "a network" that includes the separate communities circumscribed by each dominant male's home range. In other words, you have a male interacting with his overlapping

Sharing a meal

females, who tolerated not only the male, but each other as well. This social pattern turned out to be the dominant structure of puma interactions. The neighboring dominant male interacted with the females in his territory as well, and although there was some exchange with the adjacent community of lions, essentially each was acting as an independent community. Since mountain lions are relatively long-lived and create stable territories, large areas could be described as networks of distinct communities. The lions in the network would have many chances to meet up with other individuals and would have repeated interaction with their neighbors.

Elbroch explains it like this. "Male mountain lions are like politicians. They're governors of fiefdoms within which mountain lions interact frequently."

The second pattern Elbroch observed was that these independent communities, constrained by the male's home range, were hierarchical, with the male benefitting the most, at least in terms of calories. Males visited more kills (of females) than they tolerated

Mark Elbroch with cougar kitten

others at their kills. Elbroch says this is important because "it means they are structuring interactions within the community at large." It's these older males who create the social structure for the entire network. In other words, they are the glue that maintain order and dictate the levels of cooperation. Although it appears on the surface that males receive far more advantages in this structure, Elbroch senses both males and females benefit equally, yet differently. Females, he says, need to have good relations with the resident male in the future, when they come into heat. Females, then, may be banking on future payoffs for their tolerance now, while the males are using them up immediately as caloric intake.

With these observations, the PTCP is breaking new ground that has enormous implications for cougar management. Overhunting trophy males in a region may be disrupting long-term social structures, something that has not been studied enough. We know that young male dispersers tend to get into more trouble than older cats. But what happens when a whole "network," not just one

"community" of cougars, is disrupted through heavy hunting of resident males who are the guardians of cougar society?

Elbroch documented one other very interesting finding. While
the team rarely found males interacting with other males, they did
document one juvenile male feeding with resident male M29 (the
father of F51's and F61's second litter of kittens) on two occasions.
The sub-adult looked sickly and in need of nutrition. Was it because
of M29's experiences of being tolerated numerous times by his family unit that prompted him to give back to this unknown male disperser in need of nutrition? No one knows, but the young male did
move on, setting up shop to the south of the study area. Several
years later, he was killed by a hunter.

CHAPTER 9

BOUND IN AN URBAN FOREST

*That night at the fire as we sat huddled in the melting
snow around the blaze, we told Homer of the lion
tracks. The first thing a lion-hunter always asks is: "Are
you sure they were cat tracks?" We had had many an
experience with even seasoned ranchers who mistook dog
or occasional wolf tracks for those of the mountain lion.*

—FRANK HIBBEN

INTRODUCTION TO THE BAY
AREA AND RESEARCH STUDIES

I grew up in a more innocent Los Angeles. Hopping the trolley
to Santa Monica Beach, or watching my mother select vegetables
from wooden crates at Eli the Grocers under an outdoor awning on
Vermont Avenue—the late 50s was a time of naïveté in a city of two
and a half million.

My childhood was spent on the edge of one of the largest urban
parks in the United States. Griffith Park is a mostly feral preserve
of chaparral slopes and deep, shaded canyons. But the Park has its
tame side as well, with a world class observatory, the outdoor Greek
Theatre, pony rides, and a merry-go-round. The Park was my refuge
and playground. Many of my childhood memories were shaped by

experiences in the Park's varied landscape. The scramble from my house to the Griffith Observatory included a rest stop at a large tree where we carved our initials. I remember my father taking me to view Saturn's rings through the Zeiss telescope and, when I was a teenager, I hung in the trees outside the Greek Theatre's wall to listen to rock concerts for free. Despite the choking smog, there still was wildness seeping through the cracks of the massive post-war building boom of the 1950s and 60s.

When a large desert tortoise lumbered into our front yard then evaporated into my father's tropical-like garden, it was not considered particularly noteworthy. I expected the coyotes to howl every night from the park ridges above our house, and I looked forward to counting dozens of song bird nests each spring. The many vacant lots were added refuge and corridors for wildlife. Maybe mountain lions coursed through those hills in the 1960s, but I never saw or heard of one.

Today Griffith Park is the home of famous male mountain lion P-22. He lives solo in this urban wildlife island of only eight square miles, and his hormones must occasionally impress upon him the need to find a mate. Amazingly, he survived the perilous journey to his present home by crossing two freeways. He wanders the Park boundaries, but it must seem to him that he is the last of his species. A cougar's "Twilight Zone." The last cat standing. In a news story, I saw P-22 on TV living under a house temporarily. I recognized the area. It was close to the Tudor style home I grew up in. That particular street used to be scrub brush, with a few older homes. Now it's a maze of contemporary houses crushed against the Park's open space boundary. What could be developed, was.

In the 1970s, I went to college at the University of California, Santa Cruz, a beach town in northern California nestled against the backdrop of dense forests of redwoods and firs, steep eroded gullies of ferns and poison oak, and narrow mountainous roads where hippies and back-to-the-land zealots holed up. I majored in surfing, poetry, and hiking in those dark hills, yet I never saw any cougars. After college, I lived in San Francisco, as well as Sonoma County and Marin County in the North Bay. I made the Bay Area my home for more than thirty years until I moved to Wyoming.

The town of Santa Cruz lies along coastal route Highway 1, south of San Francisco. Highway 17, which bisects the mountains to San Jose to the east, is a corridor for commuters and treacherous for wildlife to cross. Mountain lions may or may not have roamed those Santa Cruz mountains in the 1970s, but they do now, and they are being tracked with G.P.S. collars for one of the longest-running lion studies in the Bay Area. With time, it was evident the lion population was growing, as they became part of the "neighborhood watch" awareness. Signage appeared on the trails in the late 1990s advising hikers to take precautions; friends periodically reported seeing mountain lions; newspapers occasionally had stories of lions in the area; and everyone, children and adults, were schooled in what to do if they saw a lion during a hike.

While the Los Angeles mountain lion study has garnered much attention, a plethora of additional studies are quietly taking place in the Bay Area. I was interested to know how lions behave when they are faced with compressed habitat in an urban-wildland interface. How does a statewide no-hunt policy affect lions, their culture, and their interaction with humans? I also wanted to know what kinds of practical and political changes might be taking place to help lions live with the burgeoning human population. I decided to return to California for a month and combine family visits with interviews of people who might help me answer these questions.

The dense urban areas of the San Francisco Bay Area can be deceiving. They don't define the area's entire nine counties. More of an open, lazy, urban sprawl, the Bay Area is a patchwork of wooded, protected hills and forests, large ranches with little cover, tight exurban cities and suburbs, enormous protected watersheds, wetlands, and hobby vineyards. The heaviest population centers are around the

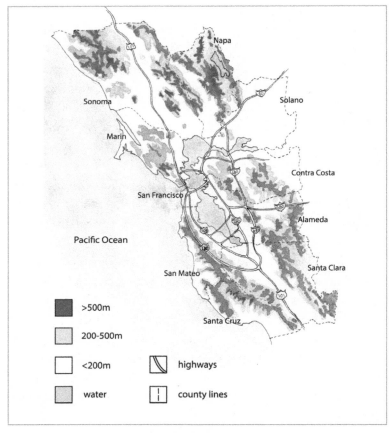

Bay Area Topography

San Francisco Bay itself and its estuaries. Unlike Los Angeles, where extremely isolated islands of natural areas are crisscrossed by river-sized freeways and an endless sea of houses and high rises, the Bay Area is more of a hodgepodge of public and private wild land next to tight urban development. No one knows how many cougars make their living here, or how they move through these enormous transition zones. Little is known about their health or their long-range chances of survival. With such a diverse medley of land ownership,

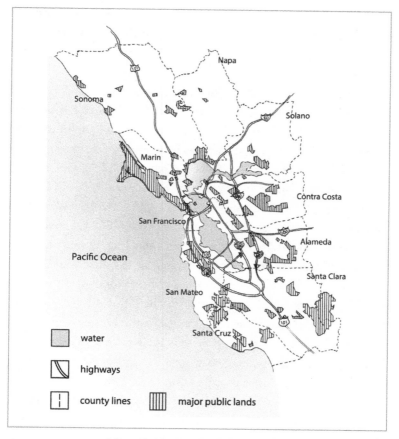

Major Public Lands in the Bay Area

cougars might have more potential for corridor dispersal—opportunities for meet and greet—than in the Los Angeles area.

Describing the Bay Area for someone who has never visited or lived there is complicated. The San Francisco Bay is enormous, with fingers to the north, south, and east, and the Pacific Coast Range has three major ridge structures running through three Bay Area counties. For the purposes of simplification, and to learn how cougars are being studied and how they might move through this area, it's helpful to divide the Bay Area into three major regions: the North Bay (Marin and Sonoma Counties); the South Bay (Santa Cruz County and Silicon Valley); and the East Bay (Alameda and Contra Costa Counties).

Sonoma County is considered an agricultural and farming community, although in the last two decades, the area has become more gentrified with hobby ranchers and people commuting to points south. Marin County, a wealthy bedroom community lying north of the Golden Gate Bridge, is home to a large amount of protected land. Golden Gate National Recreation Area (GGNRA) lies adjacent to Marin County's watershed, along with several state parks and Point Reyes National Seashore. The GGNRA, managed by the National Park Service, is a huge, sprawling, non-contiguous swath of preserved lands, mostly coastal, in the North and South Bay, and includes such diverse areas as Muir Woods and the Presidio, a former army military fort. Marin's peninsula funnels towards the water barrier that is the Bay's strait, spanned since the 1930s by the Golden Gate Bridge. So narrow is the strait's opening that Sir Francis Drake, the Spaniard to whom the discovery of California is attributed, sailed right past its mouth. East of the Marin Hills lies Highway 101, adjacent to the western wetlands of San Pablo Bay, an estuary that is the northern extension of San Francisco Bay. The freeway runs north into Sonoma County and south across the Golden Gate Bridge.

Highway 101 continues through the city, with stunning views of the Bay, and then it stretches south into the densely populated areas of the South San Francisco Peninsula, Palo Alto, and San Jose, the third most populous city in California. To the west of this tightly knit urban collage lie the Santa Cruz Mountains, bound near its eastern base by another massive freeway, Highway 280. The Santa Cruz Mountains provide a wildland respite that run northwest/southeast, dividing the coast from the inner Bay cities. This area is sometimes referred to as the Midpeninsula Open Space District.

While the GGNRA encompasses a mixed pot of old army bases, coastal properties, and isolated ridges, of particular importance is its adjacency to San Francisco's Peninsula Watershed, managed by San Francisco Public Utility Company (SFPUC). The San Francisco Watershed is cucumber-shaped with some odd land warts, encompassing 23,000 acres of woodlands and grasslands that are off limits to the public, yet vital to the South Bay's cougar population.

The East Bay, too, is a hodgepodge of open space and protected land, with East Bay Regional Park District (EBRPD) responsible for managing 66 parks and 122,880 acres. The Oakland/East Bay Hills is a highly altered area with a narrow green belt of protected parkland along a ridgeline. To the west of the ridge lie the congested towns of Berkeley and Oakland that bleed into the hills, bordered by the San Francisco Bay on the opposite side. Running east/west, and splitting the Berkeley Hills between Tilden Park to the north and Sibley Park to the south, are Highway 24 and the Caldecott Tunnel. Interestingly, in this landscape full of dog walkers, bike riders, and picnickers, EBRPD has repeatedly caught trail camera snapshots of a large tom using the tunnel overpass for a connective corridor. To the east of the Berkeley Hills lies Highway 680. If a lion could get beyond Highway 680, there is open, protected land including Mt. Diablo State Park, Contra Costa Water District, and blotches of unconnected EBRPD-managed parks. The southern portion of the East Bay is a fairly unaltered landscape encompassing Sunol and Ohlone Regional Wildernesses, part of the huge seven hundred-square-mile Alameda Creek Watershed, along with vast private ranches. In all, the Bay Area sprawl has a population of more than seven million people.

Like all western states, California once had a bounty on cougars. What makes California a unique experiment is Proposition 117, which passed in 1990 by the voters and reclassified the mountain lion as a "specially protected mammal." No other state that currently has mountain lions has a moratorium on hunting. Lions that are deemed a threat to the public, or prey on domestic animals, can be killed, but otherwise, cougars are protected. Despite the moratorium, lion protection is a complex issue. The number of yearly depredation kills could be the equivalent of a yearly sport-hunting quota. And "shoot, shovel, shut-up," otherwise known as poaching, is still a problem.

Cougars are notoriously hard to count. Secretive and solitary, most of the estimates are done by extrapolation. The Mountain Lion Foundation, based in California, uses the best available science today for an estimate of 1.7 lions per one hundred square kilometers (about thirty-nine square miles). Given available habitat, that equals about 3,100 lions for the entire state of California. Yet population pressures roil the landscape more than the San Andreas fault ever could. Reducing the cat's health and existence to a number tells no story at all. A complete picture of the California cougar's existence is complex. Los Angeles is one extreme, with isolated populations of lions whose sexual needs are at odds with intense freeway systems, while mountain lions in sparsely populated, heavily wooded, places like Humboldt County to the far north of the state tell a different story.

The beach house where I'm spending the month is in Marin County and sits tight to the ocean. It's perhaps one of the first homes built in the 1970s in this tiny, insulated community of Muir Beach, surrounded by National Park Service land and the vast Pacific Ocean. It defines a patchwork-protected corridor that runs all the way up the coast to Sonoma County—a connector that appears as if it could serve wildlife, including pumas. Occasionally a black bear travels down from Sonoma County into Marin County's Point Reyes National Seashore and surrounding environs, so why not cougars?

Koda and I take time each morning to walk the shoreline. The ocean edge keeps me connected to that slow mountain rhythm that I sorely miss. The news from home is that winter has come to Wyoming, and it's -37°F (that *negative!*), so I relish taking my morning walks on the beach barefoot, and I wear sandals to all my appointments, even during northern California downpours. The ocean water is warmer than the air. Koda—obviously as delighted as a golden retriever can be with an infinite body of water right outside his door—is magnetically drawn to the surf twenty-four hours a day. Sand and salt stick to his fur, still thick from winter in Wyoming. Every morning the surfers are out by daybreak. Their numbers ebb and flow with the daily wave conditions.

Muir Beach is a small cove, actually a double cove. Redwood Creek, flowing down from Muir Woods, snakes against the hillside and out to the ocean, forming a natural boundary. Beyond the seasonal creek outlet, rocks subjected to constant tidal flux harbor sea stars and anemones. At low tide, I walk across the rocky divide to a calmer, yet much smaller, beach. A secret resident path from above leads directly to this slender littoral strip that disappears in extreme high tides. In the afternoon, especially on stormy days, I take Koda to swim at this small cove.

Living at the beach for this month keeps me in touch with the volatility of the natural world. My nature-need is crammed into this tiny psychic island—suburbia fifteen minutes to my east over a tortuous two-lane road covering public lands—but the endless expanse of the Pacific Ocean widens my heart and mind all the way back to the expanses of Wyoming. I can rest here.

Many mesopredators seem to be very adaptive to life around the Bay Area. It's well documented that coyotes, raccoons, and skunks do well. I watch weasels, opossums, foxes, and bobcats slinking around backyards and over fences. They eat the garbage and people's cats, pull up gardens for grubs, feast on rats and mice breeding in the urban jungle. Those meso, or middle, predators don't concern me, although, surely, they provide added food for pumas. I'm curious about how that elusive top predator is doing in this urban landscape.

~~~ MARGARET OWINGS AND PROPOSITION 117

The driving force behind California's change of heart on paying bounties for mountain lions came from the untiring efforts of Margaret Owings. Owings lived in Big Sur with her husband, Nathaniel Owings, a renowned architect, in their stunning home perched on the rocky cliffs overlooking one of the most celebrated ocean views in northern California. They called their home Wild Bird, an architectural jewel encircled by the sea, the Ventana Wilderness, and Los Padres National Forest.

While walking her dog one afternoon, Owings encountered large tracks and then heard the sounds of a female lion calling for her young. Although a bit nervous, Owings was thrilled to know true wilderness surrounded her. When she later learned in the local paper that a bounty hunter received a $60 reward for killing that female lion—and was hailed as a hero—her passions were ignited. She considered mountain lions a magnificent animal. "I was just sick to hear it, and I knew then it was going to make a change in the pattern of my life, because I was going to do something about it," Mrs. Owings recalled in an interview in 1987.

Owings was already known as a conservation activist, helping to save sea lions from a state proposal to reduce their population by 75 percent. She spent decades fighting for sea otter protection from oil interests and abalone fisherman. Now she took up the fight for the last and most magnificent predator in California. Owings was well connected. She put together the forces of Olaus Murie, Ansel Adams, David Brower, Nicholas Roosevelt, along with Robert Redford and other prominent people. When she asked Rachel Carson to write a letter to a hold-out on the Fish and Game Commission, that member tipped the vote, and the bounty was finally rescinded.

With the bounty gone, the state of California reclassified mountain lions as a game animal and held its first formal hunt season in the winter of 1970-71. One hundred and eighteen lions were killed in the first two hunt seasons, which made it clear to Owings that lions still weren't really protected. Her team of conservationists could see that lion numbers in the state were dropping and there was no solid science on population sizes to support a hunt. Once again Owens used her political astuteness and pushed for a moratorium; a stay of four years was signed into law by Governor Ronald Reagan on March 1, 1972. A series of moratoriums followed, all with four- or five-year sunsets, continuing until 1986. Cougar hunting was about to begin again, but political pressure by individuals and organizations continued until Proposition 117 was passed by the voters.

By the late 1970s, when moratoriums were the only wedge between a mountain lion hunt and protection, Rick Hopkins was in graduate school at University of California, Berkeley when a mountain lion study at Fort Hunter Liggett, conducted by the California Department of Fish and Game piqued his interest. Cougars, he told me, were especially interesting because they occur regionally. He designed a unique doctoral project that lasted more than ten years in the Mt. Hamilton Range above San Jose. Hopkins spent time on the ground collaring mountain lions, attempting to understand their population dynamics, what they were eating, and their home range sizes. When I spoke with Hopkins by phone he was modest, denying his study was instrumental in helping cougars to become listed as a protected species. Sharon Negri of Wild Futures would disagree. Negri was with the Mountain Lion Foundation at that time, and as part of their campaign for Proposition 117, the Foundation invited the media on field trips with Hopkins to nearby Henry Coe State Park, melding science with the lore of an iconic symbol of wildness. Up until Hopkins's study, the longest research conducted was by the California Department of Fish and Game for only two or three years and in small areas.

Hopkins's study also provided some basic information about a lion population in an urban-interface area that had never been hunted. The Mt. Hamilton area, although surrounded by an urban area, as well as the largest state park in California, contains large ranches with few roads. His study area of 550 square kilometers harbored mountain lions that were relatively unmolested by humans, with year-round sufficient prey. Over the course of Hopkins's ten-year study, the population had a healthy density of three to five adult lions per one hundred square kilometers, stable home range sizes, an average age of five or six when collared, and a relatively mature population. The mean age at death for the Mt. Hamilton pumas (not including those under two years old) was 7.5 years for females and 6.5 for males. What stands out in Hopkins's study is an un-hunted population of mountain lions that naturally self-regulates, with older, dominant males controlling the territories and keeping their numbers stable. Hopkins notes that the mean age is older than in other studies he cites.

I was interested to know if a home range size might be altered in an urban landscape. Were they smaller because of the fragmented habitat? I learned from speaking with Hopkins that home range sizes varied depending upon prey accessibility. Hopkins explained that the size of a home range has more to do with non-migratory deer populations—deer that have no need to migrate elevationally because of snow—so Bay Area cougars spend the whole year in the same place. With no need to follow deer as they migrate up and down the mountains, the tendency is for mountain lions to have smaller home ranges, especially where deer are abundant.

CUTTING EDGE RESEARCH IN SANTA CRUZ

Hopkins's study was completed in 1989, and since that time, cougar studies in the Bay Area were sporadic and limited, until 2008, when Chris Wilmers began a study of a cougar population in the Santa Cruz Mountains that continues to this day. Wilmers's research was conducted as a partnership between the University

A pair of lions wander through the ex-urban landscape of San Mateo county

of California, Santa Cruz, and the California Department of Fish and Game, and in collaboration with Felidae Conservation Fund, a non-profit organization. Hopkins cautioned me not to compare the Santa Cruz study with his Mt. Hamilton study results from the Diablo Range. Although just a short distance apart—less than fifty miles and four major freeways—the habitat, road density, and influence of humans, along with pets, within these two areas are worlds apart. Conifer and dense redwood forests define the Santa Cruz Mountains, while the Diablo Range is largely grass and oak woodlands, with likely a higher density of deer. Scientific findings in one area can rarely be applied to another.

Although Wilmers's ongoing study is posing a lot of questions yet to be answered, some of the most practical findings to date apply to corridor connectivity. In particular, Highway 17, between Santa Cruz and San Jose—a highway named one of the most dangerous in California—has been a deadly crossing for cougars, who rarely make the jump alive. As a result of Wilmers's study, plans are underway to complete two wildlife-crossing structures across Highway 17 by 2020.

One of the most interesting findings to come out of the Santa Cruz study is how mountain lions react to human disturbance and how they use the landscape around the Santa Cruz Mountains. Like many counties in the Bay Area, Santa Cruz has a mix of public and private land, ranchland, and watershed. The study scored puma sensitivity to human disturbances on a gradient. The highest sensitivity occurred with breeding females. Females selected denning sites, where they could nurse their young, as far from humans as possible—rocky ledges, dense cover, downed trees—so they could hide their kittens. This vigilance when selecting den sites reminded me of the Jackson study, where females navigate between food sources and safe havens for kittens to protect them from the Teton's top predators—wolves. In exurban landscapes, humans substitute for wolves.

Ranked below breeding females for sensitivity to humans were males, who placed their communication sites, or scrapes, well away from human disturbances. Below that came cougar hunting activity; and the behavior least sensitive to human development was moving through the landscape. Interestingly, young dispersing males sometimes made the proximity to humans work in their favor, creeping along the fringes of populated areas to find open territory, skirting a region where a resident male might not patrol as heavily because it's close to people.

The Santa Cruz study also found that, contrary to what one might believe about a top predator in areas packed with pets and hobby livestock, cougars preferred deer. In fact, more than 90 percent of their diet was deer, with only a smattering of small, wild prey like raccoons or opossums. But this percentage of small prey changed as cougars used areas closer to human habitation. Here, approximately 37 percent of their diet, mostly in the form of raccoons and domestic cats, was the preferred menu, even though deer are also abundant near houses. Domestic cat consumption increased to 20 percent as housing development increased. So why were cougars that traveled closer to human housing choosing small prey over abundant deer?

The researchers speculated that, because cougars are nervous around housing developments, choosing small prey makes sense, as it can be devoured quickly, while consuming a deer kill requires cougars to stick around longer. Since females need larger prey to feed their young, a mosaic of housing sprawl across the landscape in wilder areas might affect kitten survival rates. This research suggests that clustering homes, while preserving large tracts of natural hunting zones and corridors, is better land planning.

I was curious about the methods by which lions are collared in a patchwork quilt of private and public land. I knew the Santa Cruz study employed a houndsman and also used cage traps. I spoke with Veronica Yovovich, who did her doctoral work on the Santa Cruz study from 2009 to 2016, and now works at the Mountain Lion Foundation, which is based in Sacramento. She explained the mechanics of how to use cage traps. The first step is to bring in a road-killed deer and place it in an area where there is evidence of mountain lions. There is also a camera trap at the site. When a mountain lion comes in to feed on the bait, a cage trap is brought in. A portion of the remainder of the bait is placed in the trap; the trap door is set open before sunset when cougars are most active. A trap beacon is installed on top of the cage, which sends out a radio signal that changes depending upon whether the door is open or shut. Biologists then set up camp about a kilometer away, checking the trap throughout the night every half hour. "If we don't catch something," Yovovich laughs, "then it's a very long night. If you do catch something, it's very exciting."

The Audubon Canyon Ranch Mountain Lion Project in northern California had a cage trap display at the Mountain Lion Conference that employed similar technology but with a different twist—the trap could be set without bait. Using an electronic sensor, the crew designed a trap that triggered only for mountain-lion-size animals. Apparently, the study was having trouble using bait, catching mostly non-target animals. Tired of trapping skunks and

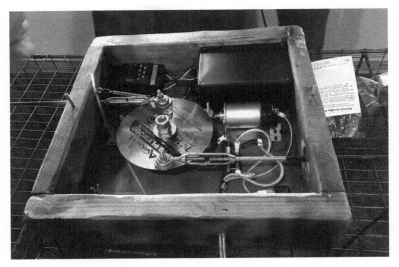

Guts of the Audubon Canyon Ranch trap that
triggers only for mountain lions

coyotes, Quinton Martins, the lead biologist, experimented with a
trap concept he pioneered in Africa for leopards and cheetahs and
found that with a few tweaks, he could make it work for cougars.

Yovovich continued with a story from one of her trapping adventures. The study team was having trouble catching a particular cat in
an area, when, finally, they had success. "The beacon had gone off,
and it was a sub-adult male in the trap. This was a pre-dispersal-age
cat, and we were really excited to get to collar him because once you
put a collar on, you can see where they go, and that kind of information is really hard to come by." With the cat drugged, and the crew
working, their flashlights revealed eye shine lurking in the shadows.
The crew presumed the mother cat was watching as they worked on
her son. Yovovich pauses to paint a picture of the scene for me—it's
3:00 a.m., pitch black in deep redwoods, a mountain lion's watching them, and they are uneasy and out of their element in the darkness. "You could look around, and one minute the shine would be

coming from over here; you'd wait a few minutes and you'd see the eye shine from the other side. But you couldn't hear anything moving. You could only tell from the eye shine that the cat was circling and probably not too pleased." The cat never approached the crew. They finished working on the young male, released him, and left the area with their gear. Back at the office, when they checked the camera card, they had a big surprise—"mom" was actually the sub-adult's brother. Apparently, the mother had left the two big kittens while she hunted. The camera video told the rest of the story. As Yovovich explained, newly collared 41M "went in the trap, steps on the trigger, the cage door closes behind him, he startles at first, then turns around and looks at the deer in front of him like, 'Sweet, ok, I've got dinner.' He lies down and starts eating. About a minute later, his brother jumps on the trap and starts playing and pawing at him through the bars, like, 'Hey, what are you doing in there? I'm gonna poke you with my paws.'"

Yovovich startles me with her next bit of information, which brought her tale full circle. "Later on, we caught 41M's brother, 46M, as well."

"Wait," I think. "I'd read about this cat!" This is the saga of 46M, the lion who dispersed blindly into the city of Mountain View, was humanely caught, and released back into the Santa Cruz Mountains.

"What happened to 46M after they moved him back to the mountains? Did he disperse successfully?" I asked.

"Unfortunately, 46M later got hit by a car and died. Most carnivore biologists' stories are going to have a sad ending. You follow these animals for a long time and too many of them end with the focal character getting shot or hit by a car."

Given the difficulties of dispersal in the Santa Cruz area across major freeways and towns, one major unanswered question is if cougars are moving from there into the East Bay, or vice versa? The southern region of the East Bay has a known, healthy population of cougars, seen on trail cameras for years by Steven Bobzien.

Bobzien is the ecologist for the East Bay Regional Park District and has had his heart set on a puma project for more than twenty years. It's now coming to fruition. The Park District, in partnership with Panthera, is moving ahead on an ambitious study, with hopes for a ten-year research arc. Bobzien explained that they have several points of interest and are planning to compare various East Bay regions for contrast. One goal is to study the depredation situation and find out if the tally is as high as livestock owners suggest it is. The District grazes 70 percent of their public land, working hard to educate ranchers as to how to guard their livestock. A special permit that allows a livestock owner to shoot the offending cougar is issued following a reported depredation. In 2015, for instance, 248 depredation permits were issued across the state.

The ultimate goal of the District's study will be to identify wildlife corridor usage. Cougars are an umbrella species. If the study reveals corridors used by dispersers and resident cougars, land connecting those corridors will be purchased. This would also help other species, such as bobcats and coyotes. By getting ahead of urban sprawl, the East Bay Regional Park District can link their diverse sections of various parks with connective corridors, as well as work with California Department of Transportation to create freeway underpasses.

⌇ WHOLE PUMA HEALTH

A line of fast-moving vehicles speeding down Marin's busy Tiburon Boulevard threatens to push me past my destination—a sharp right turn into a narrow and steep parking lot. A small office complex houses the Bay Area Puma Project, an organization guided by Zara McDonald with the mission trifecta of education, conservation, and research. I'd made an appointment with McDonald and her staff to discuss their latest projects. Knowing they are looking at puma health in these fragmented landscapes, I ask McDonald to begin with genetics. According to a DNA study done by

Zara McDonald with cougar kitten

researchers at the University of California, Davis, led by Dr. Holly Ernest of the University of Wyoming, mountain lions throughout California, separated by only a highway, have far less genetic material in common than just eighty years ago. Genetically diverse populations have better resilience to disease, climate change, and whatever else nature might throw at them.

So how are Bay Area cats faring compared to Dr. Ernest's findings in other areas of California? McDonald tells me that geneticists at U.C. Davis pulled DNA from cougars in different parts of the state. This included cats killed with depredation permits, road kills, and collared cats. Their analysis revealed that coastal lions near large urban centers, from southern California to the Santa Cruz Mountains, had much less genetic diversity than inland California populations such as those in the Sierra Nevada Mountains. "These findings raise major concerns about . . . the longer-term outlook for pumas in southern and central coastal California," says McDonald. The study emphasizes the need for connectivity across highways and development.

California's problem with genetic diversity might seem unique in this densely populated state, heavily cloaked in highways and interstates, but a study conducted in the great expanses of the northern Rockies—northwest Wyoming, Montana, Alberta, and

British Columbia—points to genetic fractures there, too. Using virus strains as a genetic marker, the research revealed eight major feline strains across those regions, marking distinct populations. In keeping with the California results, Interstate 90 in Montana was acting as a major genetic barrier. No lions had crossed that highway.

McDonald continues, "The U.C. Davis genetic study also found that almost all cats tested have percentages of rodenticide in their livers."

Rodenticide is a big issue for urban wildlife. Rodenticide poisoning killed M21 from the Jackson study. Although rare in rural and de facto wilderness, rodenticide poisoning is common in urban/suburban areas. Anticoagulant rodenticides are products specifically designed to kill rodents by causing internal hemorrhaging. Widely used by pest control agencies, these toxins travel up the food chain, becoming more lethal in larger animals as the dose accumulates. A study conducted in 2013 by the California Department of Fish and Wildlife found rodenticide in fourteen out of fourteen lion necropsies. Research conducted in the Santa Monica Mountains tested for rodenticides in bobcats and lions. Ninety-one percent of the lions tested positive—including a three-month-old-kitten—while 95 percent of the bobcats did. The famous P-22 lion in Griffith Park was seen on camera looking ragged, with a bad case of mange. His weakened condition was due to bioaccumulation of rat poison, leaving him vulnerable to disease. Researchers recaptured and treated him. Clearly, that can't be done with all wildlife.

McDonald was an ultra runner whose close encounter with a mountain lion in the Marin hills modified her professional course. "I ran every day and would frequently see coyotes, bobcats, foxes, and raptors, rain or shine, all hours of day, and into the periods of dusk—exactly the periods of day that I remind people to be cautious of when recreating alone because we are in mountain lion country.

"During one of these runs, I had this powerful encounter with a mountain lion. That very close encounter left me feeling pretty silly,

Cougar at night with the Bay Area lights in the background

because it ended benignly, as most do, but also entirely enthralled. I experienced this rush of emotion about the fate of the species. This experience transcended the knowledge I thought I had at that time about mountain lions, and led me to strongly believe that this species has a much more important contribution to this landscape than I do."

That once-in-a-lifetime encounter indirectly gave rise to Felidae Conservation Fund, a broad-reaching organization for global, wild felid research that the Bay Area Puma Project (BAPP) falls under.

Courtney Coon is one of BAPP's field research biologists. Coon has a background and interest in disease and animal health. After obtaining her Ph.D., she worked for two years in South Africa studying wild African buffalo infection and immunity as it related to nearby domestic cattle. Currently, she's working on a puma health project for BAPP in coordination with Dr. David Stoner, a cougar researcher affiliated with Utah State University and principal investigator for BAPP.

Coon shows me a Google Earth map of the study area with an overlay of what looks like a grid game board with green and red pegs. The pegs mark the location of the camera arrays. The idea is to place cameras in a variety of distinct landscapes that include a diversity of land uses, i.e. dry hillsides, golf courses, protected "wilderness," or city parks. Coon tells me they are analyzing what they call "body scoring." She likes to think of it as "Whole Puma Health."

Starting with thousands of camera images previously collected from around the Bay, and using a standardized African Lion scoring index, Coon is mapping out body scores by location. A score of one is low, while nine is high—"probably too fat"—Coon tells me, as a nine would only be found in zoo animals. Coon pulls out a colored chart with pictures of lions from the American Zoos and Aquariums manual. Forequarters, midsection, and hindquarters are described in detail for each rating: *Neck thin & shrunken; Point of hip prominent;* or *Point of hip & ischium covered.* The accompanying photos complete the story. The chart is very specific as to where the fat deposits are, correlating fat with health, which, in turn, correlates with availability of food.

Preliminary results are thought provoking. Camera trap work done on cougars living in the East Bay—the most fragmented of their study regions—show that body scores are high. Even though possibly only two or three cats are pushing these body scores higher, that's interesting to Coon.

"The difference is small, but significant," Coon says, "like between a six and a four. It's obvious looking at them, but biologically we're not sure what that difference is, for instance, if it has an effect on reproductive health. There are a lot of other aspects to health besides fat reserves, but fat reserves will show quality, especially in a wild animal.

"The studies we're planning on doing will be incredibly comprehensive. We'll also be looking at diet through scat studies, stress hormones, diseases, so we can have this whole picture of health rather than just one aspect. If we use this really deep holistic view of puma health from the few animals that we collar, then we can take a step back and put the body condition scores into context. But you have to do this holistic thing on an animal before you can do that."

In other words, by looking at puma health using a variety of tools, Coon can then return to the zoo-based body condition scores and determine if they are useful in an urban setting, or if there are other factors she can use to measure puma health.

I caught up with David Stoner at the Mountain Lion Conference in Estes Park, five months after speaking with Coon. Coon was preparing to present her research work at a conference in San Diego, and told me to speak with Stoner for an update. I had just finished listening to his presentation describing how he employed G.I.S. information on large expanses of habitat across the Intermountain West to determine its productivity quality as a predictor of mule deer abundance and cougar home range size. Land use and fertility were uppermost on his mind while describing Coon's study.

Stoner told me that the scale at which cougars operate is very important. "They are obligate carnivores that eat only meat. An animal with that life history needs a lot of space in order to meet its needs."

The Bay Area, Stoner points out, is highly productive for cougars: there are a lot of deer and no winter snowpack, so the animals don't need to move a lot seasonally. This is beneficial for cougars. We humans might consider this space sufficient, but for a carnivore that hunts deer, the large open spaces in the Bay Area are actually very small for cougars, especially when these areas are bounded by agriculture, cities, or small ranchettes.

Once she'd done all her camera analysis, Coon found that cougars using these "intermediate" areas of altered land use, such as golf courses and city parks, were doing better than the animals in more "wilderness" type settings around the Bay. "I think there's just more food," Stoner told me. "I'm talking about lightly developed spaces, not fully developed cities. We humans stabilize the variants. Where there's a lot of environmental variability, we smooth it out through irrigation. The conditions become much more stable and predictable throughout the year."

Stoner is right. Having lived in the Bay Area and worked as a landscape designer for eighteen years, I saw this first hand. Winter means rain, and with that comes the broad expanse of hillsides greening up. As moisture dries up in the spring, human landscapes are watered, city lawns turn green, domestic plants become fat with moisture. As the dry season rolls into September, deer descend from the desiccated hills to feed in our gardens. I've experienced this personally, where high fall temperatures and extended summer drought drive deer to seek water in the plants we are irrigating. All the food is sitting at the edges of our urban landscapes—pets, hobby livestock, as well as the native prey.

Stoner tells me about a study done in Africa looking at the "edge effects," where carnivores that need large habitat couldn't move very far without encountering the "edge" of a protected habitat. And that edge is where humans live, where more abundant food sources are. And that is also why animals in Coon's mixed-use zones are scoring higher, in terms of health, than cougars in what we might think of as large wild areas.

I asked Stoner if the study was analyzing why Marin County might have fewer cats than the South Peninsula. He said that kind of data might be useful for managers, but Coon is trying to tease out different information.

"We're not looking at South Bay versus North Bay, versus this place or that place," explained Stoner. "It's more about how these fundamental variables of fragmentation, primary productivity, and moisture predict animal body condition. We're trying to look at it more fundamentally. These camera sites occur along a gradient [of these conditions]; how do cougars react to these different land use types and what does that mean from an animal welfare standpoint.

"The traditional view in American society is that cougars are a wilderness animal, living in remote areas. I've always argued that's an artifact of history. We didn't tolerate them in agricultural or urban areas, so by default over generations of intensive wildlife exploitation, that's where they ended up. I think they could live in these urban interface areas, it's simply a matter of human tolerance and values."

———— ⚘ ————

It's been raining hard for several days. Some say the long drought is over, but having lived here for years, when my work was dependent upon watching the weather, I know better. Northern California is getting a moisture reprieve this year, but the trend has been toward a drier climate for a long time. Courtney Coon tells me that funding is becoming scarce for urban interface projects. Not sexy enough anymore. Climate change is where a lot of the funding is going for wildlife studies. It's much sexier.

These winter rains signal to the California orange-bellied newt that it's time to mate. I grab my torch and a jacket to head out for a newt-watch. Koda needs a nighttime adventure anyway. The ocean is wild, with a high tide coming in. The turbulence kicks up white foam that the winds carry up the cliff onto trees and bushes. The surf's edge looks like the sea is beating up egg whites. This thick weather always does something to me. It's a violence I enjoy, a surge of life force, a reminder of our smallness and our place in the universe. The winds are fierce over the exposed beach sand, but the newts won't be there. I'm heading for the dirt trails they cross on their way to the nearby marsh.

For most of the year these amphibians—*Taricha torosa*—are terrestrial, but with the strong rains, the streams start moving, and their natal vernal pools fill up. They're programmed by nature to return once a year to breed in water. They lay eggs that stick like glue to the aquatic vegetation, then they head back to dry land till next year. These funny little dinosaurs with bulging eyes are extremely toxic. Their orange bellies are a warning to anyone who might contemplate having one for dinner. *Taricha torosa* have skin glands that release neurotoxins said to be hundreds of times deadlier than cyanide.

It's pitch black. If I didn't have my flashlight I'd be stepping all over these little newts. Tonight I count more than twenty, vigorously crossing the road. The newts I see are definitely on a mission. While many are moving towards the marsh, an obvious choice, others seem to be returning toward the dry hills. Have those already mated? It is amazing to contemplate the distance these creatures travel to return to the exact pool where they were born, sometimes walking several miles. Since they live for fifteen to twenty years, that's a lot of miles on those little legs. You have to wonder how they are navigating this odyssey. No roads, no overview; their eyes must be useless in the journey. Their scenery is a tangle of brush. What's the internal homing device? It must be primarily celestial, since they always seem to be moving at night, even though tonight there is no moon. There could be earthy scents mixed in there, too. That's a mystery we humans will probably never solve. I wonder, too, if the previous droughty winters left fewer wet signals for them to start their annual walkabout.

The crash of the waves booms louder than usual, reverberating against thick cloud cover. A few coyotes howl, and I remember that only a few miles south of these coastal hills there was a known resident mountain lion that lived in Tennessee Valley, a part of the Golden Gate National Park. That was in the 1990s. The lion occasionally made the local paper and was said to have a twenty-square-mile territory, still very small for a lion.

Virginia Fifield began her foray into mountain lion work as a child when she raised a cougar kitten to adulthood for a local zoo. Beginning in the 1980s, she worked with several agencies attempting to determine if reports of eastern cougar sightings were valid.

Soon thereafter she met cougar biologist Harley Shaw who became her mentor and friend, instructing her in mountain lion field work. Fifield has done several extensive camera studies on lions here in Marin County, and she doesn't think there is a noticeable population of them. Even as far back as the mid1990s, she tells me, there's little documentation of many lions in this county. She has hard evidence of just one resident male, easy to spot on camera because he has an ocular defect, so there is eye-shine in only one eye. In a four-year study, the same cat appeared on cameras from north Marin County in Nicasio to southern Marin County near Alpine Lake, a short distance through thick scrub and rugged terrain. After inspecting hundreds of shots, she could only verify one additional lion besides this resident male, and that one was a male, too.

Fifield tells me she doesn't believe there have been any reliable sightings of females with kittens in Marin County at all. "That would be big news," she says. "We get them in Sonoma, but not down in Marin."

She's not kidding about kittens in Sonoma County. These days Fifield is working with the Sonoma Audubon Canyon Ranch Mountain Lion Project, a small pilot study that focuses on fragmentation, connectivity, and conservation on the eastern side of Highway 101. This year they discovered three ten-day-old kittens in a den, mothered by P-1, a ten-year-old female. The Ranch's fieldwork, under the leadership of African lion specialist Quinton Martins, has a collaring permit issued by the California Department of Fish and Wildlife.

Because I lived in Marin County for more than twenty years, and I know the habitat is excellent, I can't help but wonder why so few lions live here, compared to Sonoma County. Fifield speculates that Marin County, as a triangular peninsula hemmed in on three sides by the ocean and by Highway 101 is just too tiny. "The county is small and mountain lions need huge home ranges. That could mean two hundred square miles for one male. Marin County has some parameters that make it less conducive to multiple mountain lion populations. They can move in and out for sure," says Fifield.

Marin County habitat is a mix of what's found in the Mt. Hamilton and Santa Cruz Mountains area—mixed conifer forest, and large swaths of oak woodlands. I can testify that the deer population is large and healthy, along with feral cats, raccoons, opossums, and other small prey. I spent a lot of time as a designer thinking about deer-, rodent-, and raccoon-proof strategies for homeowners.

Courtney Coon, the BAPP biologist, approached my question from a different angle. "I think it's quite disturbing," she said. "Why is it that just in this little strip [of the South Peninsula], where the human population is quite dense, we see a lot of pumas, maybe six or seven? And we've had females with kittens in the South Peninsula, too, while maybe three males, at most, and no known females with kittens, in the North Bay. I think that's something we need to figure out."

What makes for good habitat? While Marin County has some of the best connected, pristine habitat in the Bay Area, pumas are just not using it much. Zara McDonald of Felidae Conservation Fund tells me that more lions were moving through Marin County and the headlands in previous years. The development of vineyards and other agriculture in northern Marin County has likely made the trip into the county riskier for lions. "Our cameras were getting lions in 2012 and 2013, and then nothing more until 2015, and now only one-eye, our only known Marin County lion," says McDonald. Coon adds that connective corridors in the South Bay are easier for a cougar to spot, while corridors from Marin County to Sonoma County are not easily found. Referring again to Google Earth, Coon shows me large stretches of ranchland, land with no cover, that cougars would have to cross to disperse. Although young dispersers don't know where they are headed, they do know the difference between cover and no cover. Coon says, "We have three criteria for good lion habitat: deer, a water source, and cover."

⟩⟩ LOOKING AT CALIFORNIA'S
LION MORTALITY HOLISTICALLY

As a native of northern California, growing up in a ranching family in the central valley, Lynn Cullins could look to the eastern slopes of California's coastal range, or east to the high Sierra Mountains, and dream of the big cats that roamed free on those mountains and hillsides. As a lover of cats and all things wild, it was only natural that when Cullins heard about the voter drive to pass Proposition 117, she quit her job as a computer systems analyst and volunteered full time for the Mountain Lion Foundation gathering signatures for the ballot initiative. After Proposition 117 passed, Cullins spent the next decade working for a series of environmental campaigns and ballot initiatives related to wildlife and habitat, only to return full-time to the Mountain Lion Foundation in 2001 as an employee. In 2015, she became their executive director.

I asked Cullins about the depredation count in California. I was under the impression that the one hundred cougars killed every year through legal permits had the same additive effect as trophy hunting in other states. Although several hundred permits might be issued by the California Department of Fish and Wildlife in any given year, many livestock owners choose not to use their "legal take." I wanted to know who the bulk of these permits were going to and where most of the predations were taking place.

"People characterize depredation as a conflict between mountain lions and ranchers, but the reality is that, in California, it isn't about cattle, it's about all the other kinds of animals that we have scattered throughout our landscape," Cullins tells me. "Less than 5 percent of the mountain lions killed on depredation permits are found to have cattle in their stomach. If we only killed mountain lions that were preying on cattle, we'd have fewer than five mountain lions killed a year. The rest [of these depredations permits] are related primarily to goats, then sheep, then a variety of other animals like llamas or alpacas. The other misconception is that there are a large number of domestic cats and dogs killed on depredation permits. But it's again less than 5 percent."

It's customary for the California Department of Fish and Wildlife to perform necropsies on mountain lions that are killed for depredation. In 2015, of 107 animals killed for depredation, eighty-three were necropsied. Of these, 52 percent had what the Department characterized as "domestic animals" in their stomach, while 5 percent had deer and 9 percent had empty stomachs. The balance could not be identified. Keeping in mind that these necropsies were done on only a handful of the 3,000 cougars in the state, and only on cougars targeted for preying on livestock, clearly 14 percent of these kills were for the wrong lion, destroyed for no reason at all.

On February 14, 2016, an article entitled, *"Study finds mountain lions are feasting on house pets,"* written by outdoor writer Tom Stienstra, appeared in the *San Francisco Chronicle.* Stienstra used the Department's necropsy results to distort facts. Stienstra's article focused on pets, writing, "A pet owner's nightmare, their dog or cat being eaten by a mountain lion, appears to happen with some frequency, according to a new report from the Department of Fish and Wildlife." Stienstra intentionally omitted key details. First, the Department's "domestic animals" category includes all livestock as well as house pets, and second, the majority of depredation tags are issued for hobby animals, not house pets. In fact, the *Sacramento Bee* pulled all permit data dating back to 1973 and found that only 8 percent of depredation tags were issued for house pets. While the *Chronicle's* headline characterized the report as a "study," suggesting a scientific analysis, the annual depredation results are only a narrow snapshot of depredation tag mortalities. The article created enough of a stir that Panthera issued a statement about the fallacious story on their Facebook page. These kinds of false narratives are what Cullins and the Mountain Lion Foundation are working to change through public education programs.

Since Proposition 117 came into effect in 1990, California has endured a population explosion, the state bulging at the seams with almost forty million people today. Housing developments are cropping up in exurban areas; landscapes that once belonged solely to the big cats are now dotted with rural developments where homeowners might decide, for various reasons, to have a few small livestock animals. "We're seeing the proliferation of development up into mountain lion territory where you have a few acres of land, and people decide they're going to have goats, or sheep, or alpacas, or some other kind of animal as a project, or as an alternative way to keep vegetation down, or because this is part of what they want to enjoy as a rural lifestyle," Cullins tells me. These project animals are not used for ranching, but for personal use, such as milk, wool, sustainable weed suppression, or family meat.

Although Cullins may be talking about landscapes that were once strictly small, rural ranching towns, project animals are cropping up in suburban areas as well. The Bay Area hosts a mosaic of private land that juts up against public land, providing habitat for cougars, bobcats, and coyotes to move through. I tell Cullins I know of a woman in suburban Marin County who lives in a subdivision adjacent to a creek. She raises fancy chickens in her postage-stamp-size backyard. Her brood was being picked off nightly, one by one, by a bobcat. No matter what she did, the bobcat was always smarter. Finally, she bought a 12x12-foot wire pen with a roof, eliminating her bobcat problem. Cullins tells me lions are killed for raiding chickens as well.

Newcomers to raising small animals oftentimes don't have the traditional and cultural knowledge of predator coexistence that people who once lived in small mountain towns for generations did. The traditional knowledge of how and why to protect your animals is not in their working vocabulary. Compounding the problem, a community of these hobby ranchettes might bring in large numbers of livestock in total, but small numbers in each person's back yard, leaving scores of animals unprotected.

Old barn in Montana

"When you see the crumbling grey barns on our landscape, we need to remember that people had barns for a reason. When traditional barns were replaced by pole barns throughout the West, what that took away was our ability to use a barn as a protective measure for the livestock. It meant protecting only hay from the elements," explains Cullins.

As Cullins is speaking, I'm thinking of the northern Rockies, where hundreds of acres once belonging to large ranches are now chopped up into twenty- or forty-acre ranchettes and subdivisions. Crumbling barns by the highway are a common sight in Wyoming and Montana, yet people elect to leave their few chickens, pigs, or goats unprotected from a wide array of predators—not just cougars—but also grizzly bears.

"We need to remember that barns used to be a feature of ranching and farming in rural areas," explains Cullins. "Every time I see a barn, it's a reminder that the idea of protecting your animals is not a new idea. People have been able to do that successfully for thousands of years and the way they did that was to protect them from dusk to dawn in a secure enclosure. To some degree, due to our arrogance, we have abandoned the traditional measures that were used to protect livestock."

Because mountain lion predation on livestock is such a rare event, newbie exurbanites might go years without seeing any losses of their animals or their neighbor's animals. But when predation hits, the shock and trauma of the event, along with the concern for what it might mean for their neighborhood, kicks in and alarms an entire community. Communities that rely on depredation permits instead of livestock protection run the risk of high cougar mortalities. El Dorado County in northern California, a region that includes Lake Tahoe, provides an example of the overuse of depredation permits. From 2012 to 2016, more than 19 percent of the county's total estimated lion population was killed through the use of depredation permits. Numerous studies have shown that to preserve a sustainable lion population in a given area, no more than 8 to 14 percent can be hunted in a year. One California Fish and Wildlife warden, who has been involved in many legal kills, is convinced that depredation numbers would be reduced by at least 50 percent if people protected their domestic animals properly.

Lynn Cullens returns our conversation to the original misconception she felt needed to be cleared up. "Again, I want to dispel this misconception that when we talk about depredation in California, that what we're talking about is a conflict with cattle ranchers. That's just not the case."

Yet Cullins is also keen to put depredation numbers in perspective. It's important to understand the causes of lion mortality holistically, she tells me, rather than picking them out one by one.

She ticks off a list for me. Taken all together, the annual numbers are astoundingly high for a state that has outlawed hunting. Road kill, 100; depredations, 100; and poaching, estimated by the Mountain Lion Foundation to be another 100, though there are no accurate state numbers. Add in rodenticide and other poisons, and combine this with public safety kills, and the totals soar. In addition, one dead female lion represents the loss of several kittens. These mounting threats to mountain lions can be boiled down to the growth in human population, with the biggest threats being habitat loss, habitat fragmentation, and corridor disruption.

"You can take any one of these as an individual variable and discuss it in depth. But the reality is that, in an additive sense, we need to be concerned about how all these things are stacking up on one another and causing a heavy impact on not just population numbers, but also on the social structure of mountain lions. One has to realize just how much the deck is stacked against mountain lions in California. And how that deck is stacked in California is a warning to the remainder of the West in terms of the kinds of variables all related to human population growth that can cause us to raise questions about the long-term survival of mountain lions on the landscape."

Yes, California's multitude of population-caused problems is a warning for western states. But can their potential solutions possibly be a template for mitigating human-caused problems affecting mountain lions throughout the West? The Mountain Lion Foundation, along with other groups throughout the West, hope to tackle this question through a variety of approaches we will explore in the next chapter.

CHAPTER 10

GREAT THINGS BEGIN IN THE TINY SEED OF SMALL CHANGE

*The end of the wild world, the emptiness . . . is a reduction
of diverse nature into a simplified biota that is entirely
managed and dependent. It is a loss of autonomous beings,
the self-willed fauna that gave us metaphor, that shaped
human minds capable of identity with all existence.*

—ELLEN MELOY

SHARON NEGRI

"You've got to speak with Sharon Negri," houndsman Rod Bullis
told me. I recognized Negri's name from my essential reading on
mountain lions. She and Maurice Hornocker, the father of mountain lion research, co-edited the massive scientific compilation,
Cougar: Ecology & Conservation. Sharon Negri's name is well known
in the field of conservation. She was one of the main drivers behind
California's Proposition 117, which reclassified mountain lions as
a specially protected species. With politics in her blood (her father
was a California state legislator), Negri was walking the halls of the
state capital as the lead lobbyist for the Planning and Conservation
League, a nonprofit lobbying organization, when she was barely out

Sharon Negri

of college. Not many women were in the field of conservation in the 1970s and 1980s, yet Negri was a competent rising star. She went on to work for the California State Coastal Conservancy, but her heart remained with wild places and, as she puts it, "the voiceless."

After a year's hiatus traveling around Africa and other wild places with her husband, Negri returned to the states with a passion for international wildlife conservation work. But the winds of cat fortunes had other plans for her. William Newsom, father of California's Lieutenant Governor Gavin Newsom, offered Negri a job as head of a small non-profit organization, The Wildlife Conservancy. Newsom described to Negri how mountain lions were about to be hunted again in California.

"I couldn't believe it," she said. "You mean the slaughter of mountain lions is going to happen in my own backyard? I realized the same thing that was happening in Africa was about to happen in California—chasing a mountain lion up a tree and shooting it point blank for sport. It just seemed outrageous to me."

There were few studies on mountain lions in the 1980s. Rick Hopkins, who was an advocate for lion protection, had done the longest study at that time in the Bay Area. With only cursory studies statewide, "It was a no-brainer," Negri told me. "Most of the studies were short and in very small areas. They had no idea how many mountain lions existed in California at that time." Although Negri had never run a non-profit before, she took the task on with fervor, organizing the most successful grassroots effort ever in the country. With the help of Margaret Owings, as well as Bill Yeates, a new 501(c)(3) organization, the Mountain Lion Foundation, was created, with Negri as Executive Director. To jumpstart the young organization, Negri went to the legislature and identified every person who had ever written a letter on behalf of mountain lions. Within three years, the Foundation went from three hundred supporters and members to 36,000.

Negri worked tirelessly. She took the media on field trips, hosted phone banks, hired media consultants, and traveled statewide with the Foundation's message for sound science and the importance of protecting mountain lions from a trophy hunt. Thousands of letters, along with almost every major newspaper in California, condemned the hunt based on scientific, humane, and ethical grounds. A coalition of groups that Negri was part of collected enough signatures for a ballot initiative and, in 1990, the people spoke: Hunting cougars in California is illegal. Penny Maldonado of the Cougar Fund told me, "Sharon Negri showed us all what can be accomplished."

"It was the most inspiring experience I've ever had." Negri told me. "Even people who'd never seen a mountain lion wanted them protected. 'I don't care if I never see a mountain lion,' they'd tell me. 'I just want to know that they are living free and running wild.' They also understood that the cursory science being used to justify a mountain lion hunting season was absurd and had to be stopped."

The western states have never seen anything like this, before or since. The groundswell of public opinion began a new era of protection for mountain lions in California, and along with it, a quandary concerning mountain lion management in the state that continues today.

Under United States common law, the people own the wildlife, while the states hold them in trust for citizens. The lines of jurisdictional authority are complex and highly political. But, in general, state legislatures pass wildlife laws, state game commissions interpret the laws, and the state wildlife agencies implement and enforce the laws. Governors usually appoint state wildlife commissioners for a set period of time, which means they are not elected by the public and, therefore, do not have to be responsive to the wide range of public opinion on mountain lion management. The commission establishes hunting seasons, harvest quotas, and management actions. Mission and mandate statements for these state commissions are broad, allowing commissioners to accommodate non-scientifically supported decisions, such as drastically reducing cougar numbers in order to increase the deer population for recreational hunting. These kinds of decisions fit neatly in with where the majority of the funding for these agencies comes from—hunting and fishing licenses. In other words, non-consumptive users—people who just like to watch wildlife and take photos—have little say in state wildlife management.

On a rainy morning, I met Sharon Negri in Berkeley at a coffee house. Her open, personable manner made it easy for us to find common ground. Negri told me that after the initiative passed, she left the Mountain Lion Foundation and now runs her own nonprofit organization called WildFutures, a project of Earth Island Institute. Part of her week is spent providing capacity-building programs and coaching for environmental directors. But most of her week is devoted to her primary passion, protecting mountain lions. I asked Negri if she'd seen a mountain lion when she began work on the 1990 initiative, and if that was the force that guided her passion. "I had not seen a mountain lion. I didn't have to. You don't have to see something nefarious to know that it is wrong."

It wasn't until many years later that she got her first glimpse of the big cat. "It was one of the biggest highlights of my life," she said.

Negri recently produced a six-minute video revealing the intimate family bonds of mountain lions and how essential they are to their survival. After years of lobbying and working to pass legislation and statewide initiatives, as well as working on books with lead mountain lion scientists, Negri changed gears. She is now producing high-profile films, videos, and educational materials that reach a broader audience and raise awareness of the importance of protecting mountain lions. When she saw the camera footage from the PTCP taken at mountain lion dens, Negri envisioned a whole new venue to reach the public—seeing these animals up close and personal.

"I read an interview with Jane Goodall," Negri said, "and someone asked her how the Internet can change the way people regard animals. Jane replied that videos and social media are some of the best ways to change peoples' attitudes and perceptions about animals. With the click of a mouse, she said, you can reach millions of people. But Goodall said one thing that really focused my attention on doing that video. The way to reach people, she said, is not just to get to people's heads, you need to also get into their hearts."

What came out of that inspiration was *The Secret Life of Mountain Lions*. Negri will soon be releasing a Spanish translation of the short film.

"Our follow up survey revealed that the video was effective in changing people's misperceptions of mountain lions," explained Negri. "Where people had conceived of mountain lions as solitary killers, they now realized they had social structure and are compassionate animals with tight family bonds. The video is powerful because it shows that we share values in common with these wild animals: of family, safety, and freedom from persecution. And it has been incredibly meaningful for me to be able to bring these animals that are extremely rare to see in the wild into the homes and hearts of millions of people."

I told Negri it was Rod Bullis who had encouraged me to speak with her. She said, "I met Rod and Cal Ruark at a Mountain Lion Conference, maybe ten years ago, and they were carrying *Cougar Management Guidelines* around with them. They said that's their bible. I never thought I'd like a houndsman. Those two are remarkable people. Rod would call me on the phone and say, 'Sharon, I need your help.' Houndsmen get a bad rap, but here are two houndsmen who understand the importance of responsible management and hunting."

What's the next step? Not surprisingly, Negri mentioned the need to reform state wildlife management by broadening the funding base of state agencies beyond hunters and fishermen and to change the structure of fish and game commissions to include non-consumptive users. "It's important for the public to understand how their state agencies are actually managing their wildlife and, unfortunately, most people don't have a clue," she said.

Negri was part of a small group who brought together fifty diverse stakeholders in Washington State, including fishermen, hunters, wildlife advocates, wildlife agency personnel and others, for a two-day dialogue. They were tasked with creating recommendations for strengthening the ability of the Department of Fish and Wildlife to manage and conserve wildlife by broadening their funding base to include non-consumptive users. With the growing threats to wildlife and simultaneous decline in funding, there is an increasing number of stakeholders who agree that the old management models are not sufficient to address the complex issues facing wildlife today.

PREVENTATIVE METHODS

In the Bodega Bay area of California, where tracker Jim Sullivan lives, sheep have taken a hard hit from cougar predation. Sullivan said they've had four mass kills in their area in a short span of time.

The first mass killing took place in a hollow outside the town of Bodega. A hobby rancher with eight, three-hundred-pound sheep in a pen forgot to protect them in her barn one night. That night a cat jumped into the outdoor enclosure, killing all eight without eating a single one. The second incident happened at the Chanslor Ranch, a 378-acre coastal dude ranch in Bodega. The ranch uses portable electric fences for sheep enclosures, moving their grazing area every few days. One night a mountain lion jumped over the short fence and killed all thirteen sheep without eating any. Neither of these ranchers chose to obtain their entitled depredation permits from the State. Sullivan has a theory about this kind of surplus killing, which he discussed with Matt Nelson and Mark Elbroch.

"This cat is probably an old, burnt-out cat," says Sullivan. "He jumps in the pen and here are these three-hundred-pound sheep. The sheep are scared and banging around off the walls; as one sheep comes by, the cat swats that one. Now he's all excited, he's got blood on his mouth. The next one comes running by and he swats that one down, and pretty soon, it's the worst night of that cat's life. This is horrible, he just wanted to have dinner and he's got this big soap opera going on. He jumps over the fence and runs away."

Sullivan and I discuss the phenomena of how this cat became overwhelmed by a group of frenzied sheep stuck in the pen. "And there's a genetic factor too," he adds. "All the years this lion has hunted deer, he takes one, and the others run away. They take off going fifty miles an hour and crashing through bushes. And he's not used to having any spectators around. It gives him cognitive dissonance."

Among wild predator/prey interactions, surplus killing is an extremely rare event. Ideas about surplus killing in wolves, for instance, were influenced by folklore, with some reliable observations. Yet few of those observers ever returned to these carcasses over the course of a few days. If they had, they would have found these kills thoroughly consumed in the days and weeks that followed. I saw two large, dead cow elk one winter in our valley. The carcasses lay on either side of our dirt road, both killed the same night by a pack of five wolves. Two adult elk is more than enough meat for one small pack of wolves. In winter, few cars drive by, but when the wolves were disturbed by vehicles, they'd leave the carcasses, returning only after nightfall. People who saw these carcasses that day thought the wolves were wasting the meat, just killing for fun—a common myth around here. But I watched the wolves return under cover of night for more than a week until they'd finally eaten through their kills.

One rancher who did ask for a kill tag lives across the street from Jim Sullivan. In less than one year, this rancher lost forty-six sheep. I asked Sullivan where these sheep were at night. "He wasn't bringing them in, they were all out in the pasture. And therein lies the problem between modern sheep ranchers and shepherds of old," Sullivan says. He looks at it politically and asks the question on many people's minds, "What is the position of a guy who's trying to make a living on a little piece of land and this cat's living in the creek down here, and every single night it comes and takes a lamb? What do you say to this rancher? He's just gotta sit there and sacrifice all his sheep? That's a tough sell politically."

I tell Sullivan I know a bit about the different types of preventative methods that people in the Greater Yellowstone Ecosystem are employing for wolves and bears, but little about lions. Even in the GYE, where cattle and sheep mingle on public lands, grizzly bears are the common problem, not mountain lions. Guarding your livestock in non-lethal ways takes extra time, attention, and money, but it can be done. Sullivan tells me his friend Mike started using llamas for guardians, but the cougars ate them. "So, then he went to alpacas, but the mountain lions ate the alpacas. He's open though. Maybe guard dogs might work." Our conversation settled somewhere in the back of my mind, not forgotten, only to be pondered until I met the right person who could answer Sullivan's question. The answers were to come sooner than I thought.

One evening, during my short winter stay in California at the beach house, a powerful storm closed in—violent winds and high surf warnings. The storm caused a power pole to go down, leaving my rental unit devoid of heat and lights. It was one of those nights when you just wanted to crawl back in bed with a good book, hoping the power would come back on soon. But I was getting ready for an event in Mill Valley. Tonight's gala celebration was for Project Coyote, an organization founded by Camilla Fox that helps ranchers and urbanites learn to live with predators using non-lethal means. I'd met Fox several years ago, and now with my compressed schedule in Marin County happily coinciding with her organization's fund raising event, I was intent on showing my support, no matter what the obstacles.

I first became aware of Project Coyote when I read an article about the Marin County Board of Supervisors. Camilla Fox had helped convince the Board to let go of Wildlife Services and try her non-lethal methods instead. I'd never heard of such a coup before, and I considered this a monumental feat. This woman, I figured, must be exceptional in order to convince an agricultural community like Marin County to give up a service they had relied upon for years for predator control. But over time, the methods Fox proposed paid off. The transition to a non-lethal approach reduced the county's predator prevention bill from $80,000 a year to $30,000 a year. The county no longer contracts with Wildlife Services but, instead, uses county resources through a cost-share program known as the Marin Livestock and Wildlife Protection Program, working directly with ranchers. Since the transition in 2000, livestock losses have plummeted from 6 percent to 2 percent for the sheep population. Here was a model that might be used throughout the country, I thought. I'd been following Project Coyote's progress ever since.

The evening was a great success—lots of schmoozing, a presentation by author Dan Flores, and an awards ceremony. But as I was ducking out early in order to brave my drive home through the powerful storm over Muir Woods, I ran into Fox and mentioned my interest in mountain lions. Remembering Jim Sullivan's stories about sheep being picked off nightly in Bodega, I wondered what Project Coyote's approach to the problem might be. Fox said she'd put me in touch with Keli Hendricks, her Ranching With Wildlife coordinator. Hendricks was at the gala that night, receiving an award for outstanding commitment and service. We later arranged to speak by phone when I returned to Wyoming, but I remembered Hendricks from her acceptance speech—unassuming, with a sweet, gentle nature—yet clearly a woman who can mix it up with ranchers, hunters, and politicians, never deterred from advocating for wildlife.

One of nine counties in the Bay Area, Sonoma County is a rural region north of San Francisco with large family and small hobby ranches. Keli Hendricks is well suited for the job of advocating for non-lethal predator controls. She and her husband manage a five-hundred-acre cow-calf operation, and they lease additional private land for grazing. A professional horse trainer, Hendricks became interested in Project Coyote while exploring ways to solve conflicts with wildlife.

"We don't have any problems with mountain lions on our property," Hendricks said, "but we do have coyotes. They come in at calving time, eat the afterbirth, and then leave. A lot of ranchers shoot them, but we want to keep their packs stable." Young dispersers are more likely to be the culprits in sheep and calf kills. With stable packs around their ranch, Hendricks tells me, there's no predation and the canines keep the rabbit and ground squirrel populations down, leaving more grass for the cows.

"On the home ranch, my husband goes out to check the cattle frequently. Human presence is probably the most important thing you have to prevent predation. And also, it allows you to see animals that might be sick, or compromised, that you may need to bring in. I think ranching around predators can make for better ranchers, because they have to check on their animals more," adds Hendricks.

Knowing that less than 5 percent of mountain lion depredation tags are issued to cattle ranchers, I wonder how Project Coyote might be addressing predator problems with small scale livestock operators. She echoes what Lynn Cullins of the Mountain Lion Foundation told me. "The challenge with these small scale operations is they know less about livestock, so their animals are more vulnerable, and there are so many these days, you can't find them all. But generally, the new operators are more open to learning a technique they might not have heard of."

Obviously, what Hendricks is dealing with in northern California is a different situation than in the Greater Yellowstone Ecosystem, where wilderness and open spaces are vast. In northern California, the main problem is coyotes, while we have grizzlies and wolves to contend with. Yet pockets exist in northern California where people run into conflict with mountain lions, particularly with small scale hobbyists—a fairly new phenomenon that is springing up all over this formerly rural county.

Wildlife Services, a program under the USDA's Animal and Plant Health Inspection Service (APHIS), specializes in killing wild animals that threaten livestock—especially coyotes, wolves, and cougars. Although its main focus is on predator control in the West, Wildlife Services also does things like bird control at airports nationwide. APHIS has a facility in Logan, Utah, that spent millions of dollars testing non-lethal methods of livestock protections. The Predator Research Field Station keeps a stock of one hundred coyotes in pens, and tests tools like turbo fladry, noise makers, and foxlights (solar-powered, sensored LED lights that flash randomly). Fladry is a line of cord with strips of colored nylon or vinyl sewn along the strand such that the strips flap in the wind and create a visual deterrent to keep predators at bay. Turbo fladry uses an electrified wire as an additional deterrent. Fladry was used for centuries to hunt wolves, and is now used as a way to keep livestock safe. The Field Station also studies coyote personalities, and they test other methods for protecting live-stock, like sterilization and novel delivery killing systems. Recent research has shown that *non–lethal* methods are more effective at resolving conflict in the long term. In fact, lethal removal may further exacerbate the problem and increase conflict between car-nivores and livestock.

Even during my December stay here, there was an uproar when ten alpacas were killed in a small rural development in the Malibu Hills of Los Angeles. A depredation permit was issued to the live-stock owner who chose not to use it. The culprit was P-45, one of just three breeding-age males out of ten to fifteen cougars in the Santa Monica Mountains. The Mountain Lion Foundation used the incident to highlight how to protect livestock by helping the affected homeowner build a predator-proof pen. I wanted to under-stand what methods Project Coyote uses with ranchers to decrease cougar depredation permit requests. I know fladry won't work with cats. Hendricks tells me they don't use fladry in these exurban situ-ations because coyotes are just too smart, and they get used to the flagging quickly. The best prevention is pre-planning and multi-pronged. This amounts to bringing your sheep, goats, llamas, horses, or other pets and livestock in at night, putting them in a protected enclosure. Cougars can easily climb over a twelve-foot fence, so any pen must have a roof.

"Sheep, especially, need some sort of protection." Over thou-sands of years, domestic sheep have had the orneriness as well as wariness bred out of them. Hendricks has a few remedies for the sheep problem. "With hobby ranches, these predator-proof pens work well. But for people with several hundred head, you really need to get guardian dogs. In lion country, Anatolian Shepherds are probably the best bet. The only problem with guardian dogs is that it takes a year to raise a dog. You have to raise them with the livestock, replace your older dogs, and have enough dogs for the number of livestock you own. Livestock grazing in heavy brush areas or hilly terrain where predators can hide and animals become scattered from the herd, means you need more guard dogs."

For these larger ranches, guardian dogs combined with other methods can work well. New tools such as e-collars from Africa are applied, one for every ten sheep. When the sheep start to move erratically, the collars flash lights, emitting a siren. The trick for all these non-lethal methods is to hone the tools to fit the situation. Nothing is cookie-cutter. Hendricks is emphatic—a rancher needs to have a cool head and be proactive. When you see your animals being attacked or killed, that's not the best time for thinking things through.

"It's like having a jewelry store in the middle of town and not locking your doors at night," says Hendricks. "You can keep shooting people while they're coming in and stealing your stuff, but it's really not the most effective way to protect your merchandise. What's frustrating for me is that people using non-lethal tools hold them to an impossible standard. They think, if I use these tools I'll never have another problem. There's no silver bullet. If you're going to have livestock, you're going to have dead stock."

While Project Coyote may have few calls for help with cougar predation in the Bay Area, keeping their focus primarily on helping large ranchers with non-lethal protection from coyotes, the Mountain Lion Foundation has been doing community outreach for livestock protection specifically from lions since 2000, the year they received a call from a game warden in Amador County. Seven lions had been killed on one homeowner's property. The landowner wanted to crop his grass "sustainably," without the use of pesticides, so he bought a goat and staked the animal in his large front yard. Each year the vulnerable goat was eaten by a lion which, by law, allowed the homeowner to obtain a depredation permit to kill the lion. The next year, the owner bought another goat, which subsequently was eaten, a permit was issued, and the offending lion was shot. This ritual was repeated through seven goats and seven lions, until the local warden called the Mountain Lion Foundation, asking for educational outreach help. "We need to explain to the landowners," the warden told Cullins, "that it doesn't matter whether you care about the mountain lion. If you care about your livestock, killing the mountain lion is not a long term solution." This was logic all could agree upon. Thus began the Mountain Lion Foundation's first pen-building program, and it was highly successful. For the next five years, no lions were killed in Plymouth.

The Mountain Lion Foundation has been working with local 4-H clubs for many years, teaching them about predator protection and how to build lion pens, as well as educating children about other potential protection methods like foxlights and noise-making systems. In 2015, the Mountain Lion Foundation began formulating a plan to create a template that could be used throughout California for small-scale producers. They found a starting point for that model in the tiny community of Julian, population 1,500, located in San Diego County.

Julian is situated in an important corridor for lions living in the Santa Ana Mountains. These lions are genetically isolated, and they are one of the most threatened lion populations in the United States. When the Mountain Lion Foundation noticed Julian was suddenly experiencing a high number of mountain lion depredations, they mobilized their forces. Lynn Cullens, along with Winston Vickers, an expert in southern California lions, arranged to speak at the local library. When 250 people in this small town showed up for the event—business suits to cowboy hats—the Foundation knew interest was high.

Looking at where most of these depredations were taking place in Julian, Foundation representatives noticed something highly unusual—three depredations occurred on one property in Julian in a period of only six months. They contacted the homeowners, Brian and Tara Denny, and found them happy to have the Foundation help build a cougar-proof enclosure.

The Denny's lion encounters began when their chicken coup was raided one night. All but two chickens were eaten. Brian Denny attempted to reinforce the coup, but the following night he saw a lion trying to reenter it. The next morning, Tara Denny almost tripped over a lion when she went to check on her chickens. The lion was a young female, sick and emaciated. Too ill to even run away, the lion growled menacingly, unmoving, crouching against the house. Brian Denny shot the animal. Then in May of the same year, the Denny's daughter Elizabeth, who also happened to be president of the local 4-H Club, lost three show pigs to a cougar that jumped over a six-foot roofless enclosure. Degradation permits for two lions were obtained and both were killed.

Gearing up, representatives from the Mountain Lion Foundation invited everyone they could think of to observe the pen-raising demonstration to be held on the Denny's property. Attendees included employees from the library, Wildlife Services, Department of Fish and Wildlife, as well as representatives from the veterinary community, county government, the cooperative extension, the local chamber of commerce, and the ranching community. "Really it wasn't even *us* showing how to build it," says Cullens, "because at that point we had involved the local 4-H club to the extent that the kids themselves were able to communicate the information, not only about good practices in terms of animal husbandry, but also about predators." Although representatives from the Foundation discussed foxlights, e-collars, and other deterrents, their primary instructions focused on what is the sure-fire way to protect animals—enclosing animals in pens with roofs from dusk to dawn.

"Our pens are light weight, easy to put up," Cullens tells me, "and a 12x12-foot fence costs about $600. One of the things we like to tell people who say 'we can't afford a pen,' is that in many counties it costs up to $300 to have a dead animal removed from your property."

Cullens was proud of their success working hand-in-hand with the Julian community. After the enclosure demonstration at the

Julian community pen builders

Denny's, Julian's 4-H club participated in their local Fourth of July parade. The kids designed their float as a miniature pen with a mountain lion mascot and a sign that said, "Build a pen, save a lion." The truck carrying the float was driven by Mr. Denny.

The Julian event spurred the idea of creating templates, sustainable programs that could last for the long term and be used by various communities within a variety of settings—urban, suburban, exurban. The template would make it possible for communities to adopt animal protection practices without requiring the intervention of an individual or an organization like the Mountain Lion Foundation. Instead, the template would be embedded within local standing institutions that already have a relationship with homeowners and are in areas likely to come into conflict with lions. This might include city and state fire officials (who already inspect urban/wildland interface zones for brush removal), schools, or local law enforcement.

Representatives from the Mountain Lion Foundation are still active in Julian, learning lessons that will help them refine their lion protection template. Cullens tells me that the goal in Julian is to create "a team of folks in a community that lasts beyond the initial outreach. We are documenting that so any community across the West would be able to pick up that model and use that in their own community."

Of the many promising outcomes from the Mountain Lion Foundation event in Julian, one has the potential to reach a nationwide audience. An attendee from Julian's Cooperative Extension took the seminar's ideas and presented them to California's state 4-H chairman. The California 4-H is now in the process of developing a 4-H curriculum around predator protections that could be implemented throughout California as well as nationwide.

⟡ THE COUGAR FUND

I'm sitting in the tiny, upstairs office of The Cougar Fund in downtown Jackson. Located above a local bookstore, the one-room office includes a long, narrow, back closet full of boxes of literature, logo T-shirts, and other goodies they sell or give away at educational presentations. The organization has a staff of one-and-a-half persons, according to Penny Maldonado, the Fund's Executive Director. A yellow Labrador Retriever wanders the room looking for a place to settle down, while I plant myself in a cushy armchair, adjusting the tape recorder so it's focused on Maldonado. The Cougar Fund is the sole conservation group in Wyoming that concentrates exclusively on cougar advocacy. Maldonado sits in a chair by the door, across the small space between us, while behind me is her work desk. Their location may be modest, but the mission and influence of this young organization has been felt across the state of Wyoming and beyond.

I first met Maldonado in Cody at a Wyoming Game and Fish Commission meeting that focused on trapping regulations. I'd spoken with her on the phone a few times about lions in my area, and more recently I had watched a video feed where she spoke on behalf of mountain lions at another Commission meeting in Pinedale. She was expressing her appreciation to the commissioners for approving a new ruling that prohibits killing any mountain lion traveling with other lions. I was already impressed. She was being very gracious, thanking them for a tiny, yet significant, change.

Predator politics in Wyoming are fraught with old-school prejudices. Keeping your optimism, fighting the good fight, one needs to be a long-distance runner, not a sprinter, if you expect to change policy in this state. I told Maldonado I'd seen her via the YouTube feed at the meeting. It must be hard, I said to her, to go to these meetings where the attendees, as well as the commissioners, just want to kill more cats. I was fishing for hints at how she could keep up her stamina.

Maldonado replied that what was really important was not what she said at that Pinedale meeting, but that she was given equal time. After she spoke, the head of the Outfitters Association walked to the microphone and announced to the Commission, "I'm blindsided by this. As far as I'm concerned I want all the lions gone."

Now, a bit of context needs to be inserted here. Deer and elk outfitters are an important voice financially for the Commission. They host out-of-state hunters who pay enormous fees for tags to hunt deer, elk, or bighorn sheep. And many of these outfitters, along with the commissioners and legislators, adhere to a belief that lions are not only competition, but are also reducing deer populations.

Maldonado reminded me of what happened next. "The commissioner's response was, 'Did you go to any of the meetings?' And the outfitter said, 'I didn't know about them.' 'C'mon. Sorry you missed them. Come back in three years,' said the commissioner. That was respectful to us [The Cougar Fund]. All too often people comment on the result, but they don't take part in the process. They feel they're not being heard. We just had an incident where I believe conservation groups were heard. Representatives from the National Elk Refuge were presenting their new comprehensive plan for public comment. One of the options in the preferred plan was to open up hunting on the Refuge, and cougars were mentioned by name. Because of public participation and civil communication, they removed all mention of hunting on the Refuge for the next fifteen years. People are heard, they just don't get what they want all the time. We have to be part of the process, and legally, too, it gives you standing."

It's those little victories that can stack up and raise her spirits. And her job as Executive Director has taught her the necessity of being open. It doesn't mean you're disloyal to your own values, she tells me. The three maxims she adheres to are honesty, communication, and trust.

I ask Maldonado what The Cougar Fund sees as their priorities. She's the soldier in the field who is realistic, working day to day in the trenches. The Cougar Fund, inspired in 1999 by the Miller Butte mountain lion family on the Elk Refuge, was formed in 2000 and has a tridental mission: education (about 85 percent of their budget), funding and promoting the use of sound science, and monitoring state policies. Just being a constant presence and applying pressure over time hopefully pays off. In her job as an advocate, Maldonado tells me, she sees movement toward incorporating the latest science into predator management policy. "For instance, you can't work for Montana Game and Fish without a Master's degree. In Wyoming, I take pride in the fact that we even have a large carnivore department, because many states like North Dakota tuck predators into other aspects of management. We [Wyoming] have a department that's dedicated to keeping carnivores around. We might not always like the way they do it, but we have it. And they don't want to get rid of them. The legislators and the outfitters would like to get rid of them and the ungulate lobbies are extremely strong."

But it's obvious where she gets recharged in her work—it's working with children. When she starts talking about The Cougar Fund's educational mission, she lights up, her voice full of enthusiasm. The kids are our hope for future change in intractable states with anti-predator beliefs.

Maldonado points to a taxidermy cougar on top of the large bookcase behind where she's sitting and tells me the mount is about forty years old. The Cougar Fund acquired the specimen from an older couple downsizing their belongings; they couldn't bear to put it in their garage sale, so they donated it to the organization. The specimen is now part of The Cougar Fund's education program. It's a powerful tool that affects both children and adults. They not only get a chance to see what a cougar looks like, but they also hear about this particular cougar's plight in an intimate exchange.

"It's a sad story," Maldonado tells me. "She's a very small female, probably around two years old, and she was hunted in Arizona. Whoever the hunter was took her to the taxidermist and never bothered to go back for her. She was worth nothing to him alive, and even less to him dead. The taxidermist said to the couple—who loved mountain lions—'I've kept this mount for two years and I don't know what to do with it.' The couple offered to buy the cougar from him, just because they didn't want her to be thrown away. They kept her in their home as a symbolic gesture, the fact that she meant something."

The Cougar Fund's ultimate goal, of course, would be to make hunting cougars illegal across the West, and to restore lions throughout the eastern United States. But Maldonado views her work in terms of incremental victories. There is good, better, best. *Good* was when cougar management began in all the western states in the 1970s, with the exception of Texas. *Better* is passing regulations that protect lions, particularly pertaining to fair chase and protection of kittens. (Fair chase for cougar hunting would mean abandoning of the use of technology such as snowmobiles, A.T.V.'s, G.P.S. on dogs, and shooting mountain lions out of trees.)

"We work on the better," she tells me. But Maldonado is quick to point out she doesn't concentrate on being against hunting as the major focus of their operation, "because even if we stop hunting, that's not the end of the problems facing cougars.

"This is the crux of the matter. We bring this up in our talks over and over again. We do not want people to think cougars are going to be okay if hunting ends. There are too many other contingences—encroachment, habitat fragmentation, lack of optimal conflict prevention behavior, corridors."

A new and interesting twist to The Fund's work is their sponsorship of a scientific detection dog through Working Dogs for Conservation. Working Dogs for Conservation uses dogs in all sorts of unique ways: finding invasive plants, determining if a region contains endangered animals, and promoting educational outreach. It's a symbiotic relationship between the two organizations, because the dog can be used as a management tool in a variety of situations. For instance, he can detect if cougars are present in an urban-interface area, signaling the need for pro-active protection. Or the dog could determine if a lion was the culprit in a predation situation. The Cougar Fund's dog will also be the star in a lot of public events. It's no secret that when a dog shows up, more people's heartstrings get pulled.

I notice a copy of the book *Cougar Management Guidelines,* the book for state managers that Sharon Negri referred to. I hadn't read it and asked if I could purchase one. Maldonado and I walk across the street to Tom Mangelson's photography gallery. Mangelson is one of the founders of The Cougar Fund, and the front desk in his gallery has a supply of *Guidelines.* Maldonado turns to wave goodbye, leaving me with a bit of her hard-earned, hands-on wisdom. "It's so complicated, Leslie, and we have a responsibility to weave our way through the maze."

✐ THE CULTURE OF STATE GAME AGENCIES

I've come to understand that management of people, and of mountain lions, is complex, but it boils down to two things—habitat loss and overhunting. Under that umbrella falls everything from government to personal responsibility. I think Dr. David Mattson put it best.

I first met David Mattson through his advocacy work for grizzly bears in the Greater Yellowstone Ecosystem. What I didn't know then was that he had also participated in more than ten years of research in the Southwest focusing on puma ecology and puma/human interactions. Both of these experiences with megafauna have shaped his opinions about state predator management and its influence on the public.

Mattson points out that although changes in attitudes towards predators have been incorporated into state game agency policy, the essential structure and funding of the agencies themselves has not changed. What he calls the "utilitarian/dominionistic" worldview has dominated these wildlife agencies since the early 1900s, where domination and utilitarianism is the goal. Over the last forty or so years, a new approach among the public has emerged that values nature for its intrinsic beauty, focusing on ecological connection, scientific advancements, and the idea that humans have a moral responsibility to protect the earth and its wildlife. These two stances are diametrically opposite, creating increased public demands on agency management.

Yet, only one set of people holds power over wildlife decisions. Wildlife commissions and employees in wildlife management agencies almost all self-identify as hunters and supporters of groups that support hunting. Funding sources for these agencies comes primarily from hunters, trappers, anglers, and gun owners through license sales and other fees. In Wyoming, for instance, 80 percent of the funding for the Game and Fish Department is from sales of hunting and fishing licenses. North Dakota's entire budget for wildlife management is sourced from these user fees. The Pittman-Robertson Act (or Federal Aid in Wildlife Restoration Act) places an excise tax on the sale of firearms, ammunition products, and archery equipment. This act gives additional monetary support to wildlife agencies to the tune of millions of dollars a year from the sale of lethal weapons. The funding bar is heavily weighted in favor of hunting opportunity.

Mattson writes that having a homogeneous group in charge of wildlife issues makes for a uniform world-view, one that tends to be sympathetic towards that particular constituency—the hunting crowd becomes the "in-group" with preferential treatment, with livestock growers a secondary component.

Wildlife is considered a public trust asset. That means that wildlife is owned by no person, but held "in trust by governments for the benefit of present and future generations." This idea dates back to the Magna Carta in England, and was enshrined into law by the Supreme Court more than 150 years ago. The public trust doctrine provides a framework for which state and federal governments can protect, conserve, allocate, and control wildlife for the benefit of the public.

Over the last forty years, expanding urbanization has made "the internal world of the utilitarian/dominionistic subsystem increasingly out of sync" with the decline of hunters, notes Mattson. This has threatened the revenue stream for game and fish agencies, perplexing them as to how to understand and reverse these declines, as well as challenged their traditional values and identities.

The other side of the coin is what Mattson calls the "out-group," those who have no real voice in wildlife management. These include non-hunting environmentalists, animal welfare groups such as The Humane Society, and what is commonly referred to as "non-consumptive" users, those who like to take photographs and watch wildlife. This group is excluded from decision making because it has no effect on agency budgets through fees, no lobbying force in the legislature, and no influence on commissioners, who are appointed by governors rather than being elected by the people. These outsiders' perspectives are not shared by those who have dominated wildlife management for the last hundred years.

Mattson argues that the incompatibility of these two perspectives, and the fact that only one group holds all the power over what should be a representative and democratic agency, is the main obstruction to reform in management.

> Mountain lion management will continue to serve a narrow set of special interests organized around hunting as long as revenues are primarily hunting related, commissioners are deeply imbued with the ethos of hunting, and management agencies are dominated by a hunting culture. This is not to say that hunting is intrinsically bad, but rather that any policy process that patently serves narrow special interests while marginalizing all others is fundamentally incompatible with a liberal democracy grounded in civil discourse.

So how to move forward. No one person has the answer, but groups like the one Sharon Negri participates in with a variety of stakeholders in Washington State are making progress. A Predator Policy Workgroup in California has a diversified membership to include three consumptive users, three non-consumptive users, three Ag users, and Rick Hopkins as the science advisor. They are responsible for considering predator reforms and for suggesting new language or regulations that the commissioners might adopt. Shrinking revenue from hunters—even as the number of wildlife watchers and non-consumptive users is growing—is beginning to force agencies to come to the table to find new funding sources. These new funding sources must include revenue from all users—whether it is something like a tax on photographic equipment and wilderness gear, use fees, lottery proceeds, or even general tax dollars—agreed upon by members of these consensus groups. Additionally, public awareness of how these agencies currently operate, what their policies are, how they are funded, and what voices they

BIG GAME HUNTING, FISHING, AND WILDLIFE WATCHING EXPENDITURES IN WYOMING, 2016

	RESIDENT	NONRESIDENT	TOTAL
Big Game Hunting Trip Spending (1)	$36,973,770	$89,656,183	$126,629,952
Big Game Hunting Equipment Spending (1)	$72,292,451	$7,415,249	$79,707,700
Total Hunting Spending	**$109,266,221**	**$97,071,431**	**$206,337,652**
Fishing Trip Spending (2)	$57,237,300	$106,931,827	$164,169,128
Fishing Equipment Spending(2)	$22,038,739	N.A.	$22,038,739
Total Fishing Spending	**$79,276,039**	**$106,931,827**	**$186,207,867**
Big Game Hunting Licenses (3)	$5,662,502	$18,498,021	$24,160,523
Fishing Licenses (3)	$2,150,721	$4,653,372	$6,804,093
Total Licenses	**$7,813,223**	**$23,151,393**	**$30,964,616**
Wildlife Watching Trip Spending (4)	$36,888,226	$298,325,635	$335,213,861
Wildlife Watching Equipment Spending (4)	$22,929,973	$6,821,271	$29,751,244
Total Wildlife Watching	**$59,818,199**	**$305,146,906**	**$364,965,105**
TOTAL WILDLIFE RELATED SPENDING	**$256,173,682**	**$532,301,558**	**$788,475,240**

(1) Southwick Associates and WGFD Annual Harvest Reports
(2) U.S. Fish & Wildlife Service National Survey and WGFD Fishing License Sales Data
(3) WGFD Licenses Sales Data
(4) U.s. Fish & Wildlife Service National Survey estimates adjusted for inflation
INFORMATION COMPILED BY DAVID TEX TAYLOR.

are excluding is essential. When Jonah Evans, a mammalogist with the Texas Parks and Wildlife Department said to me, "If the public knew the trapping policies on mountain lions they'd be outraged," he was right. I asked a few Texans if they knew that cougars had absolutely no protection in their state, and they were more than a little surprised at that news.

To begin the conversation, all interests need to come to the table. Again, Mattson sums it up very succinctly. "Moving beyond current paradigm will likely require diversifying revenues so .at no one interest group has a lock on agency financial well-being, diversifying commission membership to represent the full spectrum of ways that people value animals such as mountain lions, and diversifying the cultures of management agencies and the academic institutions that train prospective employees."

Wildlife agencies are waking up, but relinquishing control is not easy. On the other side, conservationists and animal-rights advocates need to come to the table in good faith, with open minds. Democracy isn't about getting everything one side wants. It's about listening, honoring and respecting the interests of others, and coming to policy decisions that take not only the views of all stakeholders into account, but also, in this case, the lion's future as well. Shifting the conversation from "resource" to "intrinsic value" and the ecological benefits of lions, as well as other predators, is a good starting point. The prioritization of establishing stable, self-sustaining lion populations needs to be a first topic of conversation not only among western agencies, but where lions are absent or struggling to exist in the eastern half of the country.

State wildlife management is one piece of this multi-pronged approach. Identifying and protecting corridors (such as freeway overpasses or land purchases), preserving large tracts of habitat for a species that follows migrations of prey, banning rodenticides, introducing public education programs, eliminating predator programs like Wildlife Services, funding non-lethal livestock protection programs, developing risk maps for livestock owners—the to-do list is long.

As far as hunting management, several well-thought-out ideas have been suggested by researchers as well as hunters like Rod Bullis and Grover Hedrick. Biologists Ken Logan and Linda Sweanor have broken the mold by advocating for management zones based on geographic terrain and habitat rather than political boundaries. They envision *refugias* of large contiguous tracts of suitable lion habitat, as well as sink zones in areas with high human or livestock density. Currently, only 6 to 9 percent of mountain lion range lies in fully protected habitat. With increasing pressure from human-related activity, such as development, roads, industrial disturbances, and hunting, recent studies recommend a minimum refuge of 3,000 km^2. Optimally, these would be reserves with little human influence, good quality habitat, sufficient quantity and quality of wild prey, and enough edge habitat for lions to hunt effectively. These refuges would also contain corridor links to other occupied puma habitats. Logan and Sweanor call these areas our "biological savings account."

Not all areas of protection are equal. For instance, with an area of 9000 km2, it would seem Yellowstone National Park would pro-vide an excellent source for mountain lions throughout northwest Wyoming. Yet Wyoming cannot rely on Yellowstone National Park as their refuge-source population. Wyoming Game and Fish Biolo-gist Dan Thompson tells me "there's not as much lion habitat in Yellowstone as you'd think." The Wind River Reservation to the southeast may be the best source population for cougars traveling south, west, and east. Wyoming Game and Fish was surprised when they picked up cougars on their trail cameras while perform-ing a grizzly bear study. The cats were traveling along corridor routes from the south into Area 2, the Jackson hunt zone. "I think the dispersal you're going to see into Area 2 is going to come from the west and the south," Thompson tells me.

Gary Koehler, wildlife research scientist with the Washington Department of Fish and Wildlife from 1994 to 2011, has suggested managing hunt areas based on road density and snow conditions. More road access means easier hunter success. By distributing the hunter harvest over a wide area, hunters are not necessarily attracted to areas where it's easiest to get a cougar. Koehler is also a strong advo-cate for not disrupting the resident toms who control dispersers. "I think the key is limiting the number of older cats that are harvested in the area . . . putting a limit or a quota on the number of cats that are harvested in a particular drainage. You might take one out of the watershed, then leave two others because that area that was occupied by the cat that is killed, it's going to be occupied by a young-age tom. He's going to come in and discover this vacancy and set up shop there, and it's those other older, neighboring resident toms who are going to basically confine him and say, 'Okay, this is your territory. You stay there.'"

The Washington Department of Fish and Wildlife did adopt a new management plan in 2013 based on studies done by Robert Wielgus and his students. Wielgus's advice came in the form of his favorite adage: "Every time you kill a dominant male, three juvenile delinquents show up for the funeral. With the grown-ups gone, the young hooligans run wild." The studies also found that increased hunting of toms had a deleterious impact on females and kitten populations. The state adopted a new "equilibrium" hunting management plan statewide, limiting hunting mortalities to less than 14 percent annually in any given game management unit. Similarly, a ten-year study by Colorado Parks and Wildlife found that hunting quotas should not exceed 8 percent to 12 percent of a population.

A one-pronged approach like the Oregon voter-approved measure in 1994 to ban the use of hounds in mountain lion hunting can backfire. The state agencies responded to the decline in lion mortalities by creating year-round seasons, increasing quotas, and reducing the cost of a tag. As a result, cougar deaths soared to record highs, and these kills were all indiscriminate because hunters cannot determine the sex of the animal without treeing the cat.

Fair chase means banning the use of new technologies such as G.P.S. on dogs, banning or limiting cougar hunts by outfitters unless it's for photographic purposes, creating hunt areas for "ethical release only," seasonal road closures to snowmobile or A.T.V. use, and restricting hunt areas to walk-in only.

And what about California, a state that bans all cougar hunting? Of course, this is a viable option that any state could choose. As Rick Hopkins said to me, "There's this notion that we need to be killing cougars. That is a philosophical point of view. There's the consumptive user that says it's their right to go out and kill cougars. And while states may have developed these approaches of what they think is worthwhile doing, it's really not dictated that they should do it. They choose to do it. If they choose to quit killing cougars tomorrow, the world would not collapse on them."

California is not without its problems. But its regulations do demonstrate how people can live with mountain lions without hunting. With more livestock than any other western state outside of Texas, and one of the highest cougar populations, attacks on sheep and cattle in California rank lower than half of their counter-parts that allow hunting. As far as human attacks, California ranks eleventh in the western states and Canada. But California also has issues with road kill, freeway crossings, genetic bottlenecks, roden-ticide poisoning, and habitat fragmentation.

Clearly, we have a lot of work to do to preserve mountain lions for future generations. They have managed to survive our onslaught thus far because of their inherent secretive nature. But their ensured survival into the future now depends on how we handle our rela-tionship to America's only native lion.

EPILOGUE

To see a cougar, a person must find a fresh kill and resolve to sit in one spot overnight, watching quietly and waiting for the animal's return. Alternatively, one could locate a fresh track in snow, doggedly follow it up cliff ledges, over jagged peaks, and along hogbacks until you are so close that the cat scrambles onto a shelf or up a tree for your viewing. If this is your preferred method, plan to take all day and most of the night for your tracking adventure. Or possibly, luck will be with you while driving a car one evening at dusk, and a lion will run across the road without your hitting him. You might catch a blurry glimpse of his long tail as he flees into the bushes. More than likely though, once you've learned about their habits and preferences, and begin to *think* like a mountain lion, you'll only find fragments of their presence on the landscape.

Alan Rabinowitz, famed jaguar researcher and president of Panthera, talked about his first cougar sighting, which was, ironically, before he decided to devote his life to big cat conservation. That serendipitous encounter occurred in 1976 while he was hiking in the Florida Everglades. It was a very rare sighting indeed, for at that time few cougars remained in Florida. After that lucky observation, Rabinowitz went on to work with jaguars, tigers, and leopards for more than three decades before spotting another puma. "I have tracked pumas myriad times through the jungles of Central America, up the slopes of the Teton Range in Wyoming, and over the rocky precipices of the River of No Return Wilderness Area in Idaho," Rabinowitz recalled. "Always the cat evaded me. I would catch sight of a wild puma once more, a brief glimpse of hindquarters as the cat ran across an old timber road deep in the jungle of Belize."

The most marvelous thing about mountain lions is that we *don't* see them. Masters of concealment, their innate secretiveness has ensured their continued existence in our midst. Unlike other animals that may have changed their habits to evade humans, mountain lions have always been ghosts upon the land, their movements remaining invisible day and night.

On a cool spring morning, wandering through Cougar Flats, a rock sided gully drew my attention. Following the draw down, brushing aside juniper limbs and branches of gooseberry bushes, I encountered a cougar scrape. I continued along the thin animal path with granite cliffs narrowing on either side, and within fifty feet I saw a well-eaten deer carcass, displayed with a circle of fine fur typical of a cat kill. A little farther on there was another scrape, then several more—a male lion's territorial markings. Just a few months earlier, in February, I'd seen a mom and two five-month-old kittens on my trail camera, lounging under the big scrape tree. Here, in sign language across the landscape, was their male. I wanted his photo, and I knew that he'd be coming around again. I returned with a camera and set it up on one of the few trees that afforded a good view of the area. In two weeks, I returned. To my surprise, this wasn't just a *cat* corridor, but a well-used wildlife corridor. It seemed that everyone was interested in who was in their neighborhood. A large grizzly boar, fat on all the winter-kill deer carcasses, waddled by. He bedded near the rise of the defile, leaving a meat-scented scat nearby. A solitary black wolf trotted through several times. A grizzly mom strolled uphill; her two yearlings scampered and played, batting at tree limbs as they followed. Several deer and elk, and even a mallard duck with a dozen ducklings passed through. I was pleased to see the cougar mother from my February photo with her two kittens, now nine months old and close to her size in height. One kitten stood by the camera, making purring and chirping sounds. The kittens played hide and pounce with one another. And then there was the lion I was searching for, the resident male. He was up and down the corridor many times, day and night, patrolling. At one point, he walked up to the camera, paused, and as if on cue for the video, called and called. He was beautiful and appeared to be young, which is not surprising in a hunted environment. Yet he was definitely the king of the canyons, for this was his territory.

I may never see a mountain lion, but by trusting my instincts, I passed a crucial test and discovered this lion's haunts based on my comprehension of the landscape and my newfound understanding of cougars. I can now read the signs on the landscape where cougars pass, verifying that knowledge through trail camera photos of them. I am happy just to know they are living their lives in the wilds that we share. In fact, there is something comforting and gratifying in knowing that cougars are off most people's radar. I live next to the busiest national park in America, where thousands of people follow wolves and bears on a daily basis, telegraphing their activities by walkie-talkies across the Park, tracking movements of alpha wolves and pups with expensive scopes, and giving grizzly bears endearing names—all of this posted on social media websites daily. And yet cougars are nowhere to be seen. But cougars are there, living wild and free, like liquid ghosts.

"It's kind of nice that people don't see cougars," Colby Anton tells me, "and that is why [Yellowstone] doesn't have a management program for cougars—we don't have to manage cougars, they manage themselves." I wish everyone thought like that. Cougars do self-regulate. They don't need to be managed to "grow more deer," or to control so-called "out of control" population numbers. Lions live in low numbers across immense tracts of land. They have their own society. They hold each other in check by a big male's presence. They share meals among their domestic community made up of a big tom with his females. And they know other lion communities through a network of scents, scrapes, and occasional encounters. They make sure young toms either move on or stay within their boundaries. They prefer deer, and they hunt small game, traversing corridor edges specifically to avoid human encounters.

Humans need to practice more marvel and wonder, less knee-jerk fear. We would do well to abandon the antiquated presumption that we are managers of wild animals. Caretakers, perhaps, at best.

A volunteer researcher whose task it was to hike to a cougar-killed carcass and set up trail cameras illustrates how we can trust our own senses, and how little we have to fear from mountain lions. While tying the cameras on trees, this fellow felt uneasy, as if he were being watched. The hair on the back of his neck stood up. He completed the job and promptly hiked out. When the crew picked up the camera data days later and looked at the photos, they saw the lion emerge from the bushes just as the technician left. The lion had been there the entire time, watching him, yet he left the technician alone. With knowledge of cougar habits and their preferred habitat, being aware is more useful than succumbing to blind fear.

Michelle Peziol, researcher and tracker with the PTCP told me, "One of my great goals and successes in this project was predicting where a mountain lion will move across the landscape." Of course, she had the advantage of G.P.S. collared cats. But Peziol also put in her dirt time in the field following these collared lions. "One time," she continued, "I taught a tracking class at the Teton Science School. We were walking along and I said, 'If I was a mountain lion I'd sleep under that tree.' Not three weeks later [the Project crew] had a mountain lion make a kill. He was sleeping under the tree right next to [that same tree]. That's when it hit me. In absorb-ing this landscape and learning the behaviors of this animal, I now

have a pretty good idea of where I need to go to see a mountain lion."
Peziol had developed the ability to think like a mountain lion.

Mountain lions exist on that fine edge of human consciousness
where fears of the unseen and unknown live. Because G.P.S. collars and hair DNA will never fully reveal the lion's secrets, their
presence among us is guaranteed to border on the uncomfortable.
The human need-to-know, to make safe, and to pedestrianize the
mysteries of the universe and the natural world, are destined to be
eternally foiled by this large cat. Those who live in mountain lion
territory have been gifted with a *koan* cat, a large predator who will
rarely be seen, whose inherent mystery, like the Great Mystery, will
never be fully understood and which requires us to lean into the
thin fabric that divides the visible from the invisible. Learning to
live on that edge is our cultural paradox and challenge. It can be
done. Just enough of the veil of cougar mystery has been lifted by
science that we now possess sufficient knowledge to accommodate
and share space with cougars. And accommodate we must. While
life for the cougar has not changed since the Pleistocene, humans
possess high-powered rifles and advanced technological equipment.
We eat away at lion habitat with our cities and towns, gobbling
up the landscape year after year. Living with lions and making
space for them requires not only our full hearts, but also our careful
planning. Accommodating means being willing to give—at least a
little. The lion has already given a lot. As humans, we are called to
action—preserving large tracts of wildscapes, creating connective
overpasses and movement corridors, and learning to live peaceably
with them—even if, like me, one never encounters a lion. I breathe
a little easier just knowing mountain lions walk across our western
landscapes, keeping wildness intact, living unencumbered and free.

NOTES

CHAPTER 1
THE QUIET RAPTURE OF OBSERVATION

- I spoke with Jackson resident Lisa Robertson of Wyoming Untrapped to learn from a local about her experience of watching the Miller Butte cougar family.

- As a testament to how difficult it is to see lions without the use of dogs, consider the statement of Tolbert James "Shorty" Lyon. Lyon worked as a government trapper in and around the Gila National Forest in New Mexico during the mid-20th century. "Shorty" was a legend bear and lion hunter and trapper, who hunted with dogs and his mules. In his book of short stories, while out hunting turkeys one day without his dogs, he saw a lion leaping away into the steep hillside. Without his dogs, and with only a 12-gauge shotgun, the lion got away. Lyon states, "I have hunted lions and lived in lion country better than 30 years, and up to this time I had seen only one lion without the help of traps or dogs."

- Most of the petroglyphs at Legend Rock are in the 'Dinwoody' tradition, a style associated with the Big Horn and Wind River Basin. Usually pecked into the rock, Dinwoody petroglyphs are often large, human-like figures with, according to the brochure from the new visitor center, "an unusual amount of toes or fingers, upside down figures, and/or a pattern of interior lines in the torso." Some have headdresses, some horns, some originate or end at cracks in the rock, maybe to indicate a transition from one world to another. Theory goes that these drawings were either done directly at the vision quest site, or, upon the seeker's return, they scrawled their experiences here. The Dinwoody anthropomorphic figures are uniquely different from any I've witnessed in my personal travels to the southwest. They are otherworldly, almost cartoon like, and evoke a sense of the extramundane.

- Colby Anton, researcher in Yellowstone National Park employing new methods to understand cougar gait mechanics, uses the term 'coursing than waiting' to describe cougars. The traditionally used term is 'sit and wait'. Anton explains that cougars are not true sit and wait predators, as they move across the landscape to look for prey, sneaking up on them until close. Alan Rabinowitz, in describing jaguars, says they are 'stalk and pounce' predators, which is another way of expressing these two cat's hunting strategy.

- Mark Elbroch in "Field Guide to Animal Tracks and Scat of California" describes how to tell the difference between a female and male adult cougar track. By measuring the width of the hind track's metatarsal pad, he advises using a cut-off of 50mm, where male palm pads typically start at 53mm wide, and wider. In addition, the stride of the tracks can be measured using either left hind to left hind, or right side. Females average a 36" stride while males average about 40".

- One of the most spectacular and unexplained pieces of mountain lion rock art in the United States is found deep within Bandelier National Monument Park. Located 1/2 mile from the pueblo ruins of Yapashi, *Shrine of the Stone Lions* is a hard, thirteen-mile hike traversing several steep canyons. Not really rock art at all, these two recumbent lions were carved out of individual pieces of volcanic tuff. They lie side by side, are close to life sized figures, with a crude wall of boulders encircling them. To keep them off the grid of people's attention, the National Monument doesn't even refer to the lions on their website. Local tribes consider The Stone Lions a sacred site. Pilgrimages are made even today by Cochiti and Zunis, who leave offerings around the shrine. Although it's not known exactly what these unique carvings represent, speculation is this was a hunting shrine for ancient Puebloan peoples. Not too far from this site, another single lion shrine lies outside the Park, its location on an obscure mesa kept highly secret. Like the Shrine of the two Stone Lions, this is also a recumbent lion surrounded by a stone circle. Several years ago, the University of New Mexico used a helicopter to remove the lion and deliver it to the Maxwell Museum. Amid loud protests, the carving was returned to its original site, although the tail is now missing.

- Archaeologist Frank Hibben excavated the prehistoric Pueblo site south of Albuquerque, New Mexico called Pottery Mound. Painted along the walls of one kiva was an image of a seated jaguar alongside figures of mountain lions and humans. Hibben believed this painting was a representation of a war council. Alan Rabinowitz, in his book "An Indomitable Beast" refers to anthropologist Leslie A. White's belief that jaguars, along with mountain lions, were spirit hunters "that bestowed power on tribal hunters during the tribe's hunting ceremonies."

☞ CHAPTER 2
BROOM RIDING AND HUMAN MEDDLING

- Frank Dobie published his first version of the onza story in 1931 in the magazine *Holland's, the Magazine of the South*. In the initial version, Dobie is traveling with his friend C. B. Ruggles. While searching for the Lost Tayopa Mine in Northern Mexico, their onza tale unfolds. According to Neil Carmony's exhaustive book *Onza! The Hunt for a Legendary Cat*, it was Ruggles who actually encountered and killed the onza two years before his Mexico trip with Dobie. Ruggles relayed the tale to Dobie over a campfire on their journey together. While writing the story, Dobie inserted himself as a participant so he could enliven his story in the first person. In his book, Carmony explores in depth the accounts of onzas killed by hunting parties in Mexico. Carmony concludes that the Mexican onza is simply a smaller version of the northern mountain lion. Why didn't the onza fable ever catch on north of the border? Carmony has an astute observation based on the mystical, more indigenous roots of the Mexican people. "The onza legend survives in Mexico because it continues to fit in well with the culture of the Mexican people."

- The cougar's adaptability meant his success in deserts, mountains, tropical rainforests, and grasslands. Yet once Europeans arrived in the Americas, the animal's fortunes began to change. The old growth hardwood forests of the East were cleared so quickly that by the year 1800, residents of the Hudson Valley in New York worried about the scarcity of firewood. By the mid 1800s, 50% to 90% of the eastern landscape had been cleared for agriculture. Game were so diminished that even by 1639 hunting seasons

were closed. Between habitat and food loss, along with human persecution, cougars were effectively eliminated east of the Mississippi River by
the late 1800s. Cougars were considered a "bad animal", a varmint, to be
exterminated to protect property, people, and game animals. By the early
1900s, cougar populations in the West were also severely diminished, and
cougars now occupied less than half of their native geographical range in
North America. Cougars were relegated to the lands that humans didn't
want, couldn't farm, and couldn't easily access—the mountains.

- Individuals in early America who took matters into their own hands,
  enjoyed weaving tales that celebrated their valor, and manhood, while also
  characterizing the animals they killed as vicious and aggressive to bolster
  their reputation. As more people arrived with their livestock, individual
  efforts were soon not enough. Circle or drive hunts, in the style of the
  ancient Incas, soon emerged in eastern frontier towns. These drives killed
  many more animals in a shorter period of time with less effort. Some of
  these drives were duly recorded. In 1753 citizens of three surrounding vil-
  lages in Massachusetts combined forces to rid the forests of wolves and other
  predators. In 1810 in Vermont, a large group of men, women, and children
  used an ever enclosing circle to capture and kill six wolves. Local papers
  and fliers announced these drives, asking citizens to turn out with the
  hopes of killing sheep-eating predators. These early hunts laid the ground-
  work for the ritual of circle hunts throughout New England. The preferred
  method was a ringleader would send out an invitation to the men living in
  the surrounding areas. A description of one of these drives included over
  400 men, advancing to the center "under the direction of the local militia
  officers. When the hunters could hear the shouts of their cohorts across
  the circle, their commanders ordered a halt. . . . the best marksman among
  them, entered the ring and killed the wolves and foxes trapped there. The
  farmers scalped the wolves and marched to the town clerk's office to collect
  the bounty." Just as colonists came together for barn raising, and other tasks
  done as a community effort, the circle hunt became part of the communal
  tradition: first build the cabin, then clear the woods of predators

- A vivid accounting of a circle hunt took place in the woods of Pennsylvania in 1760. Black Jack Schwartz organized two hundred townspeople into
  a drive so wide it practically encircled the entire county. Men armed with
  guns, fire, and noisemakers began with a circle thirty miles in diameter,

slowly driving all the game towards the center, then began shooting indiscriminately for several hours. A few terrified animals escaped the ring, yet the final tally revealed a slaughter of 41 Panthers, 109 wolves, 112 foxes, 114 mountain cats, 17 black bears, 111 buffalo, 98 deer, and more than 500 smaller animals. The animals were skinned, the bison tongues taken, and all the carcasses were heaped in a pile "as tall as the tallest trees" and burned. The stench was so dreadful that settlers vacated their homes for over three miles. Black Jack's reputation with the Indians of the area, who only killed game as needed for food and clothing, was so unpopular after the drive that he was ambushed and killed while on a hunting trip. The last of these drives was held in 1849 in Pennsylvania.

- On the Pacific coast, the Spanish tradition of roping grizzlies and pitting them against bulls for sport is well-documented. These bull-bear fights included betting and even after-church festivities in arenas built specifically for the sport. In *California Grizzly* Storer and Tevis describe a bear-panther fight near Big Sur that took place after California was admitted to the Union. The gold rush brought in hundreds of thousands of new settlers, and with the arrival of these new residents, grizzlies were being killed in greater and greater numbers. The Spanish bull-bear spectacle continued for a few years until the dearth of bears caused the sport to dwindle. The event in 1865 was described by a young Frank Post who witnessed the event when he was only 6 years, yet never forgot it.

  "The lion, which seemed to have no fear, leaped onto the bear's back and while clinging there and facing forward scratched the grizzly's eyes and nose with its claws. The bear repeatedly rolled over onto the ground to rid himself of his adversary; but as soon as the bear was upright, the cat would leap onto his back again. This agility finally decided the struggle in favor of the lion."

- In *'Ben Lilly's Tales of Bears, Lions and Hounds'*, editor Neil B. Carmony notes "Ben Lilly often overestimated distances. The Foote Creek/Blue River region in Arizona, where Lilly followed a five-toed lion track in 1912, is about thirty miles west of the Saliz Mountains in New Mexico, where he killed a cat with a similar track four years later." As quoted in the text, Lilly exaggeratedly claims the lion was "a full hundred miles from where I first saw it."

CHAPTER 3
A LANGUAGE WITHOUT TONGUES

- From the Mountain Lion Foundation audio interview with Dr. Toni Ruth: ". . . wolves [scavenged] about 23 percent of cougar kills and displaced the cat from about 8 percent of those kills." Also "Wolf and Bear Detection of Cougar-Killed Ungulates on the Northern Range of Yellowstone National Park" Ruth et al "we cataloged 427 positive or probable cougar-killed ungulates. Wolves visited 87 (20%) of these kills and displaced the cougar from 27 (6%)."

- Vomeronasal organ is also called the Jacobson's organ, located on the roof of the mouth. It is mainly used to detect pheromones left in urine, and could be called a scent analyzer. It aids cats in identifying other cats, and especially in locating females who are receptive. Cougars, as well as all cats, use their tongues to flick the scent to the roof of their mouth, opening their mouth wide, curling their upper lip, and lifting their head back. This is called the flehmen response.

CHAPTER 4
A TWENTY-SEVEN-MILLION-ACRE
EXPANSE OF WONDER

- Dr. Mark Elbroch wrote an opinion piece in the Jackson Hole News and Guide in response to Wyoming House Bill 12. An excerpt:

"In reality, the connection between mountain lions and mule deer population declines is tenuous at best. The Wyoming Game and Fish Department has said that mule deer declines are largely the result of other factors, including habitat loss and disruption to migration corridors. It is also well accepted among wildlife biologists that deer dynamics are driven primarily by weather patterns and resulting forage availability, not predators. In fact, a recent intensive, long-term study from the Idaho Department of Fish and Game emphasized that removing mountain lions and coyotes did not provide any long-term benefit to deer populations."

- From the Wyoming Mountain Lion Mortality Report Harvest Year –
September 1, 2014 through August 31, 2015 documenting the effects
of the 2008 Wyoming Game and Fish Commission's efforts to decrease
the state's lion population. The term HY refers to Harvest Year. "Of note,
the proportion of adult mountain lions harvested has steadily declined in
recent years, from almost 60% adults harvested in HY 2007 to below 40%
in HY 2014 . . . Data indicate that several areas are achieving desired local
reductions, but increasing harvest pressure has also resulted in a decline in
the proportion of mature mountain lions available for harvest on a statewide level. Based on harvest data and supported by public surveys, juvenile mountain lions comprise the majority of what is currently available for
harvest in certain locales where population reduction is the objective."

◢ CHAPTER 5
CLUES FROM BEYOND THE VISIBLE

- The Colorado study site was located in western Colorado near the town of
De Beque, covering an area of approximately 1100 km². The area consisted
of a matrix of public lands managed by the US Bureau of Land Management, interspersed with private inholdings of various sizes, most notably
the approximately 800 km² High Lonesome Ranch, where the research
was focused. The study was conducted between February 2010 to March
2013. Meghan, a student at that time, accompanied Casey McFarland,
Neal Wright, and Matt Nelson from Elbroch's team, all highly skilled
trackers formally certified by CyberTracker Conservation.

- PTCP scavenger study documented more than three times the scavenger
species recorded at wolf and hunter kills in the same ecosystem just north
of our study area (Wilmers et al., 2003), but the paper notes "however,
it remains possible that our results differed due to methods rather than
reflected differences in diversity."

⟡ CHAPTER 6
THE HOUNDSMEN

- The Story of F51 and F61 can be viewed in National Geographic's film 'Cougars Undercover'. The entire story and genealogy chart was pieced together as told to the author by biologists working on the study, Cat Watch articles by Elbroch, newspaper articles, and references in Carnivore Minds by Bradshaw. I preferred to use names like 'Hippy Mom' and 'Lucky' where possible to make it easier for the reader to follow.

- Bradshaw in her book *Carnivore Minds* has a chapter on F51 and her interpretation of why she attacked, and was subsequently killed by a new male in the area. "Without extensive, hunter-free habitats, carnivores have no place to run and nowhere to hide. Human excess has penetrated the minds of the great American lion and turned the puma paw of restraint into a weapon against itself. Like high-powered bullets, such impacts don't end at their immediate targets. Because stress transmits neurobiologically and socially, violence experienced by adults rips across time."

- From the Boone and Crockette website "Almost all cougars are hunted using dogs because of the considerable difficulty in locating them without dogs. The practice is legal in many states. The Club finds that using electronic collars to ensure far-ranging dogs do not become lost is understandable and acceptable, but using electronic collars to more easily locate and access a treed cougar in order to take a shot is not an appropriate use of that technology."

- Frank C. Hibben, author of the colorful and captivating *Hunting American Lions,* was given a grant from Southwestern Conservation League to spend a year studying mountain lions. Although Hibben documented prey and collected scat, researching lions in the 1930s mainly meant hanging out with professional lion hunters and going on hunts for control kills. In one tale, while out looking unsuccessfully for lion sign with his houndsman guide Homer, the two see a fresh bobcat print and decide to change course. The description of a treed bobcat's demeanor compared with a mountain lion's is telling: "Every time a dog made a particularly high jump up the side of the tree, the [bob] cat turned for a moment and spit in the direction of the leaping animal. It was an explosive hissing noise accompanied by a strike of the forepaw

with the claws raking off bits of bark with the fury of the movement . . .
But mostly the bobcat seemed to recognize in us his principal enemies, a
very astute deduction. Mountain lions, when they are treed, seem to pay
little attention to their human adversaries and spit and strike at the dogs.
The bobcats have a justifiable reputation for attacking humans if they are
backed into a corner. Many a hunter—and Homer among them—had
told me that they would climb into a tree with a mountain lion, but
never with a bobcat."

- Logan and Sweanor found that mammary glands and distended teats are
  not a reliable clue for hunters. They are visible only during the first two
  months after the kittens are born, and since suckling empties the tissues,
  they might not be visible at all.

- "Harvest" is the term used by State wildlife management to refer to a success in a hunt as in "X amount of deer were harvested this fall".

- I'd poised this question to several people regarding hunting quotas in
  mountain lion hunt area 19, where I live, and is considered a "source"
  population. For the past three years, the quota hasn't been filled, and
  each year fewer and fewer lions are "harvested". I wondered if mountain
  lions were being over-hunted here, especially since I saw the accompanying map from Toni Ruth's summary articles on her research in the
  Greater Yellowstone's northern range. The map shows source/sink for
  female cougars, and my valley was covered with dark gray, indicating
  "sink". Only the high surrounding mountains were considered source
  populations of females.

- Wyoming Game & Fish 2014-2015 Harvest Report states: "Similar to
  previous seasons, mountain lion hunters spent an average of 3.9 days to
  successfully harvest a mountain lion, although a majority of hunters spent
  only one day in the field for a successful hunt (44.4%).

- Non-resident hunters accounted for 38.3% of all successful mountain
  lion hunters in HY (Harvest Year) 2014. Overall, 27% of hunters used an
  outfitter or guide when hunting, with 53% of non-residents using outfitters or guides for successful hunting, a slight reduction from the previous
  harvest year."

✐ CHAPTER 7
THE DEADLIEST JOURNEY

- In Desert Puma, biologists Logan and Sweanor state "As a unit, the [cougar] family has roughly three times the energy demands of an adult male cougar and up to six times that of a lone adult female."

- Howard Quigley and Maurice Hornocker, lead scientists in the early years of the Jackson Panthera study, poignantly described finding the dead mother and her kitten that died of plague: "In late October 2006, a female cougar lay down for the last time and died under a small conifer, high on a west-facing slope in the southern Yellowstone ecosystem. Sometime later, probably a day or two, her kitten also died after wedging herself under her mother, perhaps in a last pursuit of comfort and warmth. Researchers reached the site shortly afterward, alerted by the signal in the mother cougar's radio-collar. They examined the area, photographed the setting, and then packed up the carcasses to carry them out of the backcountry."

- Oddly, the mother had two kittens, but only one had the plague and died. Both kittens were already weaned, yet too young to survive on their own, so the surviving kitten was sent to a Game & Fish Wildlife Research Center. Cynthia Tate, the Wyoming Game and Fish assistant veterinarian wondered "how many exposed cougars actually get sick, and what is the ultimate outcome? What is the proportion of sick cougars that die versus those that recover?" Tate also commented that plague is an acute disease which kills rapidly. In January of 2010, the collar of F13, a six-year-old female in the Teton Jackson Cougar study, was found dead from plague. F13 was well known to local researchers for her wanderings around Jackson Hole. She also had recently starred in a local magazine article before her death was discovered. F13 had given birth to at least two kittens in recent months, but their whereabouts were not known. "If the plague is localized in the lymph nodes, Mills said, it's typically not contagious to people. If the disease spreads to the lungs, however, it can cause pneumonic plague, which can be fatal to not only the animal but humans exposed to the animal" Tate explained. University of Wyoming Press Release http://www.uwyo.edu/wyovet/disease-updates/2006/files/mountain-lion-plague.pdf

- Panthera's Teton Cougar Project field researcher Anna Kusler encapsulated the intensity of their approach. "People ask me, 'Is it true that Mark is on the ground, digging through the duff?' And I'm like 'Yup! I do it every day when I'm working. Some people just couldn't believe that we would go to clusters that were only four hours old and actually find something. Sometimes we'd walk in circles for an hour and a half until we finally found something, or nothing." Only through a long, continuous study, combined with putting in their "dirt time", did Panthera's Jackson study learn things no one else before had.

- Biologist Kerry Foresman, professor emeritus at the University of Montana and author of Mammals of Montana, enlisted Katie Mally, a graduate student in 2006, to study and compare high-elevation porcupines, now a rarity, with low-elevation porcupines. According to an article in Montana Outdoors by Ellen Horowitz in the March-April 2015 issue, "Of the 183 instances where people reported seeing porcupines in the previous decade, not a single one was at an elevation above 4,000 feet. Undaunted, Mally spent the next summer scouring western Montana mountain looking for porcupine sign. Her search came up empty. 'If she had located some porcupines, she could have radio-collared them and found out what habitats they used, what they ate, reproductive success, causes of death, that sort of thing, in order to start getting at what might behind the declines,' says Foresman."

- Mally continued working on porcupine research but restricted it to lower-elevation porcupines. She found that porcupines were most common in wetland areas containing hawthorn and cottonwoods. Dr. Foresman provided an email update with the author regarding if there were any additional study results. "The graduate student who was studying porcupines finished her research but, as is often the case, was not able to come to any conclusions about the decline in porcupine numbers, especially in forested areas."

- Biologists in California's Sierras who are trying to increase fisher population, put out a call to summer hikers to report any porcupine sightings. Their decline is of major concern since they are an important food for fishers. One twist on the threatened California fisher population is that, according to researcher Peter Stine, mountain lions are killing fishers in the Sierras, yet not eating them. Mountain lion predation is a significant factor in the decline of the fisher population there. An ongoing study is attempting to understand how fishers as well as the deer population are impacted by forest management.

• Dispersers, especially males who travel extensive distances, can wander seemingly aimless for weeks on end. Sometimes they stay within their natal range for a period, as one lion in Kenneth Logan and Linda Sweanor's ten year New Mexico study did. This male wandered first around his mother's home range for 52 days, then set off on a 207-day journey. The young male had several aborted missions, finding either occupied or unsuitable habitat, finally settling in the Guadalupe Mountains. Another of their study animals, a male who dispersed at fourteen months, spent 145 days looking for a home. His first attempt was in the Organ Mountains, where he found a resident male who wasn't happy with his presence there. For three days, the two males postured and confronted each other. On the fourth day, the young disperser escaped the older male unharmed, dispersing to the Doña Mountains. Even with no hunting in their study area, only 36% of their males lived to adulthood. In areas with no roads, and no human hunting, intraspecies mortality was their highest death factor, with disease being second.

• "Because of the great distances attained by some dispersing individuals, dispersal is viewed as the most dramatic phenomenon in cougar populations . . . [It] is a key driver of population stability and vitality . . . If attrition losses are not replaced with recruitment, the population decreases." Howard Quigley and Maurice Hornocker say it definitively.

• The fact that hunting plays an additive role in lowering a cougar population is well-documented in many studies. The Garnet Range Mountain Lion Study in Montana was set up to study the effects of hunting on a population. They achieved this through three years of intensive harvest in their hunt (study) area, then closed off 2/3 of the study area to hunting, creating a refuge in the Blackfoot watershed of 7,908 km². Hunting continued in the surrounding areas, with decreasing harvest quotas each year. Researchers found that even incremental reductions in harvest quotas outside the refuge study area did not result in any significant increase in adult survival. Only when the female quotas were reduced to *zero* was there an effect on adult survival rates. Hunting of lions, the study showed, has a "dramatic effect on mountain lion survival, and therefore population growth." When heavy hunting was allowed throughout the Garnet study area, all males were killed immediately after becoming independent from their mothers. The study concluded with several different management suggestions, with a major emphasis on full protection for females. But if a true "source" population is to be attained, in other words, where you'd have mountain lions that would live to disperse and populate other areas, then the study recommended protecting a minimum of 1000 km² of contiguous area, *and* not less than 12% of the greater landscape for a minimum of five years. Clearly, based on this and multiple other studies, if a state allows hunting throughout, even with varying quotas in different hunt zones, with no protections for females, then cougar populations will decline and dispersers will have difficulty setting up new home ranges without being harvested. At a minimum, setting up refuge areas either on a rotating basis, or permanently, might ensure a healthy and continuous cougar population through successful dispersals and emmigration.

- Robert Wielgus, in a study done in Washington State, found higher mountain lion harvests increased, rather than decreased, livestock depredations. Increased young male immigration, social disruption of cougar populations, and associated changes in space use by cougars caused by increased hunting resulted in the more complaints and livestock depredations

- In 2003, a group of seven paddlers missed one of the portages along the Box of the Clark's Fork Canyon. "All seven paddlers were swept over a fifty-foot, unrunnable cascade, flushing through a deadly series of caves and sieves in the process. Dan Crain lost his life in this incident and several others were seriously injured."

✐ CHAPTER 8
THE ZEN OF MOUNTAIN LIONS

- Toni Ruth's Yellowstone study also had a mountain lion that specialized in killing coyotes. The study was monitoring a female who had two seven-month kittens traveling with her. There was a wolf kill in the Slough Creek valley. The wolves had left a few days earlier and the female lion approached the kill site as the researchers thought "That's pretty risky behavior. She must not be doing too well." The following day she brought the kittens to the kill site. "What is she doing? This is crazy behavior because the wolves may not be at the kill but they certainly aren't too far off either," Ruth told me as they watched her collar data. When the researchers approached the kill site, they found two dead coyotes. Ruth determined that this cougar never did scavenge on the kill. Instead, she just hung out to the side of the kill, ambushed coyotes, and then went back to retrieve her kittens to feed on them. That same female lion repeated this behavior another time under the Lamar Bridge. She sat on the south side of the bridge and with the river frozen, she emerged from behind a tree, went under the bridge into a stalk, and ambushed one of a group of coyotes on the other side.

- From the 12th Mountain Lion Conference synopsis of Kyle D. Gustafson's presentation entitled *Statewide genetic analyses identify mountain lion populations and barriers to gene flow in California and Nevada*: "Populations are the main level at which demographic and evolutionary processes occur. Thus, to conserve and manage species, it is of fundamental importance to understand population structure and how geographic and anthropogenic landscape components dictate that structure. We used statewide genetic data from mountain lions (*Puma concolor*) sampled across California and Nevada to identify and characterize populations. Given that mountain lion habitat in the state of California is highly structured among several mountain ranges and possibly fragmented by a dense human population, we also assessed landscape barriers to gene flow. From 992 individuals genotyped at 42 microsatellite loci, we detected 10 mountain lion populations. Some populations are small and inbred whereas some are large and genetically-diverse. The primary factors acting as barriers to gene flow were roads, specifically interstate highways, and geographic distance. Our results identify populations of conservation priority and critical areas for population connectivity. Although our results have large-scale conservation implications for mountain lions, it is also considered an umbrella species. Thus, the strong effect of interstate highways on mountain lion population genetic structure may indicate a large-scale ecological problem

for other wildlife species and communities in one of North America's
most biodiverse and rapidly-urbanizing regions."

- The new book not yet released by Toni Ruth *Yellowstone Cougars: Ecology
  Before and During Wolf Restoration*

- Colby Anton verified for me that at 98 wolves/1000km² in 2002, this is
  the figure for number of wolves on northern range **within** the park only.
  This figure does not account for wolves on the Northern Range outside the
  Park managed by the state. The full count has varied from 98-104 for the
  ~990 km² Northern Range within the park.

- The accepted mean density of cougars, gathered from years of numerous
  studies across the West is 1.5-2.0/100km². The Bitterroot study arrived at
  a figure of 4.5 and 5.2/100 km².

- In Toni Ruth's study, about 59% of the kittens born in the YNP population survived to dispersal age, at which time 90% of surviving male
  kittens and 80% of surviving female kittens leave the protected area of
  the park in search of a home range of their own. Ruth records kitten
  survival in her summary article *Cougar Survival and Source-Sink Structure
  on Greater Yellowstone's Northern Range*. PW stands for the pre-wolf study
  conducted by Kerry Murphy 1987-1994. DW stands for during wolf phase
  conducted by Toni Ruth 1998-2005. "Estimates of kitten survival in New
  Mexico (0.59–0.66, Logan and Sweanor 2001) were higher than ours
  (0.46) in the PW phase and similar to those (0.59) in the DW phase.

- In correspondence between lead biologist of Panthera Teton Cougar Project Mark Elbroch and the author, Elbroch describes the final math on kitten survival in 6-month increments: 51%, 88%, 71%. "What that means is
  if you start with 100 cats, 51 live to 6 months, of the 51, 88% survive to 1
  year, and of those remaining, 71% last till 18 months . . . so at 18 months,
  32 remaining of the 100."

- In the PTCP, this is Elbroch's analysis of kitten predation by wolves.
  "Kittens experienced extremely high predation rates in the hunting season
  (0.31 vs. 0.16 in the non-hunting season). Every instance of predation by
  wolves on puma kittens, but one, occurred during winter, and predation
  by wolves was four times higher than that of infanticide by male pumas
  during the hunting season."

- In the final study of puma decline during the PTCP of 47%, Elbroch attributes the decrease to three human management interventions. First and foremost is hunting in and around the Jackson area. "Specifically, human-caused mortality rates in the hunting season were 3.5 times higher for adult pumas and 4.0 times higher for juveniles, as compared with the non-hunting season . . . Higher kitten and juvenile starvation in the hunting season may also have been influenced by the harvest of females that orphaned kittens too young to forage and defend themselves." Second, was the decision around year 2000 to reduce the elk herd from 16,000 to 11,000 through liberalized hunting, impacting puma food sources during the winter. And third was the re-introduction of wolves who influenced pumas directly (killing of cubs and running pumas off kills) and indirectly (resource competition). Elbroch has several recommendations coming out of their analysis for wildlife management. He recommends "reducing mountain lion hunting in areas where wolves are rebounding—the cascading effects of their presence are apparently too much for the cats to handle when already under pressure from human hunters. Finally, this study shows the need for managing whole ecosystems in complex areas like the West where various stakeholders hold different objectives for wildlife, sometimes complimentary, sometimes contradictory."

- Colby explains the enormous task it takes to interpret his data from the accelerometer. First, he takes the raw data which has movement signatures in three axes. Then he takes that data, and sums it, and that gives him a different value, called ODBA, Overall Dynamic Body Acceleration.

   "This basically tells you how much that animal moved across all three of those axes, into one unit. That ODBA value has a really good correlation to volume of oxygen consumed, called VO2. If you look at VO2, that has a correlation to calories consumed, which allows you to do all these equations along the way to make all these correlates."

✒ CHAPTER 9
BOUND IN AN URBAN FOREST

- Before the sea of settlers arrived, California had it all—mountains, desert, ocean, redwoods to dunes—with near perfect climate where even grizzlies had no need to hibernate. Bird migrations so dense the skies turned dark. Carcasses of whales washed ashore, drawing wildlife to feed. Salmon spawned by the millions in the estuary streams. Tule elk ran in large herds. The gold rush, although lasting just a short decade or so, changed the face of California forever. First came the rough and tumble miners, then the settlers followed seeking new prospects. Political pressure, applied through Congress and a variety of state laws, forced the vast tracts of Spanish and Mexican land grants, called Ranchos, to be divvied up for the American farmers and ranchers coming from the east. The grizzly bear, now relentlessly hunted, soon disappeared shortly after California became a state in 1850. A new era had begun.

- East Bay Regional Park District (EBRPD) divided their project into three "zones" that define three different "eco-regions", transected by three major freeways. The section encompassing Tilden Park, called the Oakland/East Bay Hills, is a highly altered area with a narrow green belt of protected parkland along the ridgeline. It is bordered to the west by congested towns like Berkeley and Oakland that bleed into the hills. Full of hikers, dog-walkers, and weekend park activities, Bobzien showed me photos of a male who uses the crossing above the Caldecott Tunnel, highway 24, for a connective corridor. To the east of the park is highway 680. If a lion could get beyond highway 680, there are open protected lands that include Mt. Diablo State Park, Contra Costa Water District, as well as other EBRPD owned parks. This area is a future study site. EBRPD's "control" region they call the Mt Hamilton Range zone, a fairly unaltered landscape encompassing Sunol and Ohlone Regional Wildernesses, part of the huge 700 square mile Alameda Creek watershed, along with vast private ranches. Just north of Rick Hopkin's study area, the area has a known, healthy population of cougars and is considered a major biological hotspot for the Bay Area. Bobzien tells me he regularly sees nine adult lions, including females with kittens, on his trail cameras. The plan is to use this region to fine tune their capture methods for collaring, learn about normal mountain lion activity, dispersing areas, and population densities. They can compare that data with the Berkeley/Oakland Hills lions use of space.

- California Department of Fish and Game formally changed its name to California Department of Fish and Wildlife on January 1, 2013. I use the appropriate official name of the Department at the time referred to in the text.

- From 2008-2011, the Santa Cruz Puma Project collaborated with the Bay Area Puma Project. Although no longer working together, the Santa Cruz Puma Project continues to support the Bay Area Puma Project and their efforts to educate elementary and high school students about mountain lion behavior, ecology and conservation by bringing them into the field with their research project team members.

- Watch the videos of 46M and 41M http://santacruzpumas. org/2013/10/09/welcome-41m-goodbye-27m/

- The study that found no cougars had crossed Highway 90 in Montana was based on work by Roman Biek and Mary Poss using a virus specific to cats. For a lay person explanation see NPR link http://www.npr.org/templates/story/story.php?storyId=5175059

⟅ CHAPTER 10
GREAT THINGS BEGIN IN
THE TINY SEED OF SMALL CHANGE

- On the Mountain Lion Foundation's website, C.A.W. Guggisberg (in *Wild Cats of the World*) explains that the cats urge to pounce upon prey is constantly being reactivated by penned-in animals helplessly milling around the victim. The situation a cat finds itself in is quite abnormal, and so, of course, is the puma's reaction. It would never be able to perform a massacre of this kind among the wild animals which form its natural prey, for they take flight the moment one of a herd has been struck down.

- Camilla Fox is a dynamo who grew a grassroots organization on a shoe-string. Since their Marin success, they are ever expanding the operations and outreach. They spearheaded a successful statewide movement to ban bobcat trapping, and closed loopholes that allowed coyote wildlife-killing contests in California. Their extensive education is widening their net to other states, including New Mexico and Nevada.

- A well-known saying is "kill one coyote, and two will show up at its funeral". Coyotes mate for life, and if their pack is disrupted, they can adjust their breeding to produce more and larger litters.

- Working Dogs for Conservation worked on a study in the Centennials for several years. They were able to document for the first time that grizzlies were using the area and expanding their range.

- Mattson did the seminal research on the grizzly bear's diet in the ecosystem, and has been a staunch advocate for not delisting the Great Bear due to changing climate and loss of key foods.

- The term "non-consumptive user" has been recently coined as a label for all those enjoyers of wildlife and the natural environment that do not hunt nor fish. But it has been pointed out to me during my research for this book that it is a faulty and misleading term, as we are all "consumers" in one way or another--whether we eat animal products, use ATV's or bicycles which mar the landscape, or even are hikers who make noise and disturb wildlife in their native habitat. As humans, we plough through the landscape, leaving a wake of invisible disturbance that interferes with the daily habits of wildlife. A better term for those who do not hunt nor fish, but enjoy the outdoors needs to emerge.

- Not all freeway crossings are used equally by wildlife. A study of mountain lion movement in Southern California found they preferred nocturnal travels and routes with riparian vegetation. Along the Trans-Canadian highway, a study of the animal crossings there revealed that mountain lions used crossing structures more often in winter than summer, preferred to cross structures with forest cover, and favor underpasses as compared to overpasses. Deer, elk, and grizzly bears though, prefer wide-open space.

- Humane Society of the United States, in their *State of the Mountain Lion* brochure, says this about scientific studies vs. state management: "States routinely permit much higher levels of killing by trophy hunters. Colorado, ignoring its own long-term study of the effects of trophy hunting on a mountain lion population, permits trophy hunters to kill up to 28 percent of the population in some management units. While Utah's mountain lion population has been studied for multiple decades, in 2015, the state approved a management plan permitting 20 to 30 percent offtake of its estimated entire statewide lion population in contravention to biologists' suggestion to use a more "conservative" approach. In 2016, Utah proposed to increase offtake even more, including some units with unlimited trophy hunting. In 2015, South Dakota Game, Fish & Parks suggested that over 32 percent of the entire population could be hunted. These examples show that hunting levels far exceed the eight to 14 percent recommended by three long- term studies of trophy hunting of mountain lions in various regions of the West and Midwest."

- The Garnet Study, conducted in the Blackfoot River watershed of Montana, had five levels of management recommendations. Three out of their five levels of management included full protections for females. Even one of the remaining two levels (both for sink population management) recommended low quotas on females as well. Their highest level of protections, management for a goal of a true source population, recommended "full protection of a contiguous area approximately 1000 km^2 and not less than 12% of the greater landscape, for not less than 5 years (i.e. two generations). Areas managed at this level should consist of natural age and sex distributions, high reproduction and high dispersal."

- An excellent discussion on remedial hunting can be found in William Stolzenburg's *Heart of a Lion*, in his chapter entitled "Northbound." Stolzenburg chronicles the anxieties and unfounded fears around the dangers of lions, as well as game managers and hunter's misunderstandings of cougar effects on deer populations as it plays out in South Dakota's budding lion population.

SELECTED
BIBLIOGRAPHY

Alexander, Peter D., "Comparing conventional and noninvasive monitoring techniques for assessing cougar population size in the Southern Greater Yellowstone Ecosystem." Logan, Utah: Utah State University, 2016.

Allen, Maximillan L., Helko U. Wittmer, Paul Houghtaling, Justine Smith, Mark Elbroch, Christopher C. Wilmers. "The Role of Scent Marking in Mate Selection by Female Pumas." PLOS October 2015.

Allen, Max. "How Pumas Communicate through Scent Marking" Cat Watch National Geographic Online October 22, 2015.

Allen, Maxmillian L., L. Mark Elbroch, Christopher C. Wilmers, Heiko U. Wittmer. "The Comparative Effects of large Carnivores on the Acquisition of Carrion by Scavengers." The American Naturalist vol. 185, no. 6 June 2015.

Allen, Maxmillian L., Heiko U. Wittmer, Christopher C. Wilmers. "Puma communication behaviours: understanding functional use and variation among sex and age classes." Behaviour 151: 819-840, 2014.

Andrease, Alyson, Carl Lackey, Jon Beckmann. 'Impacts on survival of cougars caught as non-targets in foothold traps.' Presentation at the 12th Mountain Lion Conference, May 2017.

Backus, Perry. "Study finds twice as many mountain lions in Bitterroot as expected." Ravalli Republic, Jan. 9, 2014.

Baron, David The Beast in the Garden. New York: W.W. Norton and Company, 2004.

Beausoleil, Richard A., Gary M. Koehler, Benjamin T. Maletzke, Brian N. Kertson, and Robert B. Wielgus. "Research to Regulation: Cougar Social Behavior as a Guide for Management." Wildlife Society Bulletin 37, no. 3 (2013) 680-88

Beausoleil, Richard A., Kenneth I. Warheit. "Using DNA to evaluate field identification of cougar sex by agency staff and hunters using trained dogs." Wildlife Society Bulletin, 30 September 2014.

Bekoff, Marc, and Cara Blessley Lowe, eds. Listening to Cougar. Boulder: University of Colorado Press, 2007

Blek, Roman, Allen G. Rodrigo, David Holley, Alexel Drummond, Charles R. Anderson Jr., Howard A. Ross, Mary Poss. "Epidemiology, Genetic Diversity, and Evolution of Endemic Feline Immunodeficiency Virus in a Population of Wild Cougars." Journal of Virology, Volume 77, Issue 17: 9578-9589 September 2003.

Bolgiano, Chris. Mountain Lion: An Unnatural History of Pumas and People. Mechancisburg, PA: Stackpole Books, 1995.

Bradshaw, G.A., Carnivore minds. Who these fearsome animals really are. New Haven: Yale University Press, 2017.

Buotte, Polly C. "Wolf and Bear Detection of Cougar-Killed Ungulates on the Northern Range of Yellowstone National Park." Abstract only.

Carmony, Neil B. Onza! The Hunt for a Legendary Cat. Silver City, New Mexico: High-Lonesome Books, 1995.

Carmony, Neil B. Editor. Ben Lilly's Tales of Bears, Lions and Hound. Silver City, New Mexico: High-Lonesome Books, 2016.

Chadwick, Douglas. "Cougars: Ghost Cats." National Geographic, December 2013.

Chianese, Robert Lous. "Suburban Stalkers: The near-wild lions in our midst." American Scientist, volume 105, number 5, pg. 278 September-October 2017.

Coleman, Jon T., Vicious. Wolves and Men in America. New Haven: Yale University Press, 2004.

Cougar Management Guidelines Working Group. Cougar Management Guidelines, First Edition. Washington: WildFutures, 2005.

Curtis, Sam, Tom Dickson. "A Close Look at Mountain Lions." Montana Outdoors July-August, 2008.

Dayton, Kelsey, "Yellowstone cougars quietly thriving." WyoFile, May 6, 2016.

Dobie, J. Frank. The Ben Lilly Legend. Austin, TX: University of Texas Press, 1997

_____ "Tiger Claws" Tongues of the Monte, Boston: Little, Brown and Company, 1947.

Edwards, Melodie. "Taking a Peek into the intimate lives of Mountain Lions." Wyoming Public Radio, Mar 18, 2016.

Elbroch, L.M., Lendrum, P.E., Alexander, P., Quigley, H. "Cougar den site selection in the Southern Yellowstone Ecosystem" Mammal Research Institute, Polish Academy of Sciences, Bialowieza, Poland 2015

Elbroch, L. Mark, Rafael Hoogesteijn, Howard Quigley. "Cougars Killed by North American Porcupines" The Canadian Field Naturalist, Vol 130 pg. 53-55 The Ottawa Field-Naturalist's Club 2016

Elbroch, L. Mark, Maximilian L. Allen, Blake H. Lowrey, Heiko U. Wittmer "The difference between killing and eating: ecological shortcomings of puma energetic models" Ecosphere Vol 5(5) Article 53 May 2014.

Elbroch, L. Mark, Howard B. Quigley, Anthony Caragiulo "Spatial associations in a solitary predator: using genetic tools and GPS technology to assess cougar social organization in the Southern Yellowstone Ecosystem" ACTA Ethologica June, 2014.

Elbroch, L. Mark, Patrick E. Lendrum, Howard Quigley, Anthony Caragliulo. "Spatial overlap in a solitary carnivore: support for the land tenure, kinship or resource dispersion hypotheses?" Journal of Animal Ecology 2015.

Elbroch, L. Mark, Patrick E. Lendrum, Maximilian L. Allen, Heiko U. Wittmer. "Nowhere to hide: pumas, black bears, and competition refuges. Behavioral Ecology, October 2014.

Elbroch, L. Mark, Patrick E. Lpendrum, Hugh Robinson, Howard B. Quigley. "Population-and individual-level prey as determined with two estimates of prey availability." Can. J. Zool. Pg. 275-282 Vol. 94, 2016 NRC Research Press

Elbroch, L. Mark, Lucile Marescot, Howard Quigley, Derek Craighead, Heiko U. Wittmer. "Multiple anthropogenic interventions drive puma survival following wolf recovery in the Greater Yellowstone Ecosystem." Ecology and Evolution, Wiley Online Library 25 June 2018.

Elbroch, L.M., Feltner, J., Quigley, H.B. "Stage-dependent puma predation on dangerous prey" Journal of Zoology, The Zoological Society of London 2017

Elbroch, L. Mark, Patrick E. Lendrum, Jesse Newby, Howard Quigley, Derek Craighead. "Seasonal Foraging Ecology of Non-Migratory Cougars in a System with Migratin Prey." PLOS ONE Volume 8 Issue 12, December 2013

Elbroch, L. Mark, Howard Quigley. "Social interactions in a solitary carnivore." Current Zoology, Oxford University Press, July 2016.

Elbroch, L. Mark, Patrick Lendrum, Jesse Newby, Howard Quigley, Daniel Thompson. "Recolonizing wolves influence the realized niche of resident cougars." Zoological Studies 54:41 2014.

Elbroch, L. Mark "Letter to the Editor Opinion Piece." Jackson Hole News & Guide Feb. 10, 2016.

_____ "Fumbling Cougar Kittens: Learning to Hunt." Cat Watch, National Geographic. October 22, 2014.

_____. "Overlapping Mountain Lions." Cat Watch, National Geographic. October 22, 2015.

_____. "Mountain Lions Versus Porcupines." Cat Watch, National Geographic. Dec. 28, 2014.

Ernest, Holly. "Mountain Lion Research shows what's possible when wildlife genomics and disease ecology laboratory brings to bear its ample expertise on Wyoming wildlife." Reflections College of Agriculture and Natural Resources Research Report. University of Wyoming. 2016

Ernest, Holly B. T. Winston Vickers, Scott A. Morrison, Michael R. Buchalski, and Walter M. Boyce. "Fractured Genetic Connectivity Threatens a Southern California Puma (*Puma concolor*) Population." PLOS ONE, October 8, 2014.

Ernest, Holly B., Walter M Boyce, Vernon C. Bleich, Bernie May, San J. Stiver & Steven G. Torres. "Genetic structure of mountain lion populations in California." Conservation Genetics 353-366, 2003.

Evans, Tony. "Lending hope for big cats. Maurice Hornocker has spent decades among feline carnivores." Idaho Mountain Express and guide. Dec. 30, 2009.

Fifield, Virginia L., Aviva J. Rossi, and Erin E. Boydston. "Documentation of mountain lions in Marin County, California, 2010-2013. California Fish and Game 101 (1):66-71; 2015

Gilad, Oranit, Jan E. Janeeeka, Fred Armstrong, Michael E. Tewes, Rodney L. Honeycutt. "Cougars in Guadalupe Mountain National Park, Texas: Estimates of Occurrence and Distribution Using Analysis of DNA." The Southwestern Naturalist, 56(3):297-303. Southwestern Association of Naturalists. 2011

Gross, Liza. "Pumas Trained to Run on Treadmill help explain Big Cat's Ambush Strategy." Cat Watch. National Geographic, Oct. 2, 2014

Hamashige, Hope. "Virus Used to Track Elusive Cougars" National Geographic News, Jan. 27, 2006.

Hansen, Kevin, Cougar, the American Lion. Flagstaff, AZ: Northland Publishing, 1992

Hatch, Cory, "Well-Known female cougar dies from plague." Jackson Hole News & Guide, Jan. 13, 2010.

Hibben, Frank C. Hunting American Lions. New York: Thomas Y. Crowell Company, 1948

Hopkins, Rick A. Ecology of the Puma in the Diablo Range, University of California at Berkeley 1989.

Hornocker, Maurice, and Sharon Negri, eds. Cougar Ecology and Conservation. Chicago: University of Chicago Press, 2009.

Horowitz, Ellen. "Where have all the Porcupines Gone? Montana Outdoors March-April 2015.

Humane Society of the United States. "State of the Mountain Lion. A call to end trophy hunting of America's Lion."

Keefover-Ring, Wendy. "Mountain Lions, Myths, and Media: A Critical Reevaluation of The Beast in the Garden." Environmental Law 35, no. 4 (2005): 1083-93.

_____ "Re: Utah's Cougar Management Plan" Letter from The Humane Society of the United States to Gregory Sheehan, Utah Division of Wildlife Resources. July 2015.

" . . . it is virtually impossible to get an accurate count of an actual lion population." Pinedale Roundup, June 19, 1999.

Kling, Julie Fustanio. "Curious about cougars." Planet Jackson Hole. July 16, 2014.

Koshmri, Mike. "Orphaned lion kittens fascinate biologist." Jackson Hole News & Guide, May 7 2014.

_____. "Lions still lurk in Buffalo Valley." Jackson Hole News & Guide, Dec. 15, 2015.

_____. "Lions say 'what up' more than thought." Jackson Hole News & Guide, Aug. 10, 2016.

_____. "Study finds cougars avoid wolf territory." Jackson Hole News & Guide, Jun 18, 2014

_____. "Wolves, cold, hunters all threaten cougar kittens." Jackson Hole News & Guide. Mar 19, 2014.

_____. "Orphaned lion kittens fascinate biologist." Jackson Hole News & Guide, May 7, 2014.

_____. "Cougars not so solitary, Teton researchers find." Jackson Hole News & Guide, Jul 23, 2014.

_____. "Lives of mountain lions unfold in nighttime videos." Jackson Hole News & Guide, Apr 17, 2013.

Laelaps "Did False Cheetahs Give Pronghorn a Need for Speed?" Phenomena, A Science Salon. National Geographic, Jan. 8 2013.

Lawrence, R. D.., The Ghost Walker. Holt, Rinehart, and Winston 1983

Lendrum, P.E., L.M. Elbroch, H. Quigley, D.J. Thompson, M. Jimenez, D. Craighead. "Home range characteristics of a subordinate predator: selection for refugia or hunt opportunity? Journal of Zoology, The Zoological Soiety of London 2014.

Lowrey, Blake, L. Mark Elbroch, Len Broberg. "Is individual prey selection driven by chance or choice? A case study in cougars." Mammal Research Institue, Polish Academy of Sciences, Bialowieza, Poland 2016

Logan, Kenneth A., Linda L. Sweanor. Desert Puma: Evolutionary Ecology and Conservation of an Enduring Carnivore. Washington D.C.: Island Press, 2001.

Lyon, Tolbert James "Shorty." Lyon Hunts and Humor, True Life Hunting and Adventure Stories. Santa Fe, New Mexico: Sunstone Press, 1990.

Mangelsen, Thomas D., Cara Shea Blessley "Spirit of the Rockies: The Mountain Lions of Jackson Hole." Thomas D. Mangelsen, Inc. 2000.

Mattson, David J. "State-Level Management of a Common Charismatic Predator. Mountain Lions in the West." Large Carnivore Conservation, Chapter 2, University of Chicago Press 2014.

Mattson et al. "Spatial responses to climate across trophic levels. Monitoring and modeling plants, prey, and predators in the Intermountain Western United States." Nasa 2011 Climate & Biological Response: Research & Application 2012-2013 Annual Report.

Mattson, David, Kenneth Logan, Linda Sweanor. "Factors governing risk of cougar attacks on humans." Human-Wildlife Interactions 5, No. 1 (2011): 135-58.

Mattson, David J. "Cougars of Zion and Capitol Reef 2006-2008 Report" U.S. Department of the Interior, U.S. Geological Survey.

Mattson, David, Kirsten Ironside. "To Fuss or not to Fuss?" Southwest Biological Science Center. Grand Canyon National Park. 2011.

Mattson, David J., Erin Savage, Susan G. Clark. "Intractable Conflict? Mountain Lion Depredation in East-Central Arizona, USA" Yale School of Forestry & Environmental Studies, CT

Mattson, David, Zachary Bischoff-Mattson, "Effects of simulated Mountain Lion caching on decomposition of ungulate carcasses." Western North American Naturalist 69 (3) pp. 343-350, 2009.

Mattson, David J., Susan G. Clark. "The discourses of incidents: cougars on Mt. Elden and in Sabino Canyon, Arizona" Policy Sci, Springer, June 2012.

Mattson, David J., Elizabeth J. Ruther. "Explaining reported puma-related behaviors and behavioral intentions among northern Arizona residents." Human Dimensions of Wildlife, 17:91-111, Taylor & Francis Group 2012.

Mattson, David J. "The Problem of State Wildlife Management Institutions" April 16, 2013, given to me by the author.

Montgomery, Rutherford. Yellow Eyes. Idaho: Caxton Classic Series, 2001.

Mountain Lion Website "Survival Chances Getting Slimmer for Wyoming Lions." http://mountainlion.org/newsstory.asp?news_id=1510

National Park Service Grand Canyon. "Remembering Eric York 1970-2007." https://www.nps.gov/grca/learn/nature/puma-eric-york.htm

Negri, Sharon, David Mattson. "A Three-Part Report to The Summerlee Foundation" WildFutures. 2014.

Panterapumas, Instagram, Panthera Teton Cougar Project.

Peebles, Kaylie A., Robert B. Wielgus, Benjamin T. Maletzke, Mark E. Swanson "Effects of Remedial Sport Hunting on Cougar Complaints and Livestock Depredations." PLoS ONE 8, no. 11(2013): e79713. Doi:10.1371/journal.pone.0079713

Puckett, Karl. "Lion makes epic trip from Canada to Montana." Great Falls Tribune, Dec. 8, 2015.

Quenqua, Douglas. "A Threat is Seen in Pumas' Isolation" New York Times, Oct. 13, 2014.

Rabinowitz, Alan. An Indomitable Beast. The Remarkable Journey of the Jaguar. Island Press, Washington, 2014.

Reed, Drew. "Cougar Home Range Shifts and Apparent Decrease in Cougar Abundance in the Southern Greater Yellowstone Ecosystem." Abstract Only

Reid, Elwood. "Stalker." Outside Magazine, May 1, 2003.

Robinson, Huge, DeSimone, Rich. "The Garnet Range Mountain Lion Study. Characteristics of a hunted population in West-Central Montana." Final Report 2011. Montana Fish Wildlife and Parks Wildlife Division. Helena, Montana.

Robinson, Huge, Richard Desimone, Cynthia Hartway, Justin A. Gude, Michael J. Thompson, Michael S. Mitchell, Mark Hebblewhite. "A test of the compensatory mortality hypothesis in Mountain lions: A management experiment in West-Central Montana." The Journal of Wildlife Management 78 (5): 791-807, 2014.

Rosato, Joe Jr., "New Cameras Reveal Wildlife Above Caldecott Tunnel." NBC Bay Area News, March 8, 2017.

Ruth, Toni K. "Ghost of the Rockies". Yellowstone Science Volume 12. No. 1. Winter 2004.

Ruth, Toni K., Douglas W. Smith, Mark A. Haroldson, Polly C. Buotte, Charles C. Schwartz, Howard B. Quigley, Steve Cherry, Kerry M. Murphy, Dan Tyers, Kevin Frey. "Large-carnivore response to recreational big-game hunting along the Yellowstone National Park and Absaroka-Beartooth Wilderness boundary." Wildlife Society Bulletin 2003, 31 (4):1-xxx

Ruth, Toni K, Polly C. Buotte, Howard B. Quigley. "Comparing Ground Telemetry and Global Positioning System Methods to Determine Cougar Kill Rates." Journal of Wildlife Management 74 no. 5:1122-1133; 2010

Ruth, Toni K., Mark A Haroldson, Kerry M. Murphy, Polly C. Buotte, Maurice G. Hornocker, Howard B. Quigley. "Cougar Survival and Source-Sink Structure on Greater Yellowstone's Northern Range." Journal of Wildlife Management 75, no 6 (2011):1381-98

Ruth, Toni K. "Cougar Reproduction and Survival Pre- and Post-wolf Reintroduction in Yellowstone National Park." Abstract Only.

Sawaya, Michael A., Toni K. Ruth, Scott Creel, Jay J. Rotella, Jeffrey B. Stetz, Howard B. Quigley, Steven T. Kalinowski. "Evaluation of Noninvasive Genetic Sampling Methods for Cougars in Yellowstone National Park." The Journal of Wildlife Management 75, no. 3 (2011): 612-622

Seton, Ernest Thompson. Lives of Game Animals, Vol. 1. New York: Doubleday, Doran, 1925.

Shaw, Harley. Soul among Lions: The Cougar as Peaceful Adversary. University of Arizona, 2000.

Schaafsma, Polly. Indian Rock Are of the Southwest University of New Mexico, 1980.

Stolzenburg, William. Heart of a Lion. New York: Bloomsbury, USA, 2016.

Storer, Tracy I., Lloyd P. Tevis, Jr., California Grizzly. University of California Press, 1996.

The Province "Trophy Hunting of cougars may increase cougar-human conflict, study finds." Oct. 24, 2016

Thomas, Heather Smith. "Predators a growing problem in Wyoming." Tri-State Livestock News, Oct. 15, 2009.

Wielgus, Robert B., Dana Eleanor Morrison, Hilary S. Cooley, Ben Maletzke. "Effects of Male Trophy Hunting on Female Carnivore Population Growth and Persistence." Biological Conservation 167 (2013): 69-75.

Williams, Terrie M., Traci Kendall, Caleb M. Bryce, Christopher C. Wilmers. "Instantaneous energetics of puma kills reveal advantage of felid sneak attacks." Science 346, 81 (2014).

Woodroffe, Rosie, Joshua R. Ginsberg. "Edge Effects and the Extinction of Populations Inside Protected Areas." Science July 1998.

Wright, Bruce S., The Ghost of North America: The Story of the Eastern Panther, New York, Vantage Press, 1959.

INDEX

ACKNOWLEDGEMENTS

A big thank you to Lorna Owen and Lynn Pipet, two very fine editors, who helped flush out what needed to be said.

The list is long of people who consented to be interviewed by a little-known, yet curious and enthusiastic, writer. Each took a leap of faith, opening up regarding their knowledge of pumas, all without knowing the trajectory of the book. From conservationists to houndsmen to researchers, their common bond is their love of this magnificent animal and desire for its preservation.

Biologist Mark Elbroch generously gave me his valuable time through interviews and correspondence. His work is breaking new ground in our understanding of pumas. Anna Kusler, Jen Feltner, Michelle Peziol, Peter Alexander, and houndsman Boone Smith patiently explained findings from the PTCP, retelling interesting personal stories of their interactions with pumas.

Toni Ruth taught one of the best classes I've ever taken at the Lamar Buffalo Ranch. Our phone conversation helped me better understand her work on cougar and wolf interactions in the Park. Dan Stahler gave me precise instructions on how to collect and preserve cougar scat. Colby Anton patiently conveyed his pioneering work with accelerometers even as we were shuffled from occupied room to room at the Mountain Lion Conference.

During my brief visit over the winter holidays in the Bay Area, many people opened their schedules to help me understand the lives of urban cougars. Zara McDonald, Courtney Coons, Joe Acampora, Sharon Negri, Jim Sullivan, Scott Davidson and Camilla Fox. Many others, working in fields as diverse as research, conservation, and tracking, filled in the California pieces by phone. These included Virginia Fifield, Steven Bobzien, David Stoner, Peter Stine, Matt Nelson, Meghan Walla-Murphy, Veronica Yovocich, Keli Hendricks, and Rick Hopkins.

Jim Halfpenny always has a full satchel of great tracking stories. Peter Coppolillo with Working Dogs for Conservation told me wonderful tales of dogs finding invasive fish and weeds, along with cougar scat. WDC's dogs are presently helping with a new Panthera puma study in South America.

A whole new perspective was gained, along with new friendships, through houndsman Rod Bullis. He and his wife Carol opened their home, while Rod took me on a tour of the Blackfoot Mountains. Through Rod I gained a visual understanding of lion country in the Garnet Range. Thank you Rod for visiting the Helena office of the Montana FWP to finagle an out-of-print copy of the Garnet Range Study for me. Rod also made certain I visited Cal Ruark by personally driving me to Missoula. As Cal and I spoke about his adventures chasing lions in the Bitterroots, he described watching a lion from his kitchen window one evening kill a deer. I can't thank Grover Hedrick enough for enduring all my phone calls. First for several interviews. Then to garner his expertise on MFWP's conclusions from the Bitterroot study.

Penny Maldonado was an invaluable resource on research and conservation efforts, especially in Montana and Wyoming. Lynn Cullens helped critique and improve my California chapter. Lisa Robertson, friend to wildlife and myself, inspired me with her story of the Miller Butte family. Dan Thompson of Wyoming Game and Fish began his sit-down interview by telling me he's always excited to talk about mountain lions. Many others gave me tidbits of valuable information by phone or email, including Orie Gilad,

Koda & Leslie

Jonah Evans, David Mattson, Larry Loendorf, Gary Koehler, Kerry Foresman, as well as an unnamed staff member of the Texas Lone Star Sierra Club chapter.

Photographers Robert Martinez and Denis Callet are producing groundbreaking, unparalleled trail camera footage of Southern California mountain lions. I wholeheartedly thank them for allowing me to use a few of their photographs. Thanks as well to Panthera and Felidae for amazing color images. Other photographers who contributed their work are Bonnie Smith, Scott Davidson, Meghan Walla-Murphy, and Jim Sullivan. Thank you, Lynne Bama, our local Cody poet and writer, who contributed her poem on mountain lions and special thanks to Tara McBride and Melissa Rohm, both of whom read through earlier drafts for feedback.

One of the highlights of researching and writing this book was an unexpected meeting with Harley Shaw and his wife Patty. They generously hosted me at their casita. Patty took me on a prized, bird watching excursion with an expert birder, while Harley read through and critiqued my manuscript. I much appreciate this new friendship.

My amazing golden retriever, Koda, accompanied me on all these hikes. Many of the cougar kill sites I'd never have found without his nose. He's too old now to hike, but his spirit on the trail is always with me. Although I don't have his smell sensitivity, his natural instincts and vigilance instilled in me a reservoir of deep instruction only a dog—a bridge to our own human wildness—can offer.

ABOUT THE AUTHOR

Leslie Patten has an extensive background in horticulture, along with a life-long interest in the natural world. She is the author of *The Wild Excellence: Notes from Untamed America* and *BioCircuits: Amazing New Tools for Energy Health* as well as several eBooks on gardening. She presently lives in a small cabin in northwest Wyoming.

CPSIA information can be obtained
at www.ICGtesting.com
Printed in the USA
FSHW02n0003290918
52400FS